THREE PLAYS

THREE PLAYS

by
GABRIEL MARCEL

INTRODUCTION BY RICHARD HAYES

A MERMAID DRAMABOOK

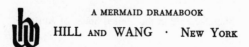

HILL AND WANG · NEW YORK

FIRST DRAMABOOK PRINTING SEPTEMBER 1965

842.91
M314t

Manufactured in the United States of America
234567890

CONTENTS

Introduction

"IT IS a principle of French thought," the composer Mr. Virgil Thomson has observed, "that analysis and reflection are not inimical to spontaneity, that art, indeed, represents all these collaborating towards a single action." To the animation of this paradox, the philosopher and dramatist M. Gabriel Marcel has borne a testimony singular in the range of contemporary letters, exploring that elusive tension between intellectual lucidity and delicate sensuous import we have come to regard as the special province of Gallic sensibility. In his stance vis-à-vis those moral solicitations which constitute the crisis and career of modern spirituality, he has maintained a prophetic intimacy, urgent, yet wholly void of the imperial tone of *J'exige:* an exemplary witness, in "this time of universal sacrilege" he has somewhere indicted, with unwonted polemic vehemence, "to the being full of weakness and hope which in spite of everything and for ever—we are."

It has been an equilibrium achieved against the grain of his age, and even, not inconsiderably, of his temperament. Bred to the *inquiétude* and "extraordinary disposition toward holocaust" Mr. Wallace Fowlie sees as Baudelaire's legacy to French letters, M. Marcel retained from the feverish interlude of *fin de siècle* its violent thrust to sincerity, which others would diminish and exploit as a blasphemous invective. In concert with his philosophic peers and contemporaries, Heidegger and Jaspers, he moved toward the radical assumption of *vertigo* as "a positive condition of all metaphysical thought worthy of the name"; like the innovators of Surrealism, he shared a distrust of exterior reality and the conscious self as transitory, impure. He might claim kinship with the later generation of M. André Malraux, who would announce, *"Nous avons été formés dans l'absurde de la guerre"*—"We were formed in

5

the absurdity of war"—and he will stand, even, with those darkling angels of the Resistance, Camus and M. Jean-Paul Sartre, at the brink of that "shimmering lagoon which perpetually sends us back the reflection of our own dereliction."

Yet he is not to be fixed, Marcel, even in schematic equilibrium, and the speculative and dramatic enterprise he would have us take as "two slopes of the same height," must be read as less a doctrinaire Existentialism than a new lease on Socratic thought. Neither the "man of congresses" nor manifestoes, he is rather *homo viator*—man the wayfarer, to whom the metaphor of landscape is habitual and the language of exploration and terrain inevitable: a vocabulary of *frontier* and *chasm* and *vista* and *zone;* now of "the sinuous road I have had to follow," and always of the supremely intuitive truth, stifled in every generation by one mode or another of scholastic aridity, that *being* necessarily means "being on the way (*en route*)." Faithful to an interior conviction—"scandalous to the scientist or the technician"—that "in the real world . . . the stage always remains to be set; in a sense everything always starts from zero," he has come to see in the dramatic work which has occupied him for more than half a century "an underground stream whose overflow, often scarcely perceptible, irrigates, as it were, my speculative thought. . . . I am convinced that it is in drama and through drama that metaphysical thought grasps and defines itself *in concrete.*" If Marcel's plays disclose a meditative dimension, in Mr. James Collins' graceful statement of the paradox, his philosophical treatises remain close to the drama of the person and his choices. Both take their honorable place in that ancient, sophisticated, and continuous tradition of French spirituality which M. Marcel has elsewhere so happily illumined as the attempt "to introduce a maximum of lucidity and at the same time a maximum of compassion."

The theatre of Gabriel Marcel has been variously characterized as a drama of sincerity, of conscience in tension and ambiguity, or—the dramatist's own metaphor—of the soul in exile. It may be seen in higher relief, I hazard to suggest, if we contemplate it as a theatre of pilgrimage: journeys to the interior undertaken in a climate of magnetic silence charged with memory and affectivity. The trio of plays gathered here—all salient instances of M. Marcel's theatrical *oeuvre*—do not invite a rhetoric of extremity; their stylistic commitment is rather to a certain mode of bourgeois Gallic verity which may seem arid, and even dour, to imaginations habituated to the scintillant and sometimes meretricious *poésie du théâtre* of the Parisian stage *entre deux guerres*. The limits of one's language are the limits of one's world, in Wittgenstein's aphorism, and it is perhaps Marcel's luckless chance that the temper of his time should have demanded Caravaggio as architect of its life-décor, and neither Ingres nor David. Meditations in *grisaille*, we might say of this playwright's method; there is something here of the pressure and draughtsmanship of drawings, or that fastidious *tenue* of a particular music—late Fauré, as an instance, or the Beethoven quartets—which Marcel sees commanding the entire development of his thought: "musical consciousness, completely transcending the realm of Eris—that of arguments and disputes in which everyone is revealed as being fundamentally selfish, harboring demands and claims on others."

Within the bourgeois *ambiance* and pensive, even monochromatic, tonality of his dramatic investiture, Marcel affirms a distinguished Gallic habit of vigilant self-inquisition. The Pastor Lemoyne of *A Man of God* (1925) would seem alien to neither Molière nor Gide, quite as the spiritual avarice of *Ariadne* (1936) is in essence a modulation on its passionate precedents in *Les Liaisons Dangereuses*. The "family relations" which compose the human matter of Marcel's theatre, and which he sees, sadly, as "unable to offer any consistency or guarantee of solidity . . . like human things in general," are ever those labyrinthine domestic crises and collusions out of which Dumas *fils* will make a geometry of intrigue, Feydeau a mathematics of farce, and Racine a syllogistic pavane of immolation and destiny. ("What is fate for the Frenchman?" Giraudoux reflects. "He admits only one of its forms: family fate. . . . The French Olympus is the entire family . . . grouped in front of the notary for the reading of the will." Or the more acrid Anouilh: "Life is one long dinner with the family.")

Mundane bourgeois figures, then, we may say—deluded egotisms, moving toward predictable revelations of the masked self. Yet as in our passage, by inconstant light, through a land unmarked, the ambient air is freighted with *presences,* reverberant. Here is M. Marcel on a certain motif from *Ariadne:*

> "The most terrible thing in life is that the possessions of which we have been deprived are not only missing, but they exist in us like upside-down shadows, nocturnal and devastating powers." In other words, in a very profound sense, *we are also what we are not;* there is a counter-reality to ourselves which is not embodied directly in our acts, but which may hover over them like a shadow. . . .

It is the encounter with these nocturnal and devastating powers that gives to M. Marcel's theatre its subtle insinuation and urgency. Creatures of *le monde cassé*—his metaphor of this broken world which has seen "the rupture, or more exactly the loosening, of the ontological bond uniting each particular being to Being in its fullness"—they can only echo Pastor Lemoyne's inarticulate prayer *to be known as one is.* Yet as exiles from "a sort of metaphysical Atlantis," they conspire in strategies of egotism and complicity—the moral imperialism of Pastor Lemoyne and the grieving Aline Fortier of *The Votive Candle* (1931), Ariadne's mirages of prophetic consciousness—all constituting "a form of concupiscence by which the world is brought to myself and compelled to submit to a set of techniques considered suitable for dominating it." In the formal language of Marcel's speculative thought, they have diminished a *mystery* to a *problem,* and their anguish issues not so much from a failure in self-knowledge—for "self-consciousness, far from being an illuminating principle, as traditional philosophy has held, on the contrary shuts the human being in on himself and thus results in opacity rather than enlightenment"—as it does from a certain defective "docility to the solicitations of the real."

Disponibilité—the quality of spiritual availability with which we welcome or rebuff the unmistakable reality of "presence"—determines, in Marcel's view, the essence of our inner freedom, of grace, even. ("It does not seem possible," he writes of Ariadne Leprieur, "to think of grace without reference to a certain breadth and inner readiness.") These hushed yet dramatic chronicles of pilgrimage echo with that same elegiac "witness to the spiritual" M. Marcel most values in the achievement of Rilke: "There is nothing in the way of demonstration or even exposition here; it is all questioning, invocation and also evocation, it is the inward debate of a soul which in a sense acknowledges the charge of the universe and, as it were, the mission of making it grow or even of repeopling it." One is reminded of the late plays of Mr. T. S. Eliot, to which M. Marcel's theatre bears more than a casual affinity of temperament and strategy—two dramatists for whom the secular, bourgeois world is the *donnée* and ground of a quest for lost authenticity, point of departure for spiritual transformations of a most intricate and perilous subtlety. (Ironically, too, the French philosopher and the Anglo-American poet, whose critiques of technological society elsewhere coincide in dismay at the reduction of man to a brutal agglomeration of functions, both implicitly invoke from players who would give the substance of being to their dramatic personages, a kind of specific gravity which our theatre, no less than our culture, either deviously subverts or actively discourages.) Each would assent to the numinous *pensée* of Mr. E. M. Forster: "It is private life that holds out the mirror to infinity; personal intercourse, and that alone, that ever hints at a personality beyond our daily vision." And the tragic sonority of their drama arises from the poignant music of figures in aspiration toward transcendence and liberation—release not only from the social pressures to inauthenticity, but equally from their less tangible private conditions of psychological servitude. If Marcel the speculative mind would acquiesce in Fichte's dictum that "we philosophize out of need for our redemption," Marcel the artist would surely submit that we dramatize out of need for transfiguration. And the medium of liberation will be that fluent *disponibilité*—ever alert to the hazards of misconstrued being no less than to the "solicitations of the real"—which we need conceive as only another modulation of love: the love, in M. Marcel's view, without which no genuine observation is possible.

"What we want," Mr. Eric Bentley proposes in his salient gloss on the drama's hazardous dialectic of thought and feeling, "is not philosophy but (to use a traditional if not scientific distinction) wisdom. The German term *Lebensweisheit* says a little more: what we want is a wisdom that bears upon our being alive (and about to be dead) as men, a thought that relates itself to our pleasure, suffering, and mortality." It is not an irrelevance that M. Marcel should have called one of his major speculative works *The Decline of Wisdom,* quite as it is instructive to reflect on how rarely his dramatic figures attain to that truth of Revelation which Marcel himself, in middle life, personally affirmed by his entrance into the Roman Catholic communion. In this, he stands somewhat apart from those notable contemporary writers of religious disposition for whom the shock of theological paradox is the summoning agent to "ultimate concern." For Marcel, grace must inhabit one "not only as radiance, but as humility," and never can it absolve us from "seeking to understand, with a lucidity which must never exclude compassion, how life appears to those who are enlightened by no belief of a transcendental nature."

A calculated trap for meditation is M. Denis de Rougemont's image of the work of art in essence. No phrase could better suggest the metaphysical design of M. Marcel's theatre,

quite as the order of its spiritual energy is nowhere so deli-
cately intimated as in M. de Rougemont's later figure of art
as "an invocation (more often than not unconscious) to the
lost harmony. . . ." The dramatist Marcel mourns this lost
harmony: he laments in his own work the absence of that
"nourishing soil which has given birth to so many of the
creations I admire"—the theatres of Lorca, Chekhov, Synge.
What his time and his vision have yielded is rather the realm
of Eris, idolatrous, barren, and vulnerable: this "inextricable
entanglement of the willed and the suffered" which brings
home to us the force of Mr. Cyril Connolly's prophecy that it
is to Civilization, not to Nature, that man must be recalled.
Yet above this savaged landscape, Marcel would bid us recog-
nize—as did Proust at certain great moments, and incompar-
ably in *La Prisonnière*—"the existence of fixed stars in the
heaven of the soul."

All that can be said is that everything in our life happens as
though we entered upon it with a load of obligations con-
tracted in a previous existence. There is no reason arising from
the conditions of our life on this earth for us to consider ourselves obliged to do good, to be tactful, even to be polite, nor
for the cultured artist to consider himself obliged to begin
again twenty times; the admiration his work will arouse cannot
matter much to his body eaten by worms, as for instance the
space of yellow wall painted with so much knowledge and taste
by an artist forever unknown and scarcely identified under the
name of Vermeer. All these obligations whose sanction is not
of this present life, seem to belong to a different world,
founded on kindness, scruples, sacrifice, a world entirely different from this one, a world whence we emerge to be born on
this earth, before returning thither, perhaps, to live under the
empire of those unknown laws we have obeyed because we
bore their teaching within us without knowing who had taught
us, those laws which all deep work of our intelligence brings
closer to us, and which are only invisible (and scarcely even
then!) to fools.

Richard Hayes

June 1965

Preface

THE DRAMA OF THE SOUL IN EXILE

(A lecture given in July, 1950, by Gabriel Marcel at the Institut Français *in London. To preserve as far as possible the vividness of the original, the translation has been kept in colloquial form.)*

NEVER more than today have I felt the risk run by an author when he tries to present his own work to the public. To begin with, it is scarcely possible for him to be as impartial, as objectively impersonal about it, as about the work of another man; and yet to give the slightest impression of crying his own wares would be ridiculous. But there is also another and far deeper contradiction inherent in the intimacy of a writer's relation to his own work. I am quite prepared to say that this is always either too close to him or too distant: too close if he has not yet detached himself from it, if he is still partially involved in the inner struggle of which it is the painfully won fruit; too distant if he feels that he has passed beyond it and left it behind. The relation of a father to his child is not more precarious or unstable. In view of these difficulties I shall today attempt no more than to throw a little light on what the theatre has never ceased to represent for me, and to indicate the apparent general trend of my own plays, when considered chronologically.

I have lately been reading some profound comments by that great dramatist Gerhart Hauptmann, which could well be used as a heading to these few remarks on my own work. "Drama," he says, "is one of the many attempts made by the human mind to create a cosmos from chaos, attempts which begin in early childhood and continue throughout life. From year to year the mental stage grows larger and more actors

13

join the company, so that soon its director, the intellect, can no longer survey them all at once, for their numbers have become infinite ... To a child, the first actors in this universal theatre, which is at the same time so great and so small, are his mother and father, his brothers, sisters and relatives and all the other people surrounding him in the exterior world. To begin with, he imitates his mother and father and the members of his own family, and then, gradually, his instinct of imitation finds more and more scope. In this way he founds and builds his own dramatic universe." "The origin of drama," Hauptmann says again, "is the self dividing itself into two, three, four and so on ..." And I cannot resist one more quotation of what is to me his most profound remark. "We must distinguish," he says, "between thought in the process of being thought, and thought which has been thought already. It is the first of these which must express itself, thought at the very moment of birth, before the umbilical cord is broken. It is perhaps like the thought of a man born blind, when his eyes are opened to the light for the first time."

This observation, which any dramatist worthy of the name will endorse, is enough in itself to dispose of that type of philosophical drama whose champion I, by some woeful misconception, have at times been taken to be, whereas in fact I have always been its most determined opponent.

Ever since I can remember I have felt the urge to express myself in dramatic form, but I cannot easily translate into words the profound necessity behind this instinct. Yet it is clear to me that it was a vital one, resulting from my comparatively solitary existence as an only child. Looking back, I can still see myself peopling many a dreary walk in the *Plaine Monceau* with imaginary brothers and sisters with whom I could have long conversations, and here we have a perfect example of that divisibility of the self of which Hauptmann speaks.

So then, we can say, that in the beginning the theatre was for me a means of peopling an inner emptiness with a host of presences. Of course my early characters were based on those in plays I had heard or read. Like nearly everyone else, my first desire was to write tragedy, and after that romantic drama, and then I passed on to Ibsenian drama and to the French drama of the end of the XIXth century. As I see it now, this evolution seems like a kind of accommodation, in the optical sense of the word. I mean that I seem to have made a persistent and coherent effort to place my characters where I could grasp them not only most directly, but also and especially from *within*, though, of course, by doing this I inevitably incurred the reproaches of those in whose opinion drama should always seek to escape from realism into a poetic and stylised world. But the real reason why I have always taken such pains to make my characters as like as possible to ourselves, to make them live in the same world and share the same experiences, is because by so doing what may be called the metaphysical design became more clear to me, and because I felt that by substituting symbols or intellectual puppets or even legendary figures for the creatures of flesh and blood whose fate I was trying to determine, I would weaken or betray that design. In this I could hardly be more unlike the classical dramatists, who have always felt compelled to place their tragic action either in the distant past or in some remote spot, such as the Turkey of *Bazajet*. Indeed, I seem always and in every way to have needed the most immediate human realities from which to leap towards the most distant spiritual horizon, towards what I am driven to describe by an obscure and much abused term, the transcendental. Nothing could be more misleading, in some ways, than the images I have been forced to use here. What I have called a leap is more like a groping and anxious approach; and again, in the order of things we are considering, the most distant is also and essentially the nearest, although this nearness is not that of objects which we can stretch out our hands towards and grasp, provided we obey certain well-established rules. It can never be said too clearly that there exists a *near* side to any possible action which is also in a sense its *far* side—though, of course, these figures of speech, which are meant to apply to a spatial world, are here quite inadequate. What I mean is that to the extent that we have no sense of perspective with regard to ourselves or our immediate companions, their very nearness becomes the equivalent of the most impassable distance. This we have all at times experienced with painful intensity, and in it lies the key to the somewhat disconcerting title I have given to these remarks on my plays. It was, in fact, only a few weeks ago, while seeking for some general yet reasonably accurate designation for my dramatic work, that it occurred to me to call it *The Drama of the Soul in Exile*. That this title is open to serious misunderstanding I fully realise, for to Platonists throughout the ages the soul in exile has always been the soul sunk, after some scarcely imaginable spiritual disaster, in the darkness of the world of sense and aspiring to expand once more in some intelligible empyrean. It is more than evident that this theme—than which, perhaps, there is none less dramatic—is entirely absent from my work. For me, the soul in exile is the soul who has become a stranger to itself, who can no longer understand itself, who has lost its way. But, of course, this general theme can take innumerable shapes. It is certainly true that most of my heroes are unaware of what they are and of their own worth, and that they could echo the wish of Claude Lemoyne at the end of *Un Homme de Dieu*—to be known as he really is; yet obviously this uncertainty about ourselves, however tragic, and however painful the light it throws on our condition, could not in itself constitute the basic principle of drama. But we are *not* alone, and only too often our uncertainty takes the virulent form of misunderstanding our own intentions and our own behaviour to other people. Once this happens, our misunderstanding inevitably becomes contagious and tends to spread misery and bewilderment.

We find an example of this in *La Chapelle Ardente* (*The Votive Candle*), which is, I think, one of the most significant plays I have written, and which was a favourite with that great critic, Henry Bidou, whose premature death we so deeply deplore.

The central theme here, as in nearly all my plays, is a living relationship seen at work in a particular situation. Aline Fortier is the wife of a colonel in the regular army, who retired shortly after the 1914–18 war. Her son, Raymond, whom she adored, was killed during a particularly dangerous reconnaissance, which he had asked to undertake while serving as a volunteer in his father's regiment. Aline has always felt inwardly convinced that her husband is really responsible for the death of their son; did he not, by word and example, awaken in the boy a patriotic fervour not quite natural to him? Left to himself, Raymond would never have thought of anticipating his call-up. So Aline has made a cult of the memory of her son and her grief has become inflexible. (Nothing, incidentally, could be less of a pose than this shrivelling of the soul.) Aline is passionately sincere, but all the same everything happens as if she is making it a point of honour to suffer as much as possible, and as if she feels a kind of contempt for those who react against their sorrow and try to live it down. In her eyes a genuine sorrow will never allow itself to be overcome, and, as a result, her scale of values gradually becomes different from that of ordinary people. Her son, Raymond, was engaged to an orphan, Mireille Pradol, who now lives with the Fortiers. A special link has grown up between her and Aline, who in normal circumstances would have been her mother-in-law, and Aline sincerely believes that she has transferred to the girl something of the love which she felt for her own son. The truth is probably far more complex. It is doubtful whether Aline really loves Mireille for herself; she loves her only to the extent that Mireille remains faithful to her lost fiancé, perhaps because she has an obscure feeling that this fidelity in some sense enables him to survive. He is, she thinks, in a way immortalised by the great love he has inspired. Mireille's feeling for Aline is almost impossible to define; it is a kind of admiration mingled with fear. So fascinated is she by the whole-heartedness of Aline's grief that she regards her as a model to be copied, a fact which can only be explained by

Aline's very powerful influence over her, which is all the stronger because she is so alone in the world. But Mireille does not identify herself with that part of herself which tries to model itself on Aline. She is young, with her whole life still to live, whereas for Aline everything is already in the past. So there comes between the two women a basic asymmetry, which for different reasons they try to hide from each other.

How will this situation evolve? An attractive and wealthy young man, Robert Chanteuil, has come to live near the Fortiers' country house. We shall not see him, for his personal characteristics do not affect the situation. From the point of view of the drama, the reactions caused by his presence in the two women and in Colonel Fortier are what matter. Aline, by a kind of infallible instinct, realises at once that he is a danger. She reasons, though this is veiled to her conscious mind, that if Mireille marries Chanteuil, whom she would be quite ready to love if she were—if she could be—left to her own devices, it would be for Aline as if Raymond had died a second time. But obviously Aline would never *consciously* dream of preventing the marriage or of coercing Mireille in any way, and besides, her real desire is for Mireille to refuse to marry Chanteuil of her own accord. She must therefore find Mireille herself an ally against the incipient love which threatens to throw the girl into the arms of this dangerously alive newcomer. Her problem, therefore, is to find, or more precisely to stir up, in Mireille herself an accomplice against this new-born secret Mireille, who is hoping perhaps to rebuild her life. Only, of course, since Aline can never visualise the situation so frankly, she must persuade herself that the new Mireille does not really exist, or in other words that the whole danger she is trying to avert is itself non-existent. (One could not, may I say in passing, find a more vivid illustration of that bad faith of which Jean-Paul Sartre has just given us an incomparable analysis in his book, *L'Etre et le Néant.*)

This situation must inevitably deteriorate, for two reasons.

To begin with, the instinctive attitude of Octave, Aline's husband, is diametrically opposed to her own. True, he is still profoundly unhappy owing to the death of his son, but something in him rises up against Aline's grief, which appears to him morbid and even sacrilegious. Is it only his feelings as a patriotic officer which revolt against a sorrow so unbalanced, so little sublimated by pride? No, there is more than this: his wife's grief is like an accusation aimed at *him*; her whole attitude seems to proclaim *his* responsibility for Raymond's death. Is he not involved to the limit in that infernal game of war and patriotism, which crushes personal feelings and tears apart personal ties, destroying everything that for an emotional being gives its meaning to life? To the extent that Aline has Mireille in tow, she treats her as an ally against Octave. This distresses him, but it also arouses a combative mood and a desire to challenge his wife's influence over the girl, whom he feels to be weak and likely to give in to her. So Mireille becomes the stake in a kind of internecine war between husband and wife, which is made even more bitter by an unforeseen incident.

The Fortiers have a nephew, André Verdet, an invalid with a weak heart, who did not serve in the war. He was Raymond's friend and admired him very much. Aline has so far shown him no more than a somewhat contemptuous pity, but now she and her husband learn, first that the doctors say he cannot live long, and immediately afterwards that he is in love with Mireille.

Their reactions are in line with their inner inclinations and are therefore contradictory. Octave is indignant: how dare this miserable wreck aspire to the hand of a healthy girl like Mireille? André does not know, it is true, that he is incurable, but he must be left no illusions as to his chances with the girl. Aline's reaction is totally different. She has succeeded in persuading herself that Mireille is no longer capable of experiencing real love, and can no longer aspire to anything but a life of self-sacrifice. She is, of course, lying to herself, since in reality she is afraid of Mireille's feelings for Chanteuil,

obscure though they still are. For, I must repeat, Aline in her
heart of hearts does not want Mireille to rebuild a normal life
for herself, although a real censorship, in the Freudian sense,
prevents her being conscious of this. So she substitutes for
the affirmation which she cannot face: "I do not want Mireille
to remake her life," another, which is inoffensive: "I know
that Mireille herself does not want to remake her life, because
she has told me so." Gradually the help she needs from
Mireille becomes clear; she must activate in the girl the
capacity for voluntary self-sacrifice, which, even if latent,
really does exist, but which is being opposed by her natural
instincts. These, then, must be stifled. It is, indeed, a kind of
spiritual infanticide of which Aline is guilty, but her gravest
sin is her refusal to face the fact.

The conclusion of this play does not seem to me always
to have been well understood, at least when performed.
Mireille marries André and watches over his health, which
does not seem to be getting any worse. They do not know real
happiness, but only a pale reflection of it, behind which there
lurks a grim misunderstanding, since André has no idea of
the circumstances which brought about his marriage. But
Aline, who is not in reality a hard woman, but only a creature
tense and highly-strung and, as it were, predestined to sorrow,
is painfully over-anxious about them. Perhaps she is dimly
conscious of her own responsibility and afraid that events
will prove her wrong, for she constantly expresses almost
tactless wishes for their happiness. She is now separated from
her husband, and André, who feels her to be an ally, would
like to persuade her to come and live with him and Mireille.
But, by some indiscreet remarks and particularly by her
excessive distress on hearing that Mireille has had a mis-
carriage, she ruins the precarious equilibrium of their marriage.
For André now glimpses the truth and guesses that Mireille
was in love with Chanteuil, of whose death in a motor
accident Aline tells them with too-obvious precautions; and
Mireille, who, freed by an independent life from Aline's
domination, is now capable of judging her, cries out hysteric-

ally how much she hates her. Aline flies—but in her flight she renews her power, for both André and Mireille fear that she may take her own life. That would of all things be the most terrible, for Aline, dead, would be invincible. She *must* live, and, as the play ends, they call her back. Doubtless she will agree to come and live with them, and this, her final victory, will masquerade as a concession.

What I wanted to bring out in this last act is the kind of fatality which a human being can carry in himself and constantly discharge upon others, even when his intentions are above reproach. We are infinitely more than we are aware of wishing to be and sometimes, strange to say, the apparently most conscious and clear-headed are, in fact, most ignorant of their inner selves.

A little study of this play may help to define certain characteristics of my work. To begin with, in what sense is it a tragedy? Mireille, being a victim, will inevitably arouse sympathy, but if the play is really understood, this sympathy must be reflected on to Aline. For the damage she does is done in spite of herself and mainly because she cannot see herself as she really is. It is no doubt easy to say that her blindness is voluntary, but experience shows how hard it is to draw the line between voluntary blindness and just blindness. Now in a work like *La Chapelle Ardente*, the inner vision lacked by the characters is, as it were, transferred to the audience, in the same way that objects are sometimes illuminated by a ray of light coming from beyond an obscure and non-reflecting area. Tragic pity then, as I see it, differs essentially from the pity aroused in us by the misfortunes of others in real life, for it springs from a profound understanding, such as a higher being might feel for humanity. And the function of the dramatist, as I conceive it, is to lead the spectator to the focal point in himself where his thought can proliferate, not on the abstract level, but on the level of action, and enfold *all* the characters of a play without any decrease in their reality or in their irreducible individuality.

This individuality, on the contrary, is more evident the

more the interlinking relationships by which the characters themselves tend to become enslaved are understood from within. But magic and magic alone can lead the spectator to this vital focal point in himself, which is not merely an ideal observation post but a concentration of his whole being. Indeed, the very idea of drama from which magic has been excluded is self-contradictory and absurd. But what is the essence of this magic? I think we have gone badly astray in imagining it to lie mainly in the exterior, I mean in the extra-human element, in the visual and auditory background. In reality, their importance, when not counterbalanced by an interpretation so perfect as to be truly an incarnation of thought, may become the worst of betrayals, for it may drown the drama in pure spectacle. The converse does not hold, for the two factors are in no way equivalent. In the theatre then, effective magic can reach us only through the interpreters, and is induced by the manner in which they make their presence felt in the consciousness of the spectators, felt more authentically even than that of our daily flesh-and-blood companions. This is not to deny, of course, our direct apprehension of those companions, or even of casual passers-by, as creatures at once infinitely real and infinitely mysterious. Indeed, this impact, it seems to me, made unwittingly by strangers upon the consciousness of the dramatist, is the real seed of dramatic work; work which appears, from this point of view, like the return of something lent him to be transmuted, or, if you will, like an outbreathing in which the vital, having been commuted into spiritual, again becomes vital, with the spiritualised vitality of dramatic creation.

At this point I should like to forestall and answer one or two questions as clearly as I can. The first concerns the relation between a stage character and the person who has stimulated the author to conceive that character. In my own experience the link seems to be remote. I think I can say that people who were, so to speak, at the root of my main works, were so only to the extent that they excited my curiosity; I mean that my imperfect and fragmentary experience of them set going in my mind an imaginative activity in some ways comparable to the swarm of hypotheses generated in the scientific mind by an unusual phenomenon. But there is one great difference between the two; a scientific hypothesis unfolds itself on the plane of pure intellect, whereas in the dramatist a faculty of sympathy is aroused, in which intelligence and sympathy are inextricably mixed.

But does the dramatist see right through his puppet, as a psychoanalyst his patient? Far from it. I even think—paradoxical though it seems—that on the occasions when he best succeeds in expressing himself he is always driven to leave a margin of ambiguity. Moreover, the very fact that this ambiguity cannot altogether be got rid of may be an indication of his success and a proof that he has created an undeniable presence, without which drama is no more than a trivial game of technical skill and scenic effects. It is from this point of view that I should like to consider *Le Chemin de Crête* (*Ariadne*), which is to me the most significant of my plays and the one which best indicates the trend of my work.

Ariadne Varet, whose family belongs to the best Protestant society, has married a childhood friend, Jerome Leprieur. He is a musical critic, but his family has been ruined and he earns scarcely enough to live on. He has always been a weak, highly-strung creature and in his youth he was exposed to abnormal temptations, which he to a certain extent resisted, and from which Ariadne hoped that marriage and a normal sexual life would free him altogether. But soon after their marriage she herself fell ill with a mysterious ailment, which the doctors thought might be tubercular, so she and her husband went to live in the mountains, where she is still leading the life of an invalid when the play begins. Jerome hated life in the mountains, and Ariadne persuaded him to return to Paris without her. There he met Violetta Mazargues, a young violinist, and became her lover. Violetta had already had one liaison with another musician, Serge Franchard, a weak man who was incapable of being of any help to her, and by him she had a little girl, whom she can scarcely afford to bring up. She is anything but a light woman but, although basically upright and generous, it seems to be her fate to sacrifice herself to men devoid of energy or courage, to whom she is tied by a feeling essentially maternal.

Ariadne is eventually pronounced cured by her doctors, but she will not admit this and returns to Paris for no more than short visits. She grows to suspect the liaison between her husband and Violetta, and the play begins when she decides to make Violetta's acquaintance on one of these visits. So, as a means of making contact, she asks Violetta for a few lessons in accompaniment. Here she is, then, at the home of her rival, to whom she shows a strange kindness. Something fascinating and irresistible emanates from her personality. Violetta is on the rack and cannot hide her embarrassment, but Ariadne reassures her tenderly. "Then you've not realised that I know everything?" she asks with devastating sweetness. After this a peculiar intimacy grows up between the two women. But Ariadne makes Violetta promise not to tell Jerome that she knows about their liaison, saying that he would find it intolerable and disaster would inevitably follow. It is her insistence on this which creates our first doubts as to her real intentions. She tells Violetta, of course, that the liaison has done Jerome good and made a normal man of him, and in this she is certainly sincere. But Jerome is surprised and alarmed at the friendship between his wife and his mistress. Doesn't it imply a duplicity on Violetta's part which is foreign to her character? And then everything that takes place suggests that Ariadne has interposed herself between Violetta and himself. The spectator cannot fail to wonder whether this is indeed Ariadne's object and he sees the first glimmerings of suspicion begin to form in Violetta's own mind. At last Jerome, exasperated, decides to get a divorce. Violetta is torn this way and that. Her feelings for Ariadne grow more and more complex; they are compounded of admiration and pity, but also of a growing distrust, for which at times she reproaches herself. How will Ariadne react when she at last induces Violetta to tell her that Jerome seriously

intends to get a divorce? If she is concealing her real intentions, will not this new situation drive her into the open? But,
in fact, she shows little sign of emotion and none of indignation or bitterness. After a moment's silent thought, she seems
to approve of the idea and even to make it her own. But she
says that Violetta must make sure of Jerome's *real* reasons for
wanting to get a divorce and marry her; could not he, by any
chance, be jealous of her influence over Ariadne or simply
of the friendship between the two women? Also, Ariadne
points out, they would be very poor, since neither of them
have any money of their own, and she suggests that to avoid
disaster Violetta must allow her to help them without
Jerome's knowledge. Is this exceptional generosity or
supreme treachery? Violetta is a proud, straightforward
creature and she is horrified at the idea of being entangled in
further duplicity. She can no longer hide her suspicions. Isn't
Ariadne's magnanimity false, she asks her, doesn't it conceal a
deliberate plot? Ariadne gives no direct answer to this
terrible accusation. "I hope from the bottom of my heart,"
she says instead, "that you will never have to regret those
words. Whatever may happen you must remember that I have
forgiven them." May not this ostentatious clemency be her
most subtle means of domination? What is the meaning of
those enigmatic words—*whatever* may happen? Is it a tragic
premonition or, worse even, a threat of suicide? For if
Ariadne died, could any burden be greater for Violetta than
the memory of her forgiveness? What other threat could so
surely and permanently keep her in a state of subjection and
inner humiliation. Is Ariadne counting on this inverted but
permanent vengeance? What does she really think or want?

As a result of her conversation with Ariadne, Violetta
breaks with Jerome, and he, unable to understand why she
will not let him get a divorce and marry her, leaves her re-
sentfully. But Ariadne finds that her own words of forgiveness
are preying upon her own mind, and little by little she begins
to question and criticise herself. A few weeks later she meets
Violetta again, up in the mountains where Violetta has had to

bring her sick child, and she insists on accusing herself to Violetta in Jerome's presence. She is certainly sincere when she admits the partial dishonesty of her charitable behaviour to Violetta, yet how can the girl help seeing that her self-accusation might equally be an act of extreme perfidity, since it fills Jerome, who has not forgiven Violetta for running away from him, with admiration for her nobility? Moreover, its tacit implication—that Violetta has behaved abominably—finally ruins her in the eyes of her former lover. And when Ariadne goes so far as to beg Jerome to forget her and remake his life with Violetta, is she not once more acting with supreme perfidity, since the obvious result will be to strengthen her own ties with her husband? He does, in fact, become infuriated at Violetta's apparent ingratitude to Ariadne, and breaks with her for good. So Ariadne, who appeared to want her own defeat, emerges victorious from this cruel struggle. But, at the point we have reached, the words victory and defeat have lost their meanings, or rather they have exchanged them, since we do not know the ultimate desires of the leading characters. It is true that Ariadne is in despair, but a pessimist may say that only in despair can she accept herself; that, after all, despair itself is her fulfilment.

Some people will no doubt be surprised at my uncertainty about a character whom I myself conceived. "You must surely know where you are in regard to Ariadne," they will say to me, "since you created her." But it is not so easy as that. While writing this play I had far less the feeling of creation than of recognition. I found myself faced with a character so resistant and so distinct from myself that I was forced to give up the ending I had planned because she rejected it. "You can't do that with me," she said, "if you insist I shall disappear." But to the extent that this character resisted me, I am justified in saying that it contains an element which remains to me irreducible. So when I am told: "She is a sick woman; her illness explains all her anomalies," I can only reply: "But isn't her disease, which is obscure even to her doctors, basically of psychic origin? Hasn't she taken refuge in it to hide the spiritual and even carnal failure of her marriage? Doesn't it satisfy her inner need for an exterior and acceptable justification for this failure, instead of herself being its cause?" We all know actual cases where the physical and psychic are just as entangled and impossible to unravel, and I think that a dramatist would be unfaithful to reality in passing judgment on what is beyond our human means of investigation. He must be content to make apparent, and even intelligible, *qua* mystery, that inscrutable something which each of us carries within himself.

And here lies what I consider to be the chief function of the theatre: not to relate the particular to the general or to a law or to an idea, but to awaken or re-awaken in us the consciousness of the infinite which is concealed in the particular. To my mind, in this way alone can the dramatist penetrate to our centre and arrive at that zone of concrete universality which music and metaphysics reach by other convergent ways. But will not such a task drive him to make a more courageous use of transposition and poetic style than I have done? As I have said, I do not think so. I am sure that the desired metaphysical impetus can only come to the spectator from creatures like himself, whose experiences and problems resemble his own.

The two plays I have discussed in detail belong to the group of those which seem to close on a sombre note. This is also true of *Un Homme de Dieu* and *Palais de Sable*. But from others of my plays there springs at times a flash of dazzling light. Jacques Chardonneau, for instance, wrote to me of *Le Monde Cassé* that the theatre was perhaps the best of all vehicles for the truths of illumination, and he is, I believe, entirely right. That the truths which are demonstrable and susceptible to proof cannot have the freedom of the stage emerges from all I have been saying, but it is quite otherwise for those sudden flashes which now and then light up the vast and undulating landscape of our lives, a landscape through which we may have travelled for years, seeing no more than a yard or two ahead, but whose vistas at such

moments take instant shape before our inner eye. The alterna-
tion of sombre and illuminated plays was, of course, quite
unintentional. There is in it a vital rhythm which was im-
posed on me, like that of sleep and waking. But to the mature
thinker it is clear that the two types of play are on different
planes, and that if the illumination is not a mirage it must
spread into the world of the sombre plays.

I should now like to glance at *L'Iconoclaste* and *Le Monde
Cassé*. In *L'Iconoclaste*, Abel Renaudier loved Viviane, the
wife of his friend, Jacques Delorne, passionately though
platonically, but, believing her to be deeply in love with her
husband, he hid this from her. He made himself believe her
husband, Jacques, to be worthy of her and he accepted the
situation, but he grew to look upon Jacques as his debtor for
having done so. Viviane died prematurely, and Abel, while
travelling in Russia, heard that Jacques had married again.
As Aline just now identified herself with Raymond, but also
unconsciously belittled his character in retrospect, Abel from
now on identifies himself with the dead Viviane and seeks to
take vengeance on Jacques. This he does by arousing in him
suspicions about Viviane's past fidelity and by conveying
through his peculiar attitude that he himself has been her
lover. He thus arrogates to himself a right which neither he,
nor any man, may claim: the right to set himself up as an
avenger.

And nothing could in reality be less pure than his motive.
He behaves as if Jacques were his debtor, but he is, in fact, all
the time entirely mistaken about both the present and the
past situations. He ultimately learns that Viviane, though—
perhaps out of pride—she had given no sign, had in fact
returned his love, and also that Jacques' second marriage is in
no way what he thought it was. Jacques has never ceased to
adore Viviane. He all but committed suicide at her death and
only lived on because he believed himself to be aware of a
permanent psychic link between her and himself. She is, he
feels, continually at his side, and it was she, he is sure, who
advised him to marry Madeleine Chazot. Madeleine also

believes that Jacques married her at Viviane's wish, and she
accepts this strange situation with more than renunciation.
To her fine and generous temperament the important thing
is Jacques' happiness, and, if this be its price, that price must
be paid. But Abel, by making Jacques doubt Viviane's past
fidelity, unwittingly destroys the basis of his present existence,
for Jacques begins to wonder whether *all* his beliefs are not
illusory. Abel, horrified, realises too late the harm he has
done and tries by a new lie, this time a charitable one, to
revive the faith by which his friend has lived. Thus the rôles
are reversed. Abel now does all in his power to reassure
Jacques, though he has not the courage—he does not even
feel he has the right *vis-à-vis* the dead Viviane—to follow
this course to the end. So at last he confesses that he has invented a conversation which, in fact, never took place. Jacques'
world collapses under him, and he now feels that his second
marriage has been brought about by a trick of nature and that
he has betrayed his dead wife. Yet it is not on his despair that
the curtain falls. Abel, who has realised his own mistake,
suddenly sees the whole tragedy in its true light. He becomes
aware that, in a sense infinitely surpassing the still too
physical and crude image of her in Jacques' mind, Viviane's
presence remains with them. She is still there to draw them
together once more, but only by recognising this mystery
can they create the harmony in which the soul can at last
possess itself. "You could never," says Abel to Jacques,
"be satisfied for long in a world deserted by mystery. . . .
Life, without mystery, would be stifling." But the mystery
must be approached with humility. As Abel says again:
"Life itself will confound the iconoclasts and the self-
appointed judges. . . . Life, or He who is beyond words."
And now at last Jacques too—though as yet confusedly—
feels awakening like music in his soul the consciousness of
this fruitful peace.

I think that the style of this play, which was written many
years ago, is open to criticism, but to me nothing in my
dramatic work is more essential than its ending, which

anticipates conclusions that I reached much later, after my conversion to Catholicism, by a philosophic and religious route.

It will be noticed that in these plays the dead play a part at least as active as the living. This is not merely by chance. Their rôle is particularly fundamental because often the action, as in *Rosmersholm* and *The Wild Duck*, is accompanied by a progressively deeper delving into the past lives of the chief characters. At first this past is no more than an opaque factor, but eventually there filters through it a light of eternity in which the destiny of the characters adjusts itself and reveals its organic unity. For this reason the plays are seldom intelligible before the ending; they can almost be said to construct themselves in reverse. The ending is in any case always a judgment, for it decides whether or not the work *is*, and gives it its value as a work. If it weakens the play falls to pieces; it becomes, not an achievement, but an attempt. Indeed, as a critic I have come to the conclusion that a play can only be judged by its last act. This is due both to the form and the intrinsic nature of dramatic architecture, for a play with a disappointing ending leaves only the memory of an entertainment, and if it is no more than that it falls short of the spiritual goal which I believe it ought to have.

In *Le Monde Cassé* I may have pushed this principle too far. My starting point is here, as almost always, the poignant awareness of a certain relation between two characters, Laurent Chesney and his wife, Christiane. She is a gay and brilliant creature, intelligent and much admired, and lives a whirlwind life. Her husband, a civil servant, is, in contrast, dull and silent, and his wife's gay life and popularity are clearly a constant source of irritation to him. On what basis does this ill-assorted marriage rest, and why does Christiane remain so obstinately faithful to a man whom she cannot possibly love? We become aware, little by little, that before their marriage she warned him that she did not love him and that she has, in a sense, married him from despair, for the man she really loved had told her, at the moment she was about to confess her feelings for him, that he intended to become a Benedictine monk. So her marriage was a kind of spiritual suicide. But she has a loyal nature and has always been conscious of having treated Laurent badly. She gradually realises too, that he really is humiliated by her superiority to him and by the fact that it is she, not he, who receives all the notice and admiration. So she comes to the conclusion that only her abasement can restore his self-respect and she therefore gives him to understand that she has been humiliated by a Russian composer, with whom she has fallen in love and who has spurned her. This lie does to some extent renew in Laurent the feeling of superiority which he needs to prevent an inner withering. But his very revival leads Christiane to despise him, and in disgust—she is essentially impulsive—she throws herself into the arms of a young admirer. She might even have left her husband and child and gone away with him, but she learns by chance that the man she had really loved, the Benedictine she has never forgotten, had, while cloistered in his cell, become aware by some supernatural intuition of her love for him and had prayed for her. He has since died, but his sister, a childhood friend of Christiane's, finds some notes among his papers which tell the whole story. So she comes to Christiane at the decisive moment, like a messenger from beyond, and renews in her the consciousness of spiritual communion and unfailing truth.

This ending has been criticised as too improbable. I do not know its effect on an audience, for it has never been produced, but what I wanted to bring out is how the illumination—in itself a grace—emanating from a sanctified personality can retrospectively throw light on the groping efforts of Christiane, whose so-far-unpredictable course we have been following. For Christiane discovers that her soul has never informed her outward life. Her charity has been false and has only led her to falsehood, and her love, false too, would have led her to ruin. But now she can tell Laurent the whole truth and try to lead him with her into this new and miraculous world. "We are not alone," she tells him, "No one is alone.

. . . There is a communion of sinners as well as a communion of saints." And Laurent, if only for a moment—but it is a decisive one—is stirred out of his apathy by Christiane's revelations. He responds to her intuitive vision and his withered soul expands in a light he had never before imagined. Of course I cannot guarantee what will happen to these two in the future. There is little reason to hope that they can remain on so high a spiritual level, but the ending of the play is none the less *real* because it marks the acme of their two destinies, the point in their lives at which they both understand and rise above themselves.

In my later plays, which followed *Le Chemin de Crête*, particularly in *Le Dard*, *L'Émissaire*, *Le Signe de la Croix*, *La Fin des Temps* and *Rome n'est plus dans Rome*, the horizon widens; in their case the basic theme, which was already indicated in *Le Monde Cassé*, is the suffering of the contemporary world. Yet they are in no way works for a social theatre, as it was conceived at the end of the nineteenth century by naturalistic writers such as Brieux or even Gerhardt Hauptmann, for this problem lies in the inner world of the human soul. Even the word problem is hardly the right one here, for where there cannot be a solution there cannot, in exact parlance, be a problem. In any case no solution is ever more than a procedure invented by the human spirit to cope with a particular difficulty; but here we are beyond all technique and faced with an ever-deepening chasm which man, left solely to his own resources, is not only incapable of crossing but even of measuring.

What, in such a situation, is the function of the dramatist? It is certainly not to mount into a pulpit; indeed, each time he tries to preach he betrays his mission. His task is rather to place himself at the very heart of human reality, in all its poignancy and intimacy. He must, it seems to me, link himself magnetically to the strands of our most secret agonies and our most secret hopes; and the accent with which he expresses feelings we hardly dare admit even to ourselves, must be strong enough and *magical* enough to transfigure our interior landscape and illuminate it in a flash with a light that seems to come from beyond. That, for instance, is what I tried to do at the end of *Le Dard* and *L'Émissaire*, though, of course, it was not my conscious aim at the time. I only realised it after the plays had been written. But consideration of my plays in the light of such an aim makes it clear why it is invariably their last acts which are truly decisive; why the very existence of the work and its effect upon the spectator is determined in and by the last act. I am profoundly convinced that a play which weakens at the end condemns itself to non-existence instead of fulfilment.

It is when viewed in this perspective that the meaning of one of my last dramatic works, *La Fin des Temps*, which has recently been given on the Third Programme of the B.B.C., becomes apparent. Its immediate predecessors seemed already to be tending towards the idea of the imminence, either of a universal catastrophe or of some ineffable event. In *La Fin des Temps* this idea becomes conscious; it is, indeed, very much in the minds of the protagonists, Laurence and Hervé, themselves. But, by a strange paradox, this idea, which might at first sight seem to be their salvation, is here a cause of illusion and even, perhaps, of death. Laurence, because of her ardent desire to be of service in the new world which is coming to birth, fails in what are her most lowly and possibly also her most absolute duties. Here we have a reminder of the basic truth that our daily life must inevitably be passed in an environment which we have not chosen for ourselves, but which we have to accept and transfigure. We must be on our guard against the mirages of the prophetic consciousness, for the vocation of prophet is an exceptional one and can only be submitted to. Let us never believe too lightly that we ought to sacrifice the duties of our situation in life to higher obligations, which may be no more than phantoms born of our own boredom or our own pride.

I do not know whether I shall write any more for the theatre; but it seems to me today—and it is on this note that I should like to close—that the key-note of my dramatic work is ethical rather than religious. In the end it is "good-will" in the Gospel rather than the Kantian sense which is held up for admiration; the will to remain faithful to an interior light, which is too often intercepted by a coalition of powerful forces born of our own vanity.

GABRIEL MARCEL

A MAN OF GOD

English Version
by MARJORIE GABAIN

OF

UN HOMME DE DIEU

a Play in Four Acts
by GABRIEL MARCEL

CHARACTERS

CLAUDE LEMOYNE   Pastor

EDMEE LEMOYNE   His Wife

MADAME LEMOYNE   His Mother

DR FRANCIS LEMOYNE   His Brother

OSMONDE LEMOYNE   Edmée's Daughter

MEGAL

MICHEL SANDIER

FRED JUNOD

LITTLE RENE

MADEMOISELLE AUBONNEAU

FELICIE

The time is mid-December and the scene is set in Paris

ACT ONE

The Lemoyne's drawing-room. Comfortless, common-place furniture. On the walls Burnand's Parables and a reproduction of the Sistine Madonna. MEGAL *is discovered standing, in his overcoat.* OSMONDE *enters.*

MEGAL: Forgive me, Mademoiselle, I didn't realise you were still at table. I told the maid not to disturb you.

OSMONDE: It's quite all right. Sunday dinner is usually late because there are always people who want to see my father after church. We had finished, anyway. Do sit down. [*A pause*]

MEGAL: I believe you said something about taking the children out for a walk this afternoon. Can you really spare the time? I don't want to take advantage of your kindness.

OSMONDE: You're doing nothing of the kind. I am quite free this afternoon.

MEGAL: I don't know how to thank you. I didn't know what I was going to do with them. It's the maid's day out and I have to go to Equinay hospital.

OSMONDE: How is Madame Mégal?

MEGAL: Much the same. You know, with that sort of illness . . . if you can call it an illness . . .

OSMONDE: Does she suffer?

MEGAL: It's impossible to say. Of course, she's always complaining, but the doctors tell me that it is largely induced by auto-suggestion.

OSMONDE: Really?

MEGAL: Yes, and do you know, that's the one thing that reminds me of her as I knew her; otherwise she has grown

37

into a completely different person. [*Speaking lower*] If you can say that she *is* a person, now. [*A pause. Their eyes meet.* OSMONDE *looks away quickly.*]

OSMONDE: Did Suzanne tell you? At the Sunday School class this morning, she got everything right.

MEGAL: Did she really? That's good.

OSMONDE: And I'm very pleased with Yvonne as well.

MEGAL: They're good little things. Where will you take them this afternoon?

OSMONDE: I'm not quite sure.

MEGAL: Look here, if I'm not too late coming back we might perhaps meet by the Park, as we did a fortnight ago, do you remember?

OSMONDE: [*Evasively*] Well, yes . . . perhaps. We shall see when the time comes. [*A pause*]

MEGAL: [*Looking at her more closely*] Your hair looks very nice. It suits you to have it done like that. [*A pause*]

Enter EDMEE, CLAUDE, *and* MADAME LEMOYNE.

EDMEE: [*To* MEGAL, *who has risen to his feet*] No, no, please don't go. Mother, [*To* MME. LEMOYNE] this is Monsieur Mégal, who lives in the flat above. He is the father of the two little girls we met on the stairs yesterday.

MME. LEMOYNE: How do you do? I am delighted to meet you.

CLAUDE: Will you have a cup of coffee?

MEGAL: No, thanks very much, I can't stay. I have an appointment out of town this afternoon. I was just telling Mademoiselle Osmonde how grateful I am for all she has done for my two little girls. She came up last night to help them with their lessons, and now she's going to take them out for a walk.

EDMEE: [*Drily*] But why shouldn't she, Monsieur Mégal? It's perfectly natural.

MEGAL: I'm afraid I can't quite agree with you there. No, don't trouble to see me out, please. Goodbye, Sir.

CLAUDE: Goodbye.

MEGAL: Goodbye Madame, Mademoiselle. [*He bows and goes out*]

MME. LEMOYNE: He seems a nice fellow.

EDMEE: We know absolutely nothing about him.

MME. LEMOYNE: He looks you straight in the eyes and he has a very nice mouth. The lines show a great deal of kindness.

OSMONDE: Some coffee, Granny?

MME. LEMOYNE: Just half a cup, my dear. Your Uncle Francis would scold me. There . . . that's enough.

CLAUDE: By the way, why didn't Francis come to lunch, Mother?

MME. LEMOYNE: He had to see a patient some way out of Paris. But he's coming to fetch me. [*Lowering her voice, to* CLAUDE] I think he has something to tell you.

EDMEE: What did you say?

MME. LEMOYNE: I said Francis was coming to fetch me.

EDMEE: We never see him nowadays. [*To* CLAUDE] Your brother hasn't been here more than once or twice since the summer holidays.

MME. LEMOYNE: You must remember he's terribly busy. I'm beginning to realise *how* busy since I've been staying with him. There's his work at the Hospital, his private patients to be seen, his colleagues to meet, reports to be written for the Academy of Science—I don't know how he stands the strain. [*To* CLAUDE] Just like you, my dear boy. Not that I would ever blame you for doing your duty, and more than your duty, as your dear father used to say. But this parish does mean a tremendous amount of work. Do you find time to take enough exercise? Edmée, you must keep your eye on him.

EDMEE: We're all in excellent health, Mother.

MME. LEMOYNE: And then life in Paris is exhausting in itself . . . compared to Lausanne. Your coffee is very good, Edmée, what brand is it?

EDMEE: I'm afraid I can't tell you. I get it at the little grocer's across the road. Will you excuse me, Mother, I must find a book for my reading circle at the Girl's Club. [*She kneels down in front of a low bookshelf*]

MME. LEMOYNE: Now about the young man from upstairs, Osmonde, do you take charge of these little girls regularly? It's very good of you.

OSMONDE: I look after them now and again.

MME. LEMOYNE: What about their mother?

OSMONDE: She's in an asylum.

MME. LEMOYNE: How dreadful!

EDMEE: I'm rather surprised that you can spare the time this afternoon. It's only a fortnight to Christmas and you have a great deal to do before then.

OSMONDE: Not at all, I'm well ahead this year.

EDMEE: But you've hardly begun the present you're making for your godmother.

MME. LEMOYNE: It's sad to think that I shan't see your Christmas tree, but Henri and Loulette are absolutely counting on having me back. It would quite break their hearts if I were not with them. That's the worst of being such a united family!

EDMEE: Osmond, do you remember *The Little Orphan of the Priory?*

OSMONDE: Show me. [EDMEE *goes on turning the pages*]

MME. LEMOYNE: I remember it, it's charming, like so many of the books translated from the English.

EDMEE: It looks to me frightfully sentimental, and these Club girls are ready to weep over anything.

CLAUDE: Well—the main thing is to get them interested, isn't it?

EDMEE: Yes, but not at any price.

MME. LEMOYNE: A little romance in a story won't do them any harm, will it? [*To* OSMONDE] What do you think, my dear?

OSMONDE: [*Who has risen*] I've no opinion on the subject.

EDMEE: Don't forget that Mademoiselle Gentil is expecting you to read aloud to her at five.

OSMONDE: [*Irritably*] Oh, all right, Mother.

EDMEE: It's all very well to take on fresh responsibilities, but . . .

OSMONDE: Goodbye, Granny. What are you doing this afternoon, Father?

CLAUDE: I've one or two letters to write and I must prepare a funeral address for tomorrow.

EDMEE: The Simonin boy?

MME. LEMOYNE: You're marvellous, Edmée, you never forget anything.

OSMONDE: [*Bitterly*] No, Mother never forgets anything. [*She goes out*]

MME. LEMOYNE: Dear child, she seems a little bit nervy.

CLAUDE: Perhaps she feels that we don't trust her.

EDMEE: I'm quite prepared to trust her, but in spite of her quiet ways, Osmonde is lacking in self-control. I've noticed that more and more lately.

CLAUDE: I wonder if noticing people's faults so much does not make one exaggerate them. Don't you think so, Mother?

EDMEE: Then one should shut one's eyes to them?

CLAUDE: I don't say that. But it's by the way you treat people that . . .

EDMEE: I know that theory, and I know what it can lead to.

MME. LEMOYNE: Well, I'm perfectly satisfied with my grand-daughter . . . You know, Claude, they are organising Holiday Courses at Lausanne, with lectures and excursions.

CLAUDE: Oh, yes, I know what you are going to suggest.

MME. LEMOYNE: Well, of course . . .

CLAUDE: But I've no wish to part with my little daughter.

EDMEE: We'll talk about it another time. [*To* CLAUDE] Claude, what are you going to say in your letter to Monsieur Junod? [*To* MME. LEMOYNE] The Pastor at Chaux de Fonds has asked us if we know of a Pension for his son. He's coming here to work for his thesis in Theology. You know him—Fred, they call him.

CLAUDE: If you think we can decently offer him the little room . . .

EDMEE: It should be perfectly comfortable for a young man. Don't you think so, Mother?

MME. LEMOYNE: I should have been very happy there myself if Francis had not insisted on my staying with him.

CLAUDE: Very well, then. I'll write and suggest it. [*He goes out*]

MME. LEMOYNE: Fred is a very young man, Edmée. You don't think that perhaps Osmonde . . .

EDMEE: He's a perfect ninny, not at all likely to appeal to Osmonde. No, that's not what I am worried about.

MME. LEMOYNE: You mean there's something else that *is* worrying you.

EDMEE: There is and there isn't. Now, this young man who made such an impression on you just now.

MME. LEMOYNE: Don't exaggerate, my dear.

EDMEE: Well, I've been keeping my eyes open, and I shouldn't be at all surprised if he were quietly turning the girl's head.

MME. LEMOYNE [*Scandalised*] Really, Edmée!

EDMEE: Osmonde is not particularly fond of children. Her Sunday School class has always been rather an effort, so you must agree that her sudden concern for these two little girls is rather surprising.

MME. LEMOYNE: Osmonde is like her father—completely selfless. I mean that with his example constantly before her it is not in the least surprising that she should have felt sorry for those poor children. And then you know, Edmée, in life [*speaking rather solemnly*] one must always trust people.

EDMEE: Indeed?

MME. LEMOYNE: Always, and in spite of everything.

EDMEE: What do you expect me to say to that?

MME. LEMOYNE: In the course of my life, Edmée, I have come up against some very ugly things. Well, in spite of that . . .

EDMEE: [*Her voice trembling*] What are you alluding to?

Mme. Lemoyne: [*Pulling herself up*] Oh, it's ancient history now.

Edmee: Ancient history?

Mme. Lemoyne: And yet at the time things were pretty desperate.

Edmee: Considering it upset you so terribly, it's strange that Claude should never have mentioned this incident in my presence, don't you agree? It must have been a secret. A secret . . . that was not his. [Madame Lemoyne *makes an evasive gesture*]

Mme. Lemoyne: [*Changing the subject*] Of course, if this is causing you anxiety . . . [Mme. Lemoyne *looks up indicating the flat above*]

Edmee: [*After looking at her questioningly*] Oh, I see, you're talking about Osmonde again. I hadn't followed. Anxiety is putting it rather strongly. I'm forewarned, that's all.

Mme. Lemoyne: Osmonde is so like her father.

Edmee: You think so?

Mme. Lemoyne: In character, at any rate.

Edmee: [*Ambiguously*] Oh yes.

Mme. Lemoyne: As my poor husband used to say, their souls speak the same language.

Edmee: I have never had the privilege of listening to my daughter's soul. [*A pause*]

Mme. Lemoyne: But if Claude shared your anxiety in this matter he would surely have let me know . . .

Edmee: Does Claude tell you everything?

Mme. Lemoyne: Everything he has the right to tell me.

Edmee: Yes, of course. I have only to see the volumes he sends to you every week. . . .

Mme. Lemoyne: You've no idea what that correspondence of ours has meant to me. I've been re-reading Claude's old letters. Some of them are so beautiful, so moving, that I nearly copied out some passages for you. [*A short pause*]

Edmee: What is the date of those letters?

Mme. Lemoyne: They were written during the first years of your marriage.

EDMEE: And you say they are moving.

MME. LEMOYNE: At that period, Claude was going through a very painful spiritual crisis. You know that for a time he even thought of giving up the ministry?

EDMEE: What?

MME. LEMOYNE: Do you mean to say you knew nothing about it?

EDMEE: Nothing. We didn't tell each other everything when we were first married. But I must ask you again to give me the exact date of those letters. Was it, say, before 1900?

MME. LEMOYNE: Yes, they all came before 1900. Why do you ask?

EDMEE: Mother, it's no good pretending. Why, only a minute ago you gave yourself away. . . . hush.

CLAUDE *enters*.

CLAUDE: Do you remember the Junods' address? I can't find the letter anywhere. Are they still in the Rue Karl Marx?

MME. LEMOYNE: I'm afraid I've lost touch with them. They've gone completely Left Wing, like everyone else in Chaux de Fonds. Your father was horrified to see it coming.

EDMEE: I don't understand your not finding that letter. I put it in the "unanswered" file in the private correspondence drawer this morning.

CLAUDE: [*Half in mockery*] Oh, I see, the *un*answered file. . . .

EDMEE: Really, Claude, I've told you over and over again we must have method in this house.

CLAUDE: Well, method carried to that point drives me to madness! I'll finish the letter, then, and I'll come back.

MME. LEMOYNE: Yes, dear. [CLAUDE *goes out*]

EDMEE: Now, about this spiritual crisis. Claude is not the man to go through certain kinds of anguish. Everything is clear and simple to him. Thank God it is, otherwise I don't know what would have become of me.

MME. LEMOYNE: We all owe him a great debt.

EDMEE: I'm not speaking of gratitude. You don't thank a person for being what they are. [*Speaking with great intensity*] Then you're quite sure it was before 1900?

MME. LEMOYNE: Yes, because after that date he seems to have felt more settled; as though a light had broken through.

EDMEE: A light?

MME. LEMOYNE: Yes, the light that only shines when the night is at its darkest. [*A pause*] Why are you laughing?

EDMEE: [*In a hollow voice*] Wonderful things, promises!

MME. LEMOYNE: What promises?

EDMEE: He promised me never to tell you.

MME. LEMOYNE: Oh, but Edmée!

EDMEE: Oh, it's no good trying to deceive me. That secret ... our secret ... he went and ... oh, it was a low-down trick.

MME. LEMOYNE: How dare you talk of him like that? You dare to insult Claude?

Enter CLAUDE.

CLAUDE: I've written the letter. If you're going out, my dear, you might post it for me.

EDMEE: I don't think it would go, it's Sunday. Besides, there's no particular hurry. Well, yes, give it to me all the same. What time is it? [*An unguarded gesture reveals her inner agitation*]

CLAUDE: What's the matter, Edmée?

EDMEE: Nothing ... Nothing at all.

CLAUDE: Mother?

EDMEE: Will you be in when I come back?

CLAUDE: Francis is coming, I believe, so I'll wait and see him.

EDMEE: Yes, but it's you that I ... I [*Speaking lower*] I must see you alone. I'll arrange things up at the Girl's Club. Someone else can easily take my place.

MME. LEMOYNE: Well, I shall be gone when you come back, Edmée.

EDMEE: Then ... goodbye, Mother. [*She goes out*]

CLAUDE: What has happened?

MME. LEMOYNE: Oh, Claude, I've done a terribly stupid thing. I don't know what made me. [*She is on the verge of tears*] Though really it's a wonder it didn't happen long ago. Edmée has just discovered that you told me everything.

CLAUDE: [*After a short pause*] I'm glad. Again and again I've reproached myself for having lied to her. It has weighed on me terribly. If it hadn't been for a sort of vague fear of what might happen, I would have confessed to her years ago.

MME. LEMOYNE: What a word.

CLAUDE: I had promised to say nothing to you.

MME. LEMOYNE: Because she made you. What right had she to impose secrecy on you?

CLAUDE: That is not the point. I had promised.

MME. LEMOYNE: But it is the point. Don't you remember? She threatened to run away, perhaps even to do away with herself . . . Very well, then, the promises you made to a sick woman . . .

CLAUDE: That makes no difference. Later on, when she had recovered, when I had nursed her back to sanity, I ought to have told her. She would have understood: you yourself are always saying that one must trust people. When I made that promise I meant to keep it. And then, one day . . . God knows why . . . I wasn't feeling more lonely than usual . . . I wrote and told you everything.

MME. LEMOYNE: There's no call for you to excuse or explain what you did. And anyhow, Claude, it's all so long ago.

CLAUDE: I treated her like a child.

MME. LEMOYNE: And besides, Claude, since then . . .

CLAUDE: When she went out just now she looked at me. I know that look, Mother. I may have lost in a moment all the ground I had won with such difficulty.

MME. LEMOYNE: Through my fault.

CLAUDE: No, through mine alone. I am the only one who is guilty. When she comes back I shall ask her to forgive me.

MME. LEMOYNE: You mean to say you will humiliate your-self to a woman who . . . Well, as far as I am concerned I can never forgive her.

CLAUDE: *You* forgive her? The word has no meaning except between her and me.

MME. LEMOYNE: She doesn't deserve a man like you.

CLAUDE: Yes, I forgave her. And I shall never forget what that did for me, the inner peace it brought, the sense of a Power working with me and not instead of me, strengthening my will but not supplanting it. Since that day I've seen my way clear. Before I was groping in the dark . . . The test, Mother, the test. Before those terrible months the word sounded hollow to me. But after what I went through . . .

MME. LEMOYNE: And she not even aware of it . . .

CLAUDE: Ah, but that's what *made* it a test—that she didn't understand. I was alone . . . alone with God Himself. And then, gradually, I felt her trust in me coming back. The way she looked at me when she thought I was not noticing. The dumb appeal in her eyes. It was as though I were helping something to live . . . something very frail, that might easily have died. At first, when I came home in the evening, I was always prepared to find that she had left the house and gone to him. I'm sure that for a long time she was contemplating this. But something stood between them; some force held them apart. And then one day, quite suddenly, I knew that it was over, that she was no longer thinking about him, that we had won. You mustn't cry, Mother, I ought not to have stirred up these memories.

MME. LEMOYNE: She's going to hurt you again.

CLAUDE: Not now. We couldn't hurt each other any more. In the old days, perhaps, before we had learned to suffer. But since then each has shared the other's sorrow, each has borne the other's cross. We are richer than we were before. Richer, yes, and better.

MME. LEMOYNE: [*Wiping her eyes*] You put it all so beauti-fully.

CLAUDE: I heard the bell ring twice. It must be Francis. Excuse me a minute, the maid is out, I'll have to let him in. [*He goes out*]

MME. LEMOYNE: [*Alone, to herself*] Too good, too generous.

Enter CLAUDE *and* FRANCIS

CLAUDE: What happened to you, Francis? You were supposed to have lunch with us.

FRANCIS: I had to see a patient out at Jouy-en-Josas. I only got back at two.

MME. LEMOYNE: When did you have lunch?

FRANCIS: At a snack-bar, half an hour ago. Well, how are you, old man? Do you know, I've just been seeing someone who was talking about you. He said they had spoken very highly of you at the Church Sessions. It seems you have fairly woken the people up here and they think the world of you.

MME. LEMOYNE: Why do you never come and hear him preach?

FRANCIS: Well, you know I'm not much of a church-goer. [*To* CLAUDE] Did Mother warn you that I had something to tell you?

CLAUDE: Yes, but I've no idea what it is.

FRANCIS: Now listen, Mother. As I told you, you can stay with us if you like, but I shall have to discuss rather a painful subject with Claude and I don't want to upset you unnecessarily.

MME. LEMOYNE: If I'm not in the way, I'd rather stay.

FRANCIS: It's about . . . Michel Sandier.

CLAUDE: Oh! [MADAME LEMOYNE *reacts*]

FRANCIS: Michel Sandier came to me as a patient a little time ago.

MME. LEMOYNE: How dare he!

FRANCIS: Why shouldn't he? He reads the medical journals and had found out that I was doing research on the disease from which he is suffering.

CLAUDE: Oh, then he's got . . .

FRANCIS: [*Lowering his voice*] Yes, and in our present state of knowledge he can't be cured. Besides, he had a special reason for wanting to see me.

MME. LEMOYNE: Indeed!

FRANCIS: Now, Mother, Claude is keeping perfectly calm.

MME. LEMOYNE: Much too calm. It's enough for me to hear that scoundrel's name . . .

FRANCIS: Michel Sandier has only a short time left to live. He knows that he is doomed. In fact, I was very much impressed with the way he is facing the situation. He is absolutely calm and clear-headed.

MME. LEMOYNE: Probably a pose.

CLAUDE: Mother!

FRANCIS: I asked him no details about the life he has been leading for the last few years, but, of course, it is not unconnected with his present state of health.

CLAUDE: Well?

FRANCIS: He seems to have been going back over his past life, and . . .

CLAUDE: Is it about Osmonde?

FRANCIS: Yes.

MME. LEMOYNE: You don't mean to say that you . . .

FRANCIS: He was very guarded at first, but I soon saw what he was driving at. He mentioned casually that he used to know you and had once heard you preach somewhere or other.

CLAUDE: Did he want news of Edmée?

FRANCIS: He simply asked me whether my sister-in-law was well. You see, it was very difficult for him to say much more because he had no reason for assuming that I knew what had happened twenty years ago. I could feel the poor fellow's embarrassment. I could see him struggling with the questions which were on the tip of his tongue. Can you blame me if I tried to help him out?

MME. LEMOYNE: Francis, how could you?

FRANCIS: I simply said, "Yes, I do seem to remember meeting you at Saint-Loup de Talvas when my brother was

Pastor there." Nothing more. Curious the power of a name. He turned quite pale and was silent for a moment. Then, with his eyes lowered like this he said, "Yes, I had a house at Saint-Loup." And, still acting my part, I exclaimed, "Why, of course, I remember, a big house that stood above the village. Have you still got it?" He made no answer and we were silent again. I had finished examining him, of course, and we were both standing in the middle of the room. I took a step towards the door, but he didn't move, so I asked him if there was anything more that he wanted to know. He said "yes" almost inaudibly—there was—and suddenly he seized my hands and peered into my face in a desperate effort to find out what I knew. Then he said "Have you really no idea what I want to ask you?" What was I to answer? I didn't want to prolong this pitiful farce with a dying man.

MME. LEMOYNE: I'm sure he is not as ill as you make out.

FRANCIS: He has only a few months to live and he knows it.

CLAUDE: What happened then?

FRANCIS: I simply told him that I knew everything . . . [*A pause*] Claude must do what he thinks best; he is entirely free. I personally could not have acted otherwise.

CLAUDE: [*To* FRANCIS] You were perfectly right.

MME. LEMOYNE: But you were supposed not to know anything. What you did was a breach of faith towards me.

CLAUDE: That's sheer hypocrisy!

FRANCIS: To cut a long story short—he wants to see his daughter before dying.

MME. LEMOYNE: But what right has he to the child?

FRANCIS: That is another question.

MME. LEMOYNE: It's the only one—and what's more, you had no right to take this message from him.

CLAUDE: Mother, you talk too much about people having the right and not having the right.

MME. LEMOYNE: You know what your brother is like—far too good, far too generous. I was telling him so just now.

FRANCIS: But Claude hasn't spoken yet.

MME. LEMOYNE: Oh, I know my Claude.

FRANCIS: We mustn't try to influence him one way or the other.

MME. LEMOYNE: No one can stop me from giving my opinion.

FRANCIS: But to what purpose?

MME. LEMOYNE: My considered opinion.

FRANCIS: No one can decide for him.

MME. LEMOYNE: His mother can. How can this man hope to see his daughter? He surely doesn't expect us to tell the darling child . . .

CLAUDE: He can call here and see Osmonde, like anyone else.

MME. LEMOYNE: You cannot allow that man into your house. It would be scandalous, it would be immoral. . . . Well, Francis?

FRANCIS: I didn't say anything.

CLAUDE: Mother, I forgave.

MME. LEMOYNE: Forgave her, perhaps.

CLAUDE: Her, most certainly.

MME. LEMOYNE: But you have not forgiven him.

CLAUDE: That is because circumstances have not yet challenged me to do so.

MME. LEMOYNE: If he hadn't the good fortune to be ill . . .

FRANCIS: Oh, Mother!

MME. LEMOYNE: And you think he'll be satisfied with just calling to see Osmonde? Heaven knows what further claims he may make.

CLAUDE: This is a test that has been visited upon me and from now on I must accept all that it brings with it.

FRANCIS: I'm not with you there, Claude. You don't want to be helplessly caught up in this. You must feel free to act as you wish.

CLAUDE: Look here, I can't stand any more of this. I cannot go on discussing it without Edmée.

FRANCIS: And if you tell her, my dear boy, you'll be running a hell of a risk. You'll have to watch your step. In my opinion this is a case where you—and you only—can and must decide.

CLAUDE: I don't agree.

FRANCIS: Don't misunderstand me, Claude. I don't think for a moment that when she sees the poor fellow she will feel the least shadow of any . . . what shall I say? . . .

CLAUDE: Francis!

FRANCIS: But she may feel horror, disgust; think how that would react on a temperament like hers. I'm sorry, old man, but you know as well as I do that your wife is not exactly what one would call a balanced nature and yet, there you go, calmly preparing to expose her to a shock like this.

CLAUDE: [Sadly] Osmonde is their daughter and after all . . . No, I can't shoulder this responsibility for her.

FRANCIS: Just a minute. Supposing on some pretext or other Michel were to come here to see you one day when your wife was out . . .

MME. LEMOYNE: I'm going.

FRANCIS: Mother, please . . . but when Osmonde was at home.

CLAUDE: And Osmonde would have to hide this visit from her mother?

FRANCIS: Yes, that does raise a difficulty, but I'm sure one could get round it.

CLAUDE: I shall not try to.

FRANCIS: Very well, then. I can only . . .

CLAUDE: I can't tell Edmée any more lies. I'd rather downright refuse.

FRANCIS: In that case refuse, by all means. After all, the poor devil has only . . .

CLAUDE: Our whole relationship is at stake. I have succeeded in creating a certain understanding between us, a mutual trust.

FRANCIS: Then you're running the risk of undermining the safety of all that you have built up.

CLAUDE: How?

FRANCIS: I don't know, but I feel it.

MME. LEMOYNE: Has this man taken any interest in Osmonde during all these years?

FRANCIS: My dear Mother, he had his compensations. Now things aren't so easy. Also, it's a case of a sick man's obsession.

CLAUDE: [*To* FRANCIS] You hurt my feelings just now when you spoke about Edmée as you did. Surely she has made good. Look at all the work she does, the help she gives. Could she possibly lead a fuller, more useful life?

FRANCIS: I know, and that is precisely what I find rather disturbing.

CLAUDE: How do you mean?

FRANCIS: I don't like to see a woman so austere, so wrapped up in her duties, so absorbed in good works. It gives me an impression of a sleepwalker. I sometimes feel that your wife is going through life half unconscious.

> EDMEE *enters towards the end of this speech. The others have not noticed her and suddenly realise that she is in the room.*

FRANCIS: Oh, hullo, Edmée.

MME. LEMOYNE: You're back very soon. What about the Girls' Club?

EDMEE: They weren't expecting me.

MME. LEMOYNE: Pity you put yourself out for nothing. Fortunately there are so many ways of getting about— buses, and trams and the Metro. [*A pause*] Is it raining?

EDMEE: I don't know. A few drops perhaps. I didn't notice . . . You all seemed very lively when I came in.

MME. LEMOYNE: As a matter of fact we were . . .

CLAUDE: I'll tell you later.

MME. LEMOYNE: Yes, that's right. He'll tell you.

EDMEE: [*To* FRANCIS] Oh, by the way, Francis, I may be sending you a girl who comes to my Sewing Circle at the Club. She looks tuberculous to me.

FRANCIS: I'll be very glad to do what I can. Are you coming, Mother?

EDMEE: Are you off already?

MME. LEMOYNE: When shall we be seeing you again?

FRANCIS: You must come and dine with us some day.

MME. LEMOYNE: Oh, Francis, are you sure it wouldn't upset Eugénie? She's been rather difficult lately. Three extra to dinner . . . [*The rest of the conversation is not heard as they go out of the room*]

> CLAUDE *and* EDMEE *come back immediately after seeing them out.*

CLAUDE: I'm glad you came back.

EDMEE: Claude. I want to talk to you.

CLAUDE: Yes, I know.

EDMEE: About your Mother?

CLAUDE: Yes.

EDMEE: I was completely upset at first. No, let me finish, darling. Then I thought it over and I decided I was probably wrong to have forced that promise from you. But I simply couldn't bear the thought of anyone knowing.

CLAUDE: I know, I know.

EDMEE: Especially your mother. For all her tolerant airs she's such a harsh judge.

CLAUDE: Edmée!

EDMEE: Yes, she is, but never mind. Only please don't talk about it again, that's all!

CLAUDE: It's so generous of you, darling. I was afraid you might . . .

EDMEE: "Generous"? I wish you wouldn't use that word, Claude. Obviously you felt you were under no obligation towards me. You were in the stronger position and it was foolish of me to forget it.

CLAUDE: When I undertook to keep our secret, I assure you that . . .

EDMEE: Yes, at the time. But don't let's discuss it. I've told you that I understand . . . or at least, I . . .

CLAUDE: And you forgive me?

EDMEE: Don't laugh at me, Claude.

CLAUDE: I was saying to Mother only just now . . .

EDMEE: So you were talking about it when I came in—the three of you? No, don't say anything. I'd rather you didn't answer . . . Your brother too, of course. [*A strained pause*]

CLAUDE: You reproached me just now with having taken advantage of what you called my stronger position.

EDMEE: I don't reproach you at all. When all is said and done the situation is what it *is*. [*Stressing the word*] After all, you did "forgive" me.

CLAUDE: My dear, you know what the word means in my eyes. I explained that to you.

EDMEE: Yes, you explained a lot of things to me.

CLAUDE: You make me feel so remorseful. If it hadn't been for that lie between us . . .

EDMEE: There's only one question I want to ask you. When I was talking to your mother she said you had once gone through a sort of religious crisis. I'm not going to take you to task for never having told me about it, I simply want to know at what date it took place.

CLAUDE: What did you say?

EDMEE: When exactly did you have these tortures?

CLAUDE: One can't date these things like a physical illness.

EDMEE: Is it so difficult to answer?

CLAUDE: No—not really. It must have been in 1900.

EDMEE: At a time, then, when you had no suspicion of . . .

CLAUDE: Absolutely none.

EDMEE: And after *that* had happened, your doubts were dispelled?

CLAUDE: You must realise that it didn't happen in a day or even a month. . . . It was more like a slow transformation, an inner growth.

EDMEE: Didn't *I* come into it at all?

CLAUDE: How do you mean?

EDMEE: Well—*me*, what I had done to you, the way I deceived you? . . . Was it simply a coincidence that after finding out about me you got back your faith in God?

CLAUDE: I can't possibly answer that question. A coincidence? No. It was certainly not coincidence.

EDMEE: That's all I wanted to know.

CLAUDE: I don't think things of that kind ever come to pass by chance or coincidence. [EDMEE *does not answer.*] I do so wish I could make you understand what happened to me.

EDMEE: Perhaps it's too difficult for me.

CLAUDE: When we were first married . . .

EDMEE: Need we go all over that again?

CLAUDE: [*Absorbed in his recollections.*] I used to feel I couldn't get near you. Whatever I said or did, we were miles apart. . . . You're not listening.

EDMEE: Yes, yes, I am.

CLAUDE: This lack of contact was torture to me. I felt I lacked the essential gift. And then, you remember, all the disappointment I had at Saint-Loup, how I failed with the young people who came to the confirmation class, the Genévrier girl and her sordid story . . .

EDMEE: I don't quite see the connection.

CLAUDE: But it's all connected. Those doubts and misgivings you spoke of just now were about myself, my own powers, my vocation.

EDMEE: Yes. I was . . . one of your failures.

CLAUDE: You know how little confidence I have in myself.

EDMEE: No, I don't know.

CLAUDE: And when a man loses faith in himself very soon he feels the ground giving way under his feet. There's nothing left . . . Of course I didn't feel this all the time. It came in bouts of depression that grew more and more frequent. And each time I was left inwardly diminished, weakened and terrified at my own weakness. Do you see what I mean?

EDMEE: More or less.

CLAUDE: And then came this . . .

EDMEE: This test.

CLAUDE: Then there was complete emptiness, I was absolutely alone. I had lost both wife and child. I thought I should go under—I did, really. And then little by little a light seemed to break through the darkness.

EDMEE: Well, well, well!

CLAUDE: What did you say?

EDMEE: I was just thinking that there's nothing like having these things down in black and white.

CLAUDE: But it all meant something. It was like a voice calling to the depths of my being. It had to be interpreted.

EDMEE: God was speaking to you.

CLAUDE: For the first time in my life I stood face to face with myself. I was finding out what sort of a person I was. And the thing that saved me was, I believe, the sense of my own infinite weakness.

EDMEE: And of course *you* were the only person concerned in all this.

CLAUDE: [*Oblivious to her irony*] I prayed as I had never prayed before.

EDMEE: For whom?

CLAUDE: For both of us, that God might give me strength to help you. And gradually I began to feel that my suffering was changing into a living, effective force.

EDMEE: Yes. The fact of the matter is that you . . .

CLAUDE: What did you say?

EDMEE: Nothing. I think it's all very wonderful.

A pause, enter OSMONDE.

CLAUDE: Did you have a good walk?

EDMEE: Who let you in?

OSMONDE: Félicie is back. It's begun to rain and the children were tired, so we came home.

EDMEE: What are you going to do now?

OSMONDE: I've come to fetch a book to read to them.

EDMEE: Don't forget about Mademoiselle Gentil at five . . . Osmonde!

OSMONDE: [*Irritably*] What is it, Mother?

EDMEE: Don't you think it might be suggested to this friend of yours that he should engage a governess?

OSMONDE: Really, Mother.

EDMEE: I've never seen you go to such trouble for anyone else. It's not like you.

OSMONDE: Father, will *you* please decide whether . . .

EDMEE: Those little girls are not in the least bit interesting, you said so yourself.

OSMONDE: They're awfully sweet.

EDMEE: Well, in any case, I'm going to write a note to Mr. Mégal to tell him that you are much too busy to give up any more of your time to his children.

OSMONDE: It would be a lie.

EDMEE: It would be quite correct.

OSMONDE: Father, may I talk to you for five minutes this evening? It will only take five minutes. You can spare me five minutes, can't you? [*She goes out*]

CLAUDE: What *is* all this about?

EDMEE: Surely you can see. [*A pause*]

CLAUDE: [*Unsteadily*] Edmée, there's something else I had to tell you. It's what Francis came about.

EDMEE: Well?

CLAUDE: [*As though to himself*] Oh, God, perhaps he was right. But I can't . . .

EDMEE: Is it so serious?

CLAUDE: It's terrible.

EDME: What is it, dear?

CLAUDE: Edmée, I need to feel your love.

EDMEE: [*Bitterly*] Do you? I wonder . . .

CLAUDE: Well—he has been to consult Francis. He is very ill.

EDMEE: Who is? Whom are you talking about? [*A pause*] Oh . . .

CLAUDE: He's very far gone, almost unrecognisable, according to Francis. He wants to see Osmonde—just once.

EDMEE: You must refuse.

CLAUDE: I'm not so sure.

EDMEE: [*With force*] You must refuse.

CLAUDE: Why?

EDMEE: I can't explain, but I know I'm right. It's impossible. Don't you feel that?

CLAUDE: Now listen, dear. I've no right to hide the truth from you. Francis says the man has very little longer to live. Try to understand. You may be right, I don't know. But are you absolutely sure you're not giving way to a sort of cowardice? [EDMEE *gives a kind of shudder.*] You needn't see him. He could call one day when you were out.

EDMEE: I see. You've already fixed everything in your own mind. It's terrifying. What sort of . . . ? You're not a man at all.

CLAUDE: He's dying, Edmée.

EDMEE: And the past? For you it's null and void. You've simply blotted it out? Does it mean nothing to you that this man once held me in his arms, that he pressed me to his heart, to his heart? do you hear?

CLAUDE: Be quiet.

EDMEE: I won't be quiet. I want you to hear everything. You're cold-blooded enough where I am concerned.

CLAUDE: Edmée, but that's monstrous. That's grossly unfair.

EDMEE: I'm sick of your tolerance, I'm sick of your broad-mindedness. It nauseates me. What do you expect me to do with all this generosity that cost you nothing?

CLAUDE: Nothing, when I forgave you?

EDMEE: Yes, you forgave me, but if it wasn't because you loved me that you forgave me, what was your forgiveness for? What do you want me to do with it? What good is it to me? [*She bursts into tears*]

CURTAIN

ACT TWO

Evening of the same day. It is eight o'clock. CLAUDE *is sitting reading. There is a knock on the door.*

CLAUDE: Yes? Who is it?

OSMONDE: It's me, Father.

CLAUDE: Come in, my dear.

OSMONDE *enters.*

Come in and sit down and tell me what all the trouble's about. But before we begin, do you think it is quite fair to Mother to keep her out of this? Shall we ask her to come and join us?

OSMONDE: If you do, I shall go.

CLAUDE: Osmonde!

OSMONDE: It's partly about Mother that I . . . well, about Mother and me. So you see it wouldn't be any good her being here. . . . Oh Father, I'm so miserable.

CLAUDE: My darling!

OSMONDE: So utterly miserable. You said the other day at the prayer meeting that our happiness lay in ourselves.

CLAUDE: And you know that that's true.

OSMONDE: Not for me. I'm utterly miserable. If there's anything in me but misery, it's hidden too deep for me to find. Mother knows that I'm not happy and I think she resents it.

CLAUDE: How has it come about? Is there some special reason?

OSMONDE: No—it's just everything. . . . I'm sorry, Father, I'm upsetting you.

CLAUDE: Why didn't you come to me sooner, my dear? You

must tell me everything. I can't bear to see you like this.

OSMONDE: Father, please.

CLAUDE: I ought to be able to see within you. But if our nearest and dearest close their hearts from us——

OSMONDE: That's it. It's just because you are so near to me—too near. Perhaps that's why I didn't come to you sooner.

CLAUDE: [*Bitterly*] Very likely you have no faith in me?

OSMONDE: Oh I do, Father. You're the only person I do trust.

CLAUDE: How about your mother, Osmonde?

OSMONDE: Mother is one of those people who can never help. For one thing, she is so critical of everything I say or do that it simply paralyses me. And you, Father, you're so busy, you have so many worries, so many unhappy people to comfort, I always feel I am stealing you from somebody else.

CLAUDE: You say you have every reason for not being happy.

OSMONDE: What I mean is that when I look into the future, it's a blank; life just doesn't attract me.

CLAUDE: What?

OSMONDE: Oh, I know you think of life as a gift from God, as a glorious opportunity. When you say the word "life" your voice has a special ring in it. Whereas to me it seems silly and meaningless.

CLAUDE: And yet you've so much to look forward to . . .

OSMONDE: Marriage . . . children. . . . Is that what you mean?

CLAUDE: Yes [*A pause*]

OSMONDE: Look at our friends here—Henrietta Bellanger, Jeanne Schild. . . . They are married, they have children. Well, I can see nothing particularly admirable, nothing to envy in their lives, nothing that even interests me.

CLAUDE: Isn't that judging things rather superficially?

OSMONDE: Their lives are narrow and difficult.

CLAUDE: So that's it?

OSMONDE: [*Irritably*] Do let me explain. I don't know whether they're happy or not. But, assuming that they are,

all it means is that they have husbands who are tolerably
faithful to them . . .

CLAUDE: My dear child!

OSMONDE: Children who don't give too much trouble and
only get ill three or four times a year. No, it's not good
enough. I can't see the point of lives like those, and if
mine is to be cast in the same mould——

CLAUDE: But there is no one mould; each life has its own
hidden beauty.

OSMONDE: Hidden—you've said it.

CLAUDE: Its own originality. You would have to live them
yourself to know what they really were like.

OSMONDE: Thank you, my own life is quite enough for me.
All the same, I may be right. Perhaps those women's lives
are all exactly the same, like copies of a newspaper printed
by the million, like tracts—yes, that's it, like tracts!

CLAUDE: Isn't there a certain amount of pride in all this?

OSMONDE: Well, pride is something.

CLAUDE: We must conform to the laws of life, make them
our own, and then finally want them for their own sake . . .

OSMONDE: That's only words, because whether you want
them or not——

CLAUDE: It's not only words, it's a great truth. We must
receive in order to give.

OSMONDE: Receive what? Give what? And if it simply
means passing on something to others who will pass it on
in their turn, what's the good of it all? Why rush blindly in
the dark?

CLAUDE: [*Drawing her to him*] Then really you're in a muddle
because . . .

OSMONDE: People like me need to lean on someone else's
faith. Up till now yours has kept me going, your faith.
But when one is too miserable, that's not enough.

CLAUDE: Then there is something that is making you unhappy?

OSMONDE: Not exactly unhappy.

CLAUDE: Something is frightening you, then?

OSMONDE: That's more like it.

CLAUDE: Won't you tell me what it is?

OSMONDE: You looked at your watch.

CLAUDE: You know, dear, I have an appointment later in the evening.

OSMONDE: [*Bitterly*] You have too many appointments, Father, too many obligations. One feels one has been fitted in between the unmarried mother in the Rue de l'Ouest and the paralytic in the Avenue du Maine. People are always pouring out their troubles to you, and you listen to them almost because it's your job. It's not exactly a help if one wants to unburden oneself.

CLAUDE: But my darling, you know that it's quite different with you.

OSMONDE: Oh yes, I'm a special line of goods.

CLAUDE: You talk like your mother.

OSMONDE: No, *do* I?

CLAUDE: Oh yes, and when she was your age . . .

OSMONDE: You'll probably think me horrid, but do you know I'd be afraid of marrying even someone like you with a mind like yours. And marrying a nonentity would be worse. Life is ghastly.

CLAUDE: But what is this thing that is frightening you?

OSMONDE: Well . . . I know exactly what you'll say about it. You preached a whole sermon on the subject last month.

Enter EDMEE.

EDMEE: The bell has rung. You know Félicie is out.

OSMONDE: I'll go. Who on earth can it be at this time of night?

OSMONDE *goes out. A pause.*

EDMEE: Are you going out tonight?

CLAUDE: Yes, but not yet. Forstmeyer won't be at his place till ten o'clock.

EDMEE: What an hour to fix for seeing you.

CLAUDE: He's a frightfully busy man and he never spares himself.

EDMEE: And as for the subject you are going to discuss . . .

CLAUDE: There's a big idea at the back of it.

EDMEE: Big words you mean. "The Reunion of the Churches." You don't believe in it any more than I do.

CLAUDE: If we don't believe in it, then it will certainly not happen.

OSMONDE: [*Re-entering*] It's Eugénie. She has brought round a note for you, Father, from Uncle Francis.

EDMEE: Oh?

CLAUDE: Is she waiting for an answer?

OSMONDE: She doesn't know. She's furious at having been sent out with a message on a Sunday evening. [CLAUDE *opens the letter.* EDMEE *reads it over his shoulder and starts violently*] What is it, Mother?

CLAUDE: Osmonde, will you tell Eugénie there is no answer.

OSMONDE *goes out.*

EDMEE: We daren't, Claude. Send a message down to the concierge to say you are out . . . or that I am ill . . . anything you like. But he must not be allowed to come up.

CLAUDE: We can't do that. Why tell such lies?

EDMEE: You see what has happened? He has seen your brother again. It's an obsession. The man must be mad. I won't let him come in here.

CLAUDE: Do keep calm, my dear.

EDMEE: Calm! Claude, we're behaving like lunatics. Even if I agreed to see this man it would be your duty to stop me. [*To* OSMONDE, *who has just come in*] Don't come in for a moment, dear.

OSMONDE: Were you talking about me?

EDMEE: It's nothing to do with you.

OSMONDE: Father, were you repeating what I said?

EDMEE: What is all this secrecy?

CLAUDE: No, no, no. We're discussing the letter you brought in just now.

EDMEE: There's no need to explain.

OSMONDE: You both look terribly upset.

CLAUDE: No, no, my dear. Just a little perplexed, that's all. Your mother and I don't quite agree. [OSMONDE *looks at them suspiciously and goes out*]

EDMEE: You heard what I said. I refuse to let that man into the house.

CLAUDE: I am waiting for you to calm yourself.

EDMEE: And to think that I have never once seen you lose your temper. [*She is seized with a kind of nervous trembling*] You think I can't guess what you're thinking? You despise me for getting into such a state.

CLAUDE: [*In a low voice*] My darling, I am sharing your cross with you.

EDMEE: Claude, you are my husband, you are not a priest!

CLAUDE: What is happening was meant to happen, it cannot have come by chance. Edmée, we must endure this test.

EDMEE: That horrible word again.

CLAUDE: Endure it as Christians.

EDMEE: You haven't got it in you to endure it as a man!

CLAUDE: [*Softly*] Won't you say a prayer with me?

EDMEE: [*In a tone of supplication*] Send down a message to say that you are not in. . . . Osmonde! [*She goes out. CLAUDE remains alone. He concentrates his thoughts in silent meditation. His hands are joined. There is a long silence*]

EDMEE: [*Re-entering*] I don't know where she is. I'll go down myself. [CLAUDE *does not answer*] But why, Claude, why? Is it for his sake or for ours?

CLAUDE: If we shrink from this meeting it will prove . . . that the past is not dead, that we have not overcome it. . . . It would be cowardly, it would be unworthy of us. Tell me, what is it you fear?

EDMEE: Everything.

CLAUDE: Someone once said, "Fear is the sign of duty."

EDMEE: You know that's not true. Good God, Claude, you argue and you quote and you talk about duty. What has

duty got to do with it? I'm beginning to wonder whether
you're not simply acting a part.

CLAUDE: Acting a part?

EDMEE: Yes, without knowing it.

CLAUDE: So that's what we've come to.

> OSMONDE'S *voice is heard off stage saying* "*Do come
> in, Monsieur. My father is in. I'll ask him if he can see
> you.*"

OSMONDE: [*Entering*] Father, it's someone who wants to
know if he can see you.

EDMEE: [*To* OSMONDE] What is his name?

OSMONDE: Sandier.

EDMEE: And where were you just now?

OSMONDE: I had gone up to the flat to say good-night to
Suzanne and Yvonne.

EDMEE: I see.

OSMONDE: This man was coming up the stairs just as I was
going down; I had the key, so I let him in.

EDMEE: Well, Claude, shall we see him? [CLAUDE *makes a
vague gesture*]

OSMONDE: What's the matter, Father?

EDMEE: Your father is not feeling very well.

OSMONDE: [*Tenderly*] What is it, Father?

CLAUDE: Just a giddy turn.

OSMONDE: I'll tell this man you can't see him. [*A pause*]

EDMEE: No, show him in . . . your father and I knew him
once . . . a long time ago.

> OSMONDE *goes out and is heard to say:* "*Will you come
> in? This is the way.*" *Re-enter* OSMONDE *with* MICHEL
> SANDIER, *a man of* 45 *to* 50. *He is very tall and stoops.
> His face is ravaged with illness.*

MICHEL: [*Bowing*] Good evening, Madame, good evening,
Monsieur, I must apologise for calling at this late hour.

CLAUDE: My brother told me that we might have the

pleasure of seeing you to-night. I needn't introduce you to my daughter, you've introduced yourselves already.

MICHEL: Yes, we have. It was Mademoiselle who . . .

CLAUDE: I understand that you are only passing through Paris.

MICHEL: Yes. I may be leaving again tomorrow.

EDMEE: [*With an effort*] And how long have you been here?

MICHEL: A week. But Paris doesn't suit me. I don't seem able to breathe in it.

CLAUDE: I remember it took me some time to get used to it.

MICHEL: And yet you didn't come straight here from your country parish in the Ardèche.

CLAUDE: No, I worked in Esquerchin for a time—a big industrial centre near Lille.

MICHEL: That must have been an inferno.

CLAUDE: Oh, no, we have some very happy memories of those years, haven't we, Edmée?

EDMEE: In a way . . .

MICHEL: I don't suppose Monsieur Lemoyne was referring to the beauties of the countryside.

CLAUDE: Although there was something very impressive about those melancholy stretches of land.

MICHEL: When I'm travelling through that part of the country I always pull down the blinds in the compartment.

CLAUDE: We got very fond of the working people there.

MICHEL: Really?

CLAUDE: Oh, yes. My wife and I got to know them very well. Some of them might have come straight out of that novel of Victor Hugo's. [*A pause*]

MICHEL: Mademoiselle Osmonde, you and I are old acquaintances though you may not know it. I knew you as a little girl when I lived at Saint-Loup de Talvas, in a big house that stood on a hill behind your father's. I often came to see your parents and I can remember you quite well as you were then. I went back to Saint-Loup a few months ago.

CLAUDE: I don't suppose it has changed much, has it?

MICHEL: They've built a saw-mill that completely spoils the view. In ten years' time the place won't be recognisable.

CLAUDE: But surely, just a saw-mill . . .

MICHEL: You can't get away from it.

OSMONDE: Then it must be like the gasworks at Fonville Saint-Vincent. We had a little villa upon the cliffs there one holiday. You could see the country for miles around, but the view was simply ruined by the gasometer.

CLAUDE: I never noticed it.

OSMONDE: You're lucky, Father, you only see the things you like.

MICHEL: Wait a minute. Fonville Saint-Vincent—I drove through it last year in my car. It's between Dieppe and Tréport, isn't it?

OSMONDE: That's right.

MICHEL: I thought it a horrible place. The houses looked like dusty squares of nougat lined up between two rows of fortifications. [OSMONDE *laughs*]

CLAUDE: But you enjoyed it, Osmonde.

EDMEE: Of course she did.

OSMONDE: As a matter of fact you only know whether you like a place after a certain time has passed. When I think of Fonville now, I don't feel a bit enthusiastic about it.

MICHEL: I believe she is right. It's only memory that gives us the truth, even about ourselves.

CLAUDE: We made some very nice friends there. And there was always the sea. I'm surprised at what you say, Osmonde.

EDMEE: Don't take any notice, she's just talking nonsense.

MICHEL: It's the same in music. The first impression is always deceptive.

CLAUDE: There I'm no judge.

MICHEL: Does Mademoiselle Osmonde . . . ?

OSMONDE: I'm very fond of music, but I hardly ever get the chance of hearing any.

MICHEL: And you don't play yourself? I seem to remember that your mother . . .

EDMEE: I gave it all up twenty years ago.

MICHEL: Surely you had a very fine Erard piano?

EDMEE: We gave it away.

MICHEL: In a full and busy life like yours I suppose a piano would be a temptation.

EDMEE: We shouldn't have had room for it at Esquerchin.

MICHEL: That's a pity. [*A pause*] When I was last at Saint-Loup I took one or two snapshots. They might interest you, Mademoiselle. You must have heard a lot about the place.

OSMONDE: [*Looking at the photos*] They're awfully good.

MICHEL: I have a good little camera.

OSMONDE: Do look at them, Father. [CLAUDE *looks at them over her shoulder*] That lovely transparent light. And those pine trees against the sky!

MICHEL: Do you like pine trees?

OSMONDE: I adore them. Do you remember, Father, those pines near the Chiberta lake, that line of them and their smell, and the way the branches swayed in the wind.

MICHEL: [*In an altered voice*] I like all those things too.

CLAUDE: [*Suddenly*] Good heavens! My appointment!

EDMEE: Don't go! Don't keep it.

CLAUDE: Forstmeyer is coming back specially to see me.

EDMEE: You needn't know that.

CLAUDE: But I let him down last time.

EDMEE: That wasn't your fault.

CLAUDE: No, I must go. [*Awkwardly to* MICHEL] If you have something private to say to me, we might go along together. [MICHEL *does not answer*] Of course, it's only two minutes' walk, so we wouldn't have much time . . . I'm so sorry. If I had known sooner . . . [*He seems at a loss*]

MICHEL: Perhaps we could arrange another meeting.

CLAUDE: But you're leaving Paris tomorrow.

MICHEL: I haven't quite made up my mind.

CLAUDE: Well, then, you can settle on a time with my wife. Goodbye and forgive me for going off like this. [*He goes out*]

MICHEL: Monsieur Lemoyne seems an extremely busy man.

OSMONDE: My father is far too conscientious. [*She holds out her hand to* MICHEL] Goodnight, Monsieur.

MICHEL: Good-night, Mademoiselle. I am very pleased to have renewed our acquaintance.

> OSMONDE *goes out.* MICHEL *follows her with his eyes. A pause.*

EDMEE: Why have you done this? [MICHEL *makes a vague gesture*] If I'd had my way you wouldn't have been allowed in.

MICHEL: Really?

EDMEE: And now I beg of you, go away.

MICHEL: Why?

EDMEE: In the first place because of Osmonde . . . and then . . . because . . . I can't bear the sight of you.

MICHEL: Is that because I have changed so little, or so much? You know, of course, what . . . what's ahead of me. Otherwise, I suppose, he would never have consented. . . . But things being as they are, he was obliged to, almost as a professional matter.

EDMEE: Oh, be quiet.

MICHEL: Fine fellow, your husband; in every way . . . He looks the part too—the complete parson. You say you can't bear the sight of me. Well, it's a curious thing, but being with you again has no effect on me at all, absolutely none. Novelists may say what they like, there are bits of us that are like dead skin, if you cut into them, they don't bleed. I had a curious experience the other day. I opened a newspaper and read this, "We regret to announce the death of Madame Claude Lemoyne" . . . someone with the same name as you. Well, all I can say is that I didn't . . . oh, it's all so long ago. It didn't happen to us as we are now.

EDMEE: [*Staring in front of her*] That's too easy.

MICHEL: I suppose that the whole of us will die, but that we live in bits.

EDMEE: That may be true of men. I'm still the same.

MICHEL: Are you sure?

EDMEE: Exactly the same.

MICHEL: Which means?

EDMEE: Oh, please don't jump to any conclusions. I don't suppose I have ever loved anyone.

MICHEL: I realised that long ago. You have never loved anyone, and that is perhaps why . . .

EDMEE: The announcement of my death didn't cause you a pang.

MICHEL: Lately . . . well, since my mind has been fixed on what is awaiting me . . . many faces have passed before my mind's eye. Yours was amongst them.

EDMEE: One of a crowd.

MICHEL: I didn't count. . . . It looked tense and cold, a face without pity. Without courage, either; the eyes looked down to earth. There was no light in them. Oh, I suppose they must have shone sometimes, but I didn't remember it.

EDMEE: And since, according to you and Osmonde, only what we remember is true . . .

MICHEL: Exactly.

A pause.

EDMEE: So you think I ought to have felt pity for you? That's fantastic.

MICHEL: But since it was not to *us* that it all happened, is there any point in digging up the whole story again? If you knew how utterly the magic had fled from—shall I call it that idyll of ours! I see it now in a cold, dull light.

EDMEE: That was not the light that shone at Saint-Loup.

MICHEL: Possibly not. [*A pause*]

EDMEE: Strange that after twenty years you should still feel such . . . enmity towards me. Why do you laugh?

MICHEL: Because the word is so inappropriate. You refuse to believe me when I tell you that now I . . . But I *have* felt bitter towards you, oh, bitter as death.

EDMEE: Then you did love me?

MICHEL: A part of me loved you, but it's dead now.

EDMEE: Words, words.

MICHEL: If you knew how little there is left of me that is still alive . . . barely enough to mourn over all that has already died.

EDMEE: [*Her voice trembling*] I cannot understand what you are reproaching me with. After twenty years you can still torture me.

MICHEL: Torture you? You were right; you haven't changed . . . I remember how you used to reproach me for the very words you had dragged out of me the moment before. The others were just the same.

EDMEE: So even then there were other women.

MICHEL: It pleased you to think so at the time, and I shouldn't care to disillusion you now.

EDMEE: I don't understand.

MICHEL: That scene of jealousy which you enacted for my benefit in the waiting-room of the little railway station, do you remember, when we sat and shivered there on our way back from Valence?

EDMEE: Are you inferring that I wasn't sincere?

MICHEL: Women are always sincere; but they never keep faith.

EDMEE: What wealth of experience!

MICHEL: I am sorry to have to inform you that since we parted I have not remained faithful to you.

EDMEE: Oh, you never concealed your intentions. Your letter . . .

MICHEL: In answer to yours . . . I assumed you were giving me my freedom.

EDMEE: Of which you have made generous use.

MICHEL: Most generous.

EDMEE: How little you have changed.

MICHEL: Such generous use have I made of the freedom you gave me that now I am dying of it, that's all. And please note that I say this without the slightest tremor in my voice.

EDMEE: My letter may have hurt your feelings, but there was nothing in it to leave you with such a canker.

MICHEL: The way you went and told your husband about our affair, and the cowardly urge you felt to patch things up with him.

EDMEE: Why cowardly? There was a certain danger.

MICHEL: There was no danger whatsoever and you knew it. Good God! I remember how you used to talk about your husband. No, you carefully weighed things up and you decided that for the sake of your moral security, the peace of your soul or whatever it was, you . . .

EDMEE: I weighed up nothing. I suddenly felt revolted by a life of lies.

MICHEL: Like that, all of a sudden?

EDMEE: Besides, if you had wished it . . .

MICHEL: What?

EDMEE: If you had suggested taking me away with you, I would have come.

MICHEL: And yet I did offer to do so and you refused.

EDMEE: I felt you were hesitating. If you had insisted . . .

MICHEL: Don't you think all this wrangling about our ancient love affair is rather deplorable and even grotesque? In three months' time I shall be in the Pere Lachaise Cemetery, and you . . . Good Lord, why, you're old enough to be a grandmother. [A pause]

EDMEE: A little while ago you said . . .

MICHEL: What?

EDMEE: I don't remember the exact words . . . something about what you had done with your freedom. As though you were trying to make me responsible for what is happening to you.

MICHEL: Rubbish!

EDMEE: Yes, you were, I know that tone in your voice. You didn't really mean it, did you? Tell me you didn't mean it. It's as if you had injected poison into me. If you had really cared for me you wouldn't have offered to take me away with you just once, in a moment of excitement, you would have spoken of it again.

MICHEL: [*Looking at her steadily*] Are you quite sure that it was not because you knew I was going to speak of it again that you took fright and . . .

EDMEE: Well?

MICHEL: And went and told him everything? Why were you in such a hurry to raise a wall between us?

EDMEE: I don't understand.

MICHEL: His kindness, his generosity, which you knew you could count on. . . .

EDMEE: How could I count on them?

MICHEL: Which you knew you could count on—those were the things which made it impossible for you to leave him. No. You chose the easiest way, the way of confession, because you were too much of a coward to face the music and take the only risk there was. You don't protest? Because the whole thing is as plain as a pikestaff. Oh, I assure you I no longer feel any bitterness towards you. It's far too long ago since I . . . And anyhow, love . . . [*He makes a gesture of disgust*] Before I take my final departure I want something less worn, less shop-soiled. [*He looks in the direction where* OSMONDE *has gone.* EDMEE *observes him anxiously*]

EDMEE: You didn't answer my question. . . . You can't leave me with that terrible thought.

MICHEL: What thought?

EDMEE: [*Hiding her face in her hands*] That it was partly my fault.

MICHEL: I see there's nothing you'd like better than to receive a signed certificate of innocence. I'm sorry, but I can't oblige. . . . As a matter of fact you were too utterly lacking in imagination. You didn't even realise that I loved you. Oh, you mustn't be afraid of the word. For one thing, because it all happened such a hell of a time ago, and also because love is too much like some wretched illness. But if only you'd had more guts and less virtue, who knows— we might have made something of our lives together. Whereas, naturally, after the confession—you, I suppose, went to sleep and I went to the dogs. No, it's not a very pretty story. [*He has risen to his feet*] I saw just now that you had guessed what I was hinting at. You *must* let me see the girl every now and then. Oh, please, don't put this down to sentimentality on my part. She intrigues me, that's all; the idea entertains me; and it's rather difficult at the stage I've reached to find ideas that will occupy my mind and keep it off . . .

EDMEE: You know it's impossible. On what pretext could you see her? What reason could I give her?

MICHEL: You can say anything you like. Would you like me to give her piano lessons, or teach her music? Think it over. I'm sure you'll find something that will do. Goodbye. This is the way out, isn't it; on the left? [*He goes. EDMEE does not see him out. She is in a state of great agitation. She sits down, picks up a book, puts it down again, rises and goes to the up stage door which she opens a little*]

EDMEE: Osmonde? I thought you had gone to bed. Who are you writing to? Come in here for a moment.

OSMONDE *comes in. She is wearing a dressing gown.*

OSMONDE: I can't see much point in starting a discussion now.

EDMEE: I've no intention of doing so. You've been up to the flat again without telling us.

OSMONDE: I have, and I don't mind your knowing. Who is this man who just left? Why have you never mentioned him to me?

EDMEE: He's an old friend we had quite lost sight of.

OSMONDE: Rather extraordinary of him to call at this time of night.

EDMEE: It was the only time he was free to come.

OSMONDE: Very strange. Father was quite pale.

EDMEE: He's not feeling very well to-night.

OSMONDE: Then why did you let him go out?

EDMEE: You know perfectly well that your father decides these things for himself. That's not what I wanted to talk to you about. Once and for all, Osmonde, I want to settle this Mégal business.

OSMONDE: There isn't any Mégal business.

EDMEE: Don't let's quibble, please. I have no objection to those children coming here from time to time, but I will not allow you to go up to them.

OSMONDE: In other words, you don't trust me. Don't you see that if there were anything to be afraid of, you'll only make it worse by suspecting me?

EDMEE: Who said there was anything to be afraid of? I don't think it's a proper way to behave, that's all.

OSMONDE: And what does Father think?

EDMEE: Your father doesn't realise.

OSMONDE: By which you mean he's not taking your line.

EDMEE: What line, if you please?

OSMONDE: The line of snubbing me and wounding me at every turn. Why, even this evening, in front of that old friend of yours, you made a fool of me.

EDMEE: People as completely taken up with themselves as you, always feel injured and misused. If you devoted to others one-tenth of the interest which you lavish on your precious self, you . . .

OSMONDE: Mother, I am not selfish.

EDMEE: That news to me.

OSMONDE: I'm not nearly as selfish as you are. You put no love into anything you do, and that's the only thing that matters. Sitting on committees and running Rescue Homes and knitting socks for the poor doesn't prove that a person is good. You are not good, you are not any better than I am. I can tell by the way you look when you're talking to anyone who is ill; you never smile. All the trouble you take is just—it's just . . .

EDMEE: Oh—go on . . .

Enter CLAUDE.

CLAUDE: You're still up? Look here, would you be a dear

and make me a cup of tea? I'm frozen. It was frightfully cold at Forstmeyer's.

EDMEE: I suppose it all led to nothing.

CLAUDE: We talked . . .

EDMEE: You needn't tell me that. [*To* OSMONDE] Use the electric kettle, Osmonde.

OSMONDE: Yes, I'm going to. [*She goes out*]

CLAUDE: Did he stay long after I had gone?

EDMEE: Only a few minutes.

CLAUDE: And was Osmonde there all the time?

EDMEE: No.

CLAUDE: I think that if I had foreseen what it would mean . . .

EDMEE: You see? I was right.

CLAUDE: But it would have been cowardly to have refused. All the same, the way he talked about Saint-Loup, and that cynical, disillusioned attitude to everything.

EDMEE: He's a very sick man.

CLAUDE: I had to keep telling myself that all the time.

EDMEE: Did you?

CLAUDE: Yes. Otherwise I'd have shown him the door. Did you notice the way he looked at Osmonde? That was the hardest thing to bear.

EDMEE: Oh, that was it? . . . I see.

CLAUDE: When he first came in and shook hands with you I had the feeling he was a ghost.

EDMEE: Yes.

CLAUDE: But later, when he was looking at Osmonde, and his features lit up, it was something worse.

EDMEE: [*Going to the door*] Hurry up, Osmonde.

OSMONDE: [*Off stage*] The kettle isn't boiling yet.

EDMEE: Would you like a drop of brandy in your tea?

CLAUDE: No, thanks, don't bother.

EDMEE: [*Ironically*] I was forgetting you had signed the pledge.

CLAUDE: Couldn't you tell me just a little of what he said to you? Unless, of course, you'd rather not.

EDMEE: [*Impulsively*] Claude, *be* inquisitive and petty and suspicious. I'd so much rather you were!

CLAUDE: Whatever do you mean?

> OSMONDE *enters with a cup of tea which she places on the desk.*

OSMONDE: I put in one lump of sugar. Now I'm going to bed. Good-night, Father, I hope you'll soon feel warmer.

CLAUDE: Good-night, my dear.

EDMEE: Good-night. [OSMONDE *goes out. A pause.* CLAUDE *drinks his tea*] Feeling better?

CLAUDE: Well?

EDMEE: Well, an awful thing has happened, Claude, and I need your help. A terrible thought has come into my head and it's getting a hold on me. Don't let it, Claude. We talked about the old days; you mustn't mind, Claude. It was so strange, just as though it had happened yesterday, and the twenty years between had all melted away. Then I discovered that he had been far more unhappy than I had thought; not only unhappy but desperate. And that was what drove him to the sort of life that has killed him. At least, so he believes. Of course, he may be wrong; he might have gone that way anyhow. If I could only feel sure that I did right when I told you everything. But he tries to make out. . . . Oh, it can't be true. It can't be true.

CLAUDE: What can't be true?

EDMEE: He says I was a coward, that I wasn't brave enough to face life with him, and that when I went and confessed everything to you it was to put myself in chains, to bar my own way.

CLAUDE: I don't understand.

EDMEE: Yes, you do. Once you knew everything, once you had forgiven me, there could be no question of my leaving you. Don't you understand? I had nothing to fear from you. And that's just what is so horrible. [*With growing bitterness*] When I talked to you that night I didn't think of you, inside myself, as my husband.

CLAUDE: Edmée!

EDMEE: That's why it all happened. If you had really been

my husband, if you had loved me as a man ought to love his wife, with the best in him and the worst in him——

CLAUDE: The worst?

EDMEE: You know that I would never have been unfaithful to you.

CLAUDE: You're out of your mind.

EDMEE: Now you're acting a part again. Your voice sounds quite unreal.

CLAUDE: But you showed that you trusted me.

EDMEE: Trusted? The more you love a person the less you trust them.

CLAUDE: But not people who feel as we do.

EDMEE: It cost you nothing to forgive me and you had no right to lay such a burden on me.

CLAUDE: Hadn't I the right to protect you against yourself?

EDMEE: There you are, those are words, just words. You had everything to gain by keeping me. Not that you loved me. . . . I know, I know, you'll say you loved me "in God." Perhaps you did, but there were *other* things besides me that came into it.

CLAUDE: There was nothing else that counted.

EDMEE: Wasn't there? [*With growing venom*] You're not doing yourself justice, my dear. What about your position in the parish? What about your spiritual leadership? Think of the scandal.

CLAUDE: A scandal for none but you in the end.

EDMEE: That's not what you really think. I helped you by staying on, helped you. Not only that, but I gave you a marvellous opportunity.

CLAUDE: What are you talking about?

EDMEE: An opportunity of exercising your gifts as an evangelist, my dear, of saving the soul of a poor sinner.

CLAUDE: [*He has risen to his feet, livid*] Be silent!

EDMEE: Ah! I've made you see at last, have I?

CLAUDE: Be silent, you're destroying me!

CURTAIN

ACT THREE

Ten days later.
Same set as in Act II. CLAUDE *and* FRANCIS. FRANCIS
is writing a prescription at the table.

FRANCIS: Nervous strain due to over-work, that's all that's
the matter with you. What you want is a good tonic.

CLAUDE: Then you can put Mother's mind at rest. I can't
think why she made such a fuss.

FRANCIS: I think she was afraid it might be the illness that
Father died of. But there's no connection. [*He rises*] There
you are. A tablespoonful three times a day before meals.
And now, my boy, I've got to be off.

CLAUDE: Wait a moment. As we're alone I'd like to ask you
a question. But you must promise to answer truthfully.
You will, won't you? Well—it's about what happened at
Saint-Loup.

FRANCIS: I wondered if there was something preying on
your mind.

CLAUDE: It's about myself. I want to know what you . . .
whether you thought I was right to forgive Edmée?

FRANCIS: You must know, of course, that I've never allowed
myself to pass any judgment on the matter. In a case like
that a man must obey his own feelings, or his conscience, or
whatever you like to call it. And besides, quite honestly,
your question doesn't seem to me to have any meaning.

CLAUDE: Were you . . . surprised?

FRANCIS: Oh no. Given your character, your beliefs and . . .
er, well . . . even you . . .

CLAUDE: My calling?

FRANCIS: Yes, in so far as it reflects your personality.

CLAUDE: You thought it quite natural?

FRANCIS: Yes. I still think that at that time what you did was in line with your way of life.

CLAUDE: Thanks very much. You've given me a very clear answer.

FRANCIS: Look here, what are you driving at?

CLAUDE: Nothing. You've told me all I wanted to know.

FRANCIS: [*Taking his brother's head between his hands*] Claude, old chap, what is at the back of all this? You're not by any chance ... Oh, bother my patient, he can wait. I must get this clear.

CLAUDE: It's of no interest whatever, I assure you.

FRANCIS: If you don't look out, you're going to land yourself with a first-class nervous breakdown. I was a perfect fool not to have sent Michel Sandier about his business, because that's obviously what ...

CLAUDE: If my life was based on a sham, it was far better to expose it.

FRANCIS: What do you mean by a sham?

CLAUDE: You live for years with a certain idea of yourself, and you think you are drawing strength from that idea. Then suddenly you realise you're living in a fool's paradise.

FRANCIS: But that can't apply to you and your life.

CLAUDE: Can't it? I wonder. Perhaps not, you can never be sure, and the moment you're not sure, you're lost. What I mean is that when I look back into the past, the things I used to say and think have become meaningless. They ought to be clear and familiar. I ought to recognise them as mine and feel at home with them. But I don't. I can make nothing of them

FRANCIS: You're splitting hairs, my dear fellow, and you'd better be careful; these little Protestant games can be extremely dangerous to play.

CLAUDE: Not for me. I see people every day who look upon me as their conscience.

FRANCIS: That's their look-out.

CLAUDE: But if I haven't even the courage to read in my own heart?

FRANCIS: It's not a question of courage—I really must get along. [*He has risen*] Now you be careful. Once you go in for that particular kind of tomfoolery you have to pay for it, and pay for it very dearly sometimes.

CLAUDE: Do speak to me like a man, Francis, not like a specialist.

Enter EDMEE.

EDMEE: Hullo, Francis, I didn't know you were here.

FRANCIS: Mother asked me to look in and have a look at Claude. You know how she worries about his health.

EDMEE: Well?

FRANCIS: There's nothing much the matter with him. Nerves a bit overstrained, but the blood pressure is normal and his heart is sound. [*In a comic whisper*] Has your lodger arrived yet?

EDMEE: Oh yes, he's busy trying to get his bath-tub into his room. [FRANCIS *laughs*] That's all he can think about at the moment.

FRANCIS: Well, goodbye, old fellow. Remember what I told you. Goodbye, Edmée. [*He goes out*]

EDMEE: So you're feeling ill?

CLAUDE: Not in the least. It was entirely Mother's idea.

EDMEE: You don't look well.

CLAUDE: Don't worry about me.

EDMEE: It's my fault, I'm sure it is my fault.

CLAUDE: Not at all. You told me what you really thought; I can't blame you for that.

EDMEE: What I really thought. How do I know what I really think?

CLAUDE: Then that Sunday evening?

EDMEE: Oh, I meant it at the time. But somehow things don't stay where they are. You think you're on solid ground, and you find there's an abyss.

CLAUDE: That's it, an abyss.

EDMEE: But even the abyss gradually fills up again.

CLAUDE: You mean that one turns one's head away from it.

EDMEE: No, I mean that what you thought was a shattering discovery turns out to be nothing at all, and you wonder why you ever believed in it. I've been thinking a great deal the last few days and I've come to the conclusion that when these sudden flashes of insight come, it's best to shut one's eyes. One must learn not to be too hard on oneself.

CLAUDE: Very well, then. Indulge yourself with pretexts and illusions. It's not in *my* power to do so.

EDMEE: So far, I've not been the sinner in that respect, have I? [*A pause, then speaking firmly*] You have no right to lose faith in yourself, you're there to give us strength. It's your calling, after all. I can't bear it if you give way. Remember what I'm going through myself, seeing this man again. If I can't lean on you. . . .

CLAUDE: [*With deep feeling*] When I forgave you I thought it was an act of Christian charity. But apparently I was simply running away from scandal and loneliness. It was you who forced me to open my eyes, and now you come and put your two hands over them and plunge me into darkness again. What do you want? What have I done to you?

EDMEE: I'm weak, I must have your help.

CLAUDE: But not at any price, not if it means a lie. I can't do that, I won't. [*A long pause*]

EDMEE: [*In a changed voice*] Very well. As a matter of fact you're quite right, we've got to look things in the face.

CLAUDE: We've no alternative.

EDMEE: Only, of course—it *will* mean all sorts of problems. We're not the only ones concerned.

CLAUDE: You're thinking of Osmonde?

EDMEE: Not only of Osmonde. What about this man who is going to die? We've sacrificed him, and do you know what it is we have sacrificed him to?

CLAUDE: Don't begin again.

EDMEE: I'll tell you—to our selfishness, to our cowardice. [*She is on the verge of tears*] That is the account rendered, mine as well as yours.

CLAUDE: [*As though suddenly waking up*] All the same, I saved you both, you and Osmonde.

EDMEE: Saved us from what?

CLAUDE: Sooner or later he would have let you down. Then what would have become of you?

EDMEE: Would that have been worse than your kind of faithfulness?

CLAUDE: He would have made you suffer.

EDMEE: Better that than kindness that is only a professional virtue.

CLAUDE: And Osmonde . . . we gave her a home.

EDMEE: What a home for her! Oh, I understand what it feels like to be bankrupt!

CLAUDE: [*With desperate defiance*] There's no question of bankruptcy. I may have my faults but I am what I believed myself to be . . . however much you try to annihilate me.

EDMEE: Then prove it.

CLAUDE: What?

EDMEE: Prove that you are the man you believed yourself to be.

CLAUDE: Why do you look at me with such hatred? What have I done to you?

EDMEE: Nothing. You've done nothing. You were you and I was myself, and we married, that's all. And as for what you call the hatred in my eyes, you know, after twenty years of suffering . . .

CLAUDE: Of suffering?

EDMEE: I'd ceased to realise how much I was suffering. I had forgotten. I had only known it in the early days, long before meeting Michel, when I realised what love meant to you.

CLAUDE: But I loved you in that way too.

EDMEE: No. There was a certain reserve of force in you and you spent it on me as you would have spent it on a woman of the streets. But that wasn't love, you know very well, any more than your love for my soul was. The woman in me you never even suspected of being there, and certainly didn't satisfy.

CLAUDE: The woman in you?

EDMEE: Yes. You can't understand that. It's not your fault. It's the price you have to pay for your virtue.

A pause. FRED *enters.*

FRED: I beg your pardon.

EDMEE: What is it? Would you mind knocking another time?

FRED: It won't go in.

CLAUDE: Go in?

EDMEE: The bath tub?

FRED: I don't know what is the best thing to do, so I want to ask your advice. I had to pay excess luggage on it, so it's rather annoying. Perhaps I could sell it. And there's something else I want to ask you, Sir. Do you think I ought to attend the course of lectures by Bergson? I know some people who say it's soul-shaking and Papa told me to make the most of my time here. . . . The only thing that worries me is that at exactly the same hour there's a fencing class just next door, and as Mama wants me to have plenty of exercise . . . What do you think, Sir, is it as soul-shaking as all that?

EDMEE: Which? The Bergson lectures or the fencing?

FRED: Bergson, madam. I know what fencing is like.

EDMEE: It's not a very good moment to discuss it. Later on, if you don't mind.

FRED: It's awfully . . . Thank you. [*He goes out*]

EDMEE: And in three years' time that boy will be responsible for human souls in some corner of the Jura. [*A pause*]

CLAUDE: [*In a strained voice*] What did you mean just now, when I said I still believed in myself and you wanted me to prove it?

EDMEE: You really want to know?

CLAUDE: What is it?

EDMEE: Well, I've seen him again.

CLAUDE: You! . . . You've been to his house?

EDMEE: We arranged to meet at the Lutetia Hotel. That's where he is living. We went out together, but he can't walk any distance. He gets tired at once. We sat on a bench.

CLAUDE: And then?

EDMEE: He didn't reproach me any more. That made it almost worse. He spoke about his illness. And he asked me a lot about Osmonde. He wants to know when he can see her again.

CLAUDE: [*Violently*] I don't want him to see her again.

EDMEE: [*In an ambiguous tone*] I see!

CLAUDE: Why should he? What reason could we give? The girl took quite enough interest as it was the other night. We'd have to tell her everything and it would be too much for her.

EDMEE: [*In the same tone*] You think she's so sensitive?

CLAUDE: And you, Edmée, how could you bear the thought of being judged by your own daughter?

EDMEE: So it's for my sake? No, my dear, you can't take me in with that sort of prevarication.

CLAUDE: I know what you are thinking.

EDMEE: I daresay you do.

CLAUDE: But you are wrong, it is not from cowardice. I refuse to upset the child unnecessarily.

EDMEE: That's just the point.

CLAUDE: There's no need whatever. She can do nothing for him. No one can. He's lost. The man is lost.

EDMEE: There's no need to shout. I simply asked you to answer me yes or no. All I can say now is that when for once you are asked to make a real sacrifice . . .

CLAUDE: That's not true.

EDMEE: I said a real sacrifice. . . .

CLAUDE: It wouldn't be a sacrifice.

EDMEE: You manage to find all sorts of reasons for getting out of it.

Enter OSMONDE *quickly, with a letter in her hand.*

OSMONDE: Father, you had nothing to do with sending this letter, I hope.

CLAUDE: What letter?

OSMONDE: Read it.

EDMEE: So *that* gentleman has shown you my letter. That's the finishing touch.

OSMONDE: [*To her father*] What have you to say about these insinuations?

CLAUDE: Listen, darling, even if your mother has erred on the side of caution——

OSMONDE: It's not a case for caution. I don't need to be shielded and protected like a precious object.

CLAUDE: Come now, there's nothing to get angry about. At your age it's quite natural not to realise that there are certain dangers.

OSMONDE: What dangers? Why can't you call things by their proper names?

CLAUDE: The father of those two little girls . . .

OSMONDE: I know, you're afraid that he rather enjoys my company. Well, of course he does, and he makes no bones about it. Anyway, he's a widower.

CLAUDE: Osmonde, his wife is alive.

OSMONDE: He's a widower, I tell you, and if you drive me too far, I'll . . .

EDMEE: Is that a threat?

OSMONDE: Father, tell her it was a wicked thing to do.

CLAUDE: [*In a low voice to* EDMEE] Leave us alone for a minute.

EDMEE: I don't see what can come of these confabulations. However, if you wish it, I'll leave you to yourselves.

OSMONDE: Mother is quite right, it won't do any good. [CLAUDE *has moved over to her and put his hand gently on her shoulder.* EDMEE *gives him a malevolent look and goes out*]

CLAUDE: My dear child, you're heading for danger.

OSMONDE: That word again.

CLAUDE: I'm beginning to see why you kept everything back the other day.

OSMONDE: Well, what of it?

CLAUDE: This man . . .

OSMONDE: You don't know him, Father, so you can't talk about him.

CLAUDE: The mere fact of his showing you that letter.

OSMONDE: I made him.

CLAUDE: On what sort of terms are you with him?

OSMONDE: I think he's very fond of me, and I also love him very much.

CLAUDE: But you're not a child, Osmonde, you must realise that in his feelings for you there is something . . . equivocal.

OSMONDE: You mean something physical? I don't doubt it for a moment. [*A pause*]

CLAUDE: I'm perfectly sure that if you faced things honestly you would see my point. . . . For one thing, it's a situation that can lead nowhere.

OSMONDE: I'm not so sure of that.

CLAUDE: You're banking on his wife's death.

OSMONDE: His wife? She'll outlive us all!

CLAUDE: Very well, then. [*A pause*] But what are you hoping for, my darling, what are you reckoning on?

OSMONDE: I'm not hoping for anything, I'm not reckoning on anything. I want to clear things up in my own mind.

CLAUDE: There, you see, you're not even sure of your own feelings, and thank God you're not.

OSMONDE: That's not what I mean at all. What I call clearing things up in my own mind is knowing what I consider right and what I consider wrong. I have no illusions about what this man feels for me. As a matter of fact—it may shock you—but I would much rather he felt that way than if he simply offered me his friendship. No—if I were to throw prudence to the winds and take the plunge he would probably be only too pleased to take advantage of it. All men are the same. [CLAUDE *makes an impatient movement*] It's no good, Father, you know you can't possibly judge. Either I take the plunge, or I don't. But if I do, it will be with both my eyes open.

CLAUDE: [*Controlling himself with difficulty*] You're talking like a child. And you're doing your best to deceive yourself. The fact is, my poor darling, you're hopelessly out of you're depth.

OSMONDE: I'm nothing of the kind.

CLAUDE: Your voice is trembling.

OSMONDE: The day when I feel that nothing but convention is holding me back . . .

CLAUDE: Exactly. The day has not yet come, and in the meantime it's my duty to make you see yourself.

OSMONDE: I'm sorry, but that doesn't mean anything.

CLAUDE: It's my duty to put you on guard against the sort of vanity—I say vanity, for you are flattered at the thought that a man has undesirable feelings for you.

OSMONDE: It isn't vanity. For the first time in my life I've met somebody who can think of me as I am, and not as one of a family group living a humdrum existence in a happy Christian home, with texts on the wall and family prayers every morning. What I need is to live my own life, not have it laid down for me in advance. There may be something wrong with me, but if you haven't the luck to be religious . . .

CLAUDE: You think it's a matter of luck?

OSMONDE: Yes, one's will has nothing to do with it. I know, because I've tried.

CLAUDE: [*With growing bitterness*] So you're in earnest. You are calmly, cynically weighing the pros and cons. You don't quail before this outrage you contemplate . . .

OSMONDE: It would be no outrage.

CLAUDE: You talk of our humdrum existence . . .

OSMONDE: Well, isn't it? I'm always being told about self-denial and helping other people, but the sort of sacrifices I'm asked to make are ridiculous and humiliating. Nothing has changed, nothing, I tell you, since the days when I was told to give my favourite doll to the orphans' home, or to enter my good deed for the day in a little leatherette diary. That kind of morality revolts me. I may be heading for danger, I may be on the edge of a precipice, but at any rate I . . .

CLAUDE: My dear child, you've simply fogged your brain with the worst type of literature.

OSMONDE: Literature, Father, is other people's suffering. You're lucky, you've never known certain kinds of temptation. It's a very great privilege.

CLAUDE: [*As though to himself*] This is intolerable.

OSMONDE: But you have to pay for it. There's a price to be paid for virtue.

CLAUDE: You too! [*Suddenly changing his tone*] Now look here, Osmonde, you say your life here is too monotonous, too easy, you complain of being wasted on the tasks you have to do. Well, as you have forced me to, I am going to open your eyes. To begin with . . . we are *not* just an ordinary family.

OSMONDE: What do you mean by that?

CLAUDE: You mustn't think that it's a question of judging anyone. I want you to . . .

OSMONDE: Why do you look so miserable?

CLAUDE: [*To himself*] I can't . . . I can't bear it.

OSMONDE: Is there something important that you know and that I don't?

CLAUDE: I had sworn that you would never know, and now . . . And I'm not even doing it of my own free will. [*He has got up and is walking up and down the room in a state of great agitation*] They're all taking advantage of me, they're all so unjust . . .

OSMONDE: How am I taking advantage of you, Father?

CLAUDE: I could wish this were the end of things for me.

OSMONDE: [*Bitterly*] It's never the end of things . . . for anyone.

CLAUDE: I might as well never have lived. I shall have handed on nothing. I shall have helped no one. Even you are already half corrupted.

OSMONDE: I'm not, Father.

CLAUDE: Yes you are. Just now you were calmly planning you own ruin.

OSMONDE: You can stop it all if you want to, but first, Father, you must trust me. Whatever this secret may be, I want to share it.

CLAUDE: You don't know what you are asking.

OSMONDE: I'm braver than you think.

CLAUDE: Yes, but you know nothing about life, absolutely nothing. [*Abruptly*] Osmonde, I am not your father.

OSMONDE: [*Stunned*] What did you say?

CLAUDE: You heard me. I am not your father. [*A long pause*]

OSMONDE: Then . . . Oh Father, I see now, I see. That man who came the other night and who kept looking at me.

CLAUDE: Yes.

OSMONDE: And she . . . Oh, how I hate her.

CLAUDE [*Gently*] Hush.

OSMONDE: Oh, Father. [*She is crying, he takes her in his arms and presses her to his heart*] I don't know where I am.

CLAUDE: My darling, you must forgive me. I ought never to have told you.

OSMONDE: I'll be all right in a minute. I'll get used to it.

CLAUDE: My precious.

OSMONDE: Only . . . you will explain everything, won't you? I have a right to know.

CLAUDE: My dear, it's a dreadful story, there's no need for you to know the details. And believe me, don't ask anyone else, it would only cause unnecessary suffering.

OSMONDE: And I thought I had a family.

CLAUDE: You must try and take a higher view. You have always been dearly loved.

OSMONDE: By you.

CLAUDE: By both of us. We have never allowed this misfortune to weigh on your life.

OSMONDE: Haven't you? I wonder. . . .

CLAUDE: And even now that I have told you about it . . .

OSMONDE: [*Hiding her surprise*] Do you mean that we'll go on as if nothing were changed?

CLAUDE: My dear, you must understand. I'm not asking the impossible, but one thing I have a right to demand.

OSMONDE: Well?

CLAUDE: And that is that you should refrain from passing judgment.

OSMONDE: Yes, but one can't control one's own thoughts.

CLAUDE: Up to a point one can. Don't you see how horrible it would be?

OSMONDE: It's funny, but I feel I've always known. You say I mustn't pass judgment on mother, but I believe I *have* judged her all my life. I've never been taken in by all her wonderful qualities—her kindness to other people, her good works, her self-denial. I've known all along that that wasn't her real self. I'll tell you what her real self is, it's what she shows in her face when she catches you out doing something wrong, or when . . .

CLAUDE: I can't bear to hear you talk like that about your mother.

OSMONDE: Then we are to go on pretending, even when we're alone?

CLAUDE: You owe your mother a certain respect.

OSMONDE: Do you know, Father, now you've told me, it's almost a relief. I never dared admit that my real feeling for her was one of . . .

CLAUDE: Of what?

OSMONDE: Now I shall dare . . . [*A pause*] Oh, Father, if only it had all come out long ago, if there had been a scandal, if she had gone away . . . It might easily have happened that way . . . We two could have been so happy together.

CLAUDE: Osmonde!

OSMONDE: Life would have gone on just as though she had died. It's not always a sad thing when someone dies in a family. And you're so sweet and tolerant, you'd have told me about her and made me feel that she was someone worth regretting.

CLAUDE: Osmonde, that's a dreadful thing to say.

OSMONDE: Of course, you might easily have been too kind. You might not have wanted to separate me from her. Good heavens, as though . . . Or else you might have let her stay on, because you always think people can be saved in spite of themselves. Yes, who knows, you might even have forgiven her and one would always have wondered whether . . . I'm glad that didn't happen, aren't you, Father? It didn't happen that way, did it?

CLAUDE: [*Speaking with an effort*] No, Osmonde, not that way.

OSMONDE: That's all right then, because if I thought you'd been acting a part all these years, it would spoil everything, even your love for me. Father, I hurt you just now when I was talking about myself, but I'm awfully fond of you, really, and now there's this secret between us . . .

CLAUDE: No, no, I was wrong to feel hurt. You're just a child who feels no pity for anyone. [*With a kind of desperate intensity*] Promise me, my darling, promise me that you'll never have these horrible ideas again.

OSMONDE: What ideas?

CLAUDE: If I had to lose you because of this . . . Why do you smile?

OSMONDE: I believe you're trying to take an unfair advantage . . . No, I didn't mean that. I know you're still suffering from the shock, you're not well. To think that a week ago, ten days perhaps, you didn't know.

CLAUDE: [*Speaking very low, as though ashamed*] No, I didn't know.

OSMONDE: Poor Father, darling Father! [*She kisses him*]

Enter MADAME LEMOYNE.

MME. LEMOYNE: [*Looking at them, touched*] What a pretty sight! . . . Good day, my precious. Well, Claude, you can't think how pleased I am at what Francis tells me.

OSMONDE: What, Granny?

MME. LEMOYNE: I thought your father was not looking at

all well, so I asked your Uncle Francis to come and examine him. Fortunately, it seems there was nothing wrong. [*To* CLAUDE] Your eyes look rather red, dear boy.

CLAUDE: I've got a speck of dust in one.

MME. LEMOYNE: Don't rub it whatever you do, it only makes it worse. . . . [*To* OSMONDE] Now, my pet, your mother says you simply must go and help her. I think she is making out lists of Christmas presents.

OSMONDE: Mother has absolutely no need of my assistance. However, I'll go and deal with it. See you later, Granny. [*She goes out*]

MME. LEMOYNE: Guess what Madame Hourseau has just told me!

CLAUDE: How can I possibly know?

MME. LEMOYNE: It is practically settled that you are to be offered a big parish on the Rive Droite, Chaillot.

CLAUDE: You know that I wouldn't even consider it.

MME. LEMOYNE: I have heard that the offer will be worded in the most flattering terms.

CLAUDE: I won't have my hand forced, and if ever I leave the Rue Alesia . . .

MME. LEMOYNE: Well?

CLAUDE: It will not be to go to the Avenue Marceau.

MME. LEMOYNE: My dear boy, it's not for me to advise you, but I should have thought you would have welcomed a congregation that was worthy of you.

CLAUDE: That's not the question.

MME. LEMOYNE: I'm not the only one who thinks that with your eloquence . . .

CLAUDE: I'm not a fashionable lecturer.

MME. LEMOYNE: Your dear father used always to say "Our right place in the world is where we can be of most use to others."

CLAUDE: I quite agree.

MME. LEMOYNE: Madame Hourseau was telling me that a great many people who would love to hear you are put off by having to come such a long way. People whom you could help, intellectuals.

CLAUDE: There are buses, and the Metro is five minutes away.

MME. LEMOYNE: You know how difficult it is for people in Paris to fit everything in. They have so many interests. . . .

CLAUDE: Then these people have no time to waste on me. [*Suddenly*] Besides, I may have some news for you, real news.

MME. LEMOYNE: I know . . . you're going to work on your book again, your thesis on Melancthon. Oh, Claude, I am so glad.

CLAUDE: No, not that at all.

MME. LEMOYNE: Oh, I'm sorry.

CLAUDE: I'm thinking about my ministry of the Gospel. As unfortunately I am not as convinced as you are of my spiritual gifts, or even of my . . . [*he stops short*]

MME. LEMOYNE: What are you saying?

CLAUDE: [*As though to himself*] I can't go on! I can't go on.

MME. LEMOYNE: I'm afraid Francis didn't do his job properly.

CLAUDE: That's a little too easy. . . . But you're right, Mother, I am sick, mortally sick.

MME. LEMOYNE: Don't frighten me like that, Claude; you know my heart is not up to it.

CLAUDE: I could be dying, rotten with grief and self-loathing —what would you care, so long as my digestion was good! . . . Do you know that five minutes ago I told a lie, a shameful lie.

MME. LEMOYNE: I'm quite sure that's just your way of putting it.

CLAUDE: That's right, pour out the remedy, pour the sickly stuff down my throat, as you used to when I was ten years old. . . . Oh, mother, you have a great deal to answer for.

MME. LEMOYNE: To answer for?

CLAUDE: To think that if it hadn't been for you I might have been just an ordinary man. No one would have stopped me. I should have gone into an office.

MME. LEMOYNE: Claude!

CLAUDE: Oh, the tears you would have shed at the thought of having a son working in an office—though very likely it was all that I needed. But no—you had your own little list of careers for me. First, in order of preference, to be a pastor, like Father, and grandfather, and like grandfather's father; secondly, a schoolmaster, because that means building up the boys' characters, Ernest would have been a schoolmaster if he had lived. Third, a doctor because one would still be working for the good of humanity. That's the rubbish you fed us on, that's the pious balderdash that has made me the utter failure that I am.

MME. LEMOYNE: *You* a failure!

CLAUDE: When I think of the atmosphere I was brought up in. Francis' speciality was literary composition, mine was moral scruples. Your eyes used to shine with pleasure when I trotted them out for your inspection. Francis has intellect, everyone would say, but Claude has something more, he has moral consciousness. God knows if I didn't sometimes invent my scruples just to please you. And that is what you called preparing a soul for God's service. And later on, when I was at the Theological College, a time came when I was tormented with doubts—I spoke about it to Father. Then came a transformation scene. I heard you talking as I lay in bed, talking till the small hours, and the next morning there were black looks from you both and I was treated as if I had spent a night out. That was how you set about inculcating a love of sincerity. No, Mother, honestly it hasn't been altogether my fault that I have ended in such utter bankruptcy. Yes, that's the right word. Bankruptcy, I'm spiritually bankrupt, I've been living on assets that didn't belong to me. And now . . .

MME. LEMOYNE: I won't answer your reproaches, because they are too unjust and I know you don't really mean them. But I won't let you go on torturing yourself as you are doing. You know how proud I am of you. You've sown the good seed, Claude, and in good measure.

CLAUDE: Don't use such expressions, I can't bear to hear them.

MME. LEMOYNE: You've led the life of a true Christian.

CLAUDE: I ought first to have led a man's life. But I am not a man. I wasn't even capable of loving like a man, of hating like a man.

MME. LEMOYNE: Hating?

CLAUDE: Yes, hating too. . . . But I'm nothing, I am nothing. [*He collapses into the armchair*]

Enter EDMEE.

EDMEE: What's the matter?

MME. LEMOYNE: He's very, very ill. He'll have to see another doctor. You must let me take him to Lausanne. We have some wonderful specialists there.

EDMEE: Specialists in what?

MME. LEMOYNE: Oh, in everything, everything, my dear.

CLAUDE: What are you muttering and plotting there, the two of you? Yes, that's right, take a good look at me. I am your handiwork.

CURTAIN

ACT FOUR

The drawing-room. Two days later.
OSMONDE *is sitting reading a book. Every now and then she glances at her mother who is sitting in her out-door clothes.* EDMEE *looks distraught and has not taken off her hat.*

OSMONDE: Are you going out again?
EDMEE: No.
OSMONDE: Then why don't you take off your hat? [EDMEE *slowly takes off her hat. A pause*] Are you going to keep it on your knees? [*A knock*] Come in.

Enter FELICIE.

OSMONDE: What is it, Félicie?
FELICIE: What will you be having for lunch, Madame?
EDMEE: Oh . . . you can do what you like.
FELICIE: The lodger has just been in to say he can't eat spinach.
OSMONDE: You mustn't call him "the lodger", Félicie. And you mustn't take orders from him. If he's not satisfied he can speak to Madame.
FELICIE: That's what I told him, Mademoiselle, but he said Madame frightened him. Did you ever?
OSMONDE: All right, Félicie.
FELICIE: Very well then, Madame, I'll give you the same as yesterday. But don't blame me if it doesn't make much of a change. [*She goes out. A pause*]
OSMONDE: [*Without looking up*] Has he died?
EDMEE: What did you say?
OSMONDE: I asked you if he had died.

EDMEE: Who? Whom are you talking about?

OSMONDE: Of . . . of the man who called the other day.

EDMEE: Osmonde!

OSMONDE: Well, I don't know what to make of you. You don't generally look so depressed.

EDMEE: So your father has told you.

OSMONDE: Looks like it, doesn't it?

EDMEE: Why didn't he tell me he had spoken to you? When did this happen?

OSMONDE: Two days ago.

EDMEE: And you didn't even come and . . .

OSMONDE: Well, quite frankly, I don't quite know what one says in such a case. I suppose there are suitable phrases but they don't seem to have been included in my education.

EDMEE: You're quite heartless.

OSMONDE: So I've been told before.

EDMEE: Your father has so much generosity, I'm sure he . . .

OSMONDE: He simply informed me of a fact which in my opinion does not call for any comment.

EDMEE: Would you mind closing your book?

OSMONDE: If it will please you. [*She shuts the book*]

EDMEE: There's no necessity for me to go into details.

OSMONDE: I should like to point out that I have not asked for any.

EDMEE: But what I can tell you is that through no fault of any one of them, three people have made each other suffer terribly, and that it is not over yet. Are you listening?

OSMONDE: I am. But I don't see what this has to do with me.

EDMEE: You're still young; you have all your life before you. . . .

OSMONDE: Well?

EDMEE: Surely you would like to bring a little comfort to these poor wretched people?

OSMONDE: I'm afraid I don't quite follow.

EDMEE: The person you spoke of just now——

OSMONDE: The man who called that evening?

EDMEE: Yes. Well, he has only a short time to live——

OSMONDE: That's very sad.

EDMEE: But, my dear, you know who he is. He's your . . .

OSMONDE: Well, what of it?

EDMEE: He's completely alone except for the trained nurse who is looking after him. [*Her shoulders are shaken with a convulsive sob*]

OSMONDE: Look here, mother, the Junod boy may come in any minute. If he sees you in such a state——

EDMEE: What difference should it make to me?

OSMONDE: I thought one ought always to control oneself.

EDMEE: At your age one can have no conception of what a certain kind of loneliness can be, when you're no longer young, when you're ill, and when there's not one single happy memory to dwell upon.

OSMONDE: So this man has no pleasant memories?

EDMEE: It would do him so much good if you went and sat with him sometimes. I can do nothing for him. He even says I'm bad for him. [*She can hardly control her grief*]

> *There is a knock.*

OSMONDE: Yes? Who is it?

> *Enter* FRED.

FRED: I'm so sorry to disturb you, Mademoiselle. It's not a bit important really, but I only wanted to say that . . . perhaps you didn't know . . . but I had colitis when I was a child——

OSMONDE: No, I didn't know.

FRED: Well, I did, so I'm still rather inclined to . . . I mean there are certain vegetables that I can't . . . and as I was going past the kitchen, I thought I smelt . . .

OSMONDE: All right, you can have an egg instead.

FRED: Thank you, Mademoiselle. I hope it won't give a lot of trouble, but you see my mother told me I must be careful. . . . Our family are all very delicate . . . in that way.

OSMONDE: Oh, yes. Goodbye.

> FRED *goes out.*

OSMONDE: I'm surprised at what you're asking me to do, Mother. Honestly I am. Even if I did find time now and again to go and read aloud to this man, what could we talk about? What have we got in common? I'd be sorry to awaken painful memories, and as you say he has no others. . . .

EDMEE: Oh, Osmonde, why do you talk in this mocking way? It's horrible of you.

OSMONDE: You didn't let me finish my sentence. The obvious thing to do would be to ask Father what he thinks of such visits.

EDMEE: Your father is kindness itself.

OSMONDE: He is still terribly shaken.

EDMEE: What do you mean?

OSMONDE: It's not very surprising after what he has just discovered.

EDMEE: Just discovered? Don't be absurd. He's known all about it for the last nineteen years.

OSMONDE: Oh . . .

A pause. Enter FRED.

FRED: Oh, it's only to say, Mademoiselle, that if by any chance you're having an egg done for me, it might be better not to have it boiled, because I seem to have noticed that Paris eggs . . . But of course, it's just as you wish. [*Noticing* EDMEE] Oh! Is Madame Lemoyne not feeling well? I'm so sorry.

OSMONDE: She has a very bad headache. Mother, I do think you ought to go and lie down.

EDMEE: I think I will.

FRED: If I might suggest . . . perhaps one of my cachets would relieve the headache. I have a travelling medicine chest upstairs. . . .

EDMEE: Oh, no, thank you, thank you very much, it's very kind of you. [*She goes out*]

FRED: I'm afraid I made your mother go. . . . You must think me an awful fool, making such a fuss about the spinach and

the boiled egg, as though I thought of nothing but food.
But I'm not like that a bit, really. Mother would tell you
that I never notice what I'm eating. . . . Besides, at home,
they all look upon me as an intellectual, really.

OSMONDE: Do they?

FRED: If I really minded about food and things like that, I
should never have come to stay with your parents, because
really clever people like them don't mind *what* they eat.
I'd hate to give you the wrong impression. First impres-
sions are so important, don't you think? But as a matter of
fact, you and I have met before. Do you remember that
summer you spent at Evilard, in the Soldanelles' Pension?
I was staying next door with my cousins at the Hôtel des
Cyclamens. You played an awfully good game at tennis.
Do you remember, we played a single together, and you
beat me? And then there was a party at the Pension and
you sang a little thing that was terribly good—I adore
music, don't you? I've always remembered that tune, I
could play it now if you had a piano.

OSMONDE: You have a wonderful memory. It must be a
great help in your work.

FRED: Well, fairly. There's a lot to learn that is pretty stiff.
Nowadays you're expected to be well up in all sorts of
subjects like philosophy and philology, and the whole bag
of tricks. You can't get out of it. I don't know what you
feel about it, but I don't see the need for all that sort of
thing. What matters is to have faith really. That I don't
think I need worry about, because I have faith, I have really.

OSMONDE: I congratulate you.

FRED: Oh, not at all. It's just in my nature to have faith.

Enter CLAUDE.

CLAUDE: Good morning, Fred.

FRED: [*Blushing*] Good morning, Sir. I'm so sorry to disturb
you. I was just asking Mademoiselle Osmonde about
something.

CLAUDE: That's all right, my boy. [FRED *goes out*]

OSMONDE: What a specimen! And to think that that's what I might have been landed with if it hadn't been for . . . I must write a note. I shan't be a minute . . . [*Sits down and writes*]

CLAUDE: Who are you writing to?

OSMONDE: I'll tell you in a second. [*She seals the letter and goes to the door*] Félicie!

FELICIE: [*Off stage*] Yes?

OSMONDE: Will you please take this note straight up to Monsieur Mégal?

FELICIE: [*Off stage*] Yes, Mademoiselle.

CLAUDE: What does this mean?

OSMONDE: Father, I've just found out something. Why did you let me think that you had only just heard the truth? I can't understand it, and I must say I think it was pretty rotten of you. I thought we weren't going to have any more secrets from each other . . .

CLAUDE: [*Speaking very low and without looking at her*] I was a coward.

OSMONDE: In what way?

CLAUDE: I was afraid of what you might think of me.

OSMONDE: Why afraid?

CLAUDE: Because it might have been humiliating for me.

OSMONDE: So I had guessed right.

CLAUDE: Where is your mother?

OSMONDE: She's lying down.

CLAUDE: Oh? Is your mother feeling ill?

OSMONDE: No, I think she's just letting herself go.

CLAUDE: You talked about it then?

OSMONDE: Only a few words.

CLAUDE: [*Harshly*] I told you not to.

OSMONDE: It was she who began it. She wants me to go and visit this man.

CLAUDE: [*Violently*] I won't allow it.

OSMONDE: Don't worry, I've no intention of going.

CLAUDE: You're not to go without my permission.

OSMONDE: Father! whatever's the matter?

CLAUDE: And if he ever sets foot in this house again . . .

OSMONDE: It's not likely.

CLAUDE: God knows what you might start thinking after all that has happened . . . I won't have any more of it.

OSMONDE: More of what?

CLAUDE: [*With increasing violence*] I've had enough of being humiliated and trampled on. It's my turn to hurt somebody.

OSMONDE: You—couldn't.

CLAUDE: Oh, yes I could. I could now—hurt them, knock them about, throw them out of the house.

OSMONDE: It wouldn't do you any good.

CLAUDE: [*In a changed voice*] So this is what I've come to. It's like being drunk. For the last two days it has been boiling up inside me—feelings I have never had before, the words I had never said. . . . It's terrifying! Just now I found myself talking aloud to myself. If you'd heard the things I was saying! It can't go on. Tell me it won't go on. . . . No, no, don't tell me that. I'm not sure that I want it to stop.

OSMONDE: You're not yourself now, Father, but it won't last, you'll soon be all right again.

CLAUDE: I suppose I shall.

OSMONDE: Besides, there are times when you are quite calm. This only seems to come on when you are alone.

CLAUDE: It's like a rush of blood to the head—suddenly, for no reason.

OSMONDE: You see? You're all right again.

CLAUDE: You talk to me as if I were an invalid.

FELICIE: [*Off stage*] Monsieur Mégal wants to know if he can see Mademoiselle Osmonde.

CLAUDE: What's that?

OSMONDE: [*Calling to* FELICIE] Ask Monsieur Mégal to come in.

CLAUDE: Did you ask him to come in?

OSMONDE: I did.

Enter MEGAL.

MEGAL: Good morning. Good morning, Sir.

OSMONDE: Good morning. I'm glad my father is here because I want him to hear what I'm going to say. You told me you were looking for someone who would take complete charge of your two little girls. Well, I wish to apply for the post.

MEGAL: It's very kind of you, Mademoiselle. I am extremely touched by your offer, but it's quite impossible for me to accept it. For one thing you haven't the time . . .

CLAUDE: I never heard such nonsense. What do you mean by bringing M. Mégal down on such a ridiculous pretext?

OSMONDE: My time is my own, and I need a job that will use up all my energy.

MEGAL: But you know, don't you, that I am planning to leave Paris for several months?

OSMONDE: Yes, you told me.

MEGAL: Your parents will surely not . . .

CLAUDE: I am very grateful to you, Monsieur Mégal, for realising that you cannot possibly accept my daughter's suggestion. I really don't know how the idea could have entered her head.

OSMONDE: Will you please think it over?

MEGAL: But you know . . . I haven't the right to accept.

OSMONDE: Why not?

MEGAL: I should be taking advantage of your affection for my children. It would be wrong.

OSMONDE: Wrong towards my parents?

MEGAL [*Deeply disturbed*] Not only towards your parents.

CLAUDE: [*Shaking hands with him*] Thank you, Mégal, you're a man of honour. But I think you'll agree that there is no point in prolonging this conversation. When I have made her see my reasons for . . .

OSMONDE: I know them already.

CLAUDE: You can see for yourself that my daughter is not in a normal frame of mind.

MEGAL: I can't tell you, Sir, how I wish I could accept this offer, but I can't. It's very hard for me [*his voice chokes*] terribly hard . . .

OSMONDE: Father, if you won't let me have my way about this, do you know what I'll do? I shall go straight to that . . . invalid we were talking about and I shall stay at his bedside till he dies. [*To* MEGAL] He's a relation of ours, and if *you* won't accept my offer I shall devote myself entirely to him.

CLAUDE: Monsieur Mégal, I must beg you to leave me alone with her. You'll understand my feelings, I'm sure.

OSMONDE: [*To* MEGAL] I shall see you presently.

MEGAL: [*With something approaching commiseration*] I do understand. I wish I could help. I . . . with all my heart I do. . . . [*He shakes* CLAUDE *by the hand and goes out*]

OSMONDE: You must choose.

CLAUDE: There's no question of choosing, you will stay here.

OSMONDE: Nothing on earth will make me stay.

CLAUDE: Take care, Osmonde.

OSMONDE: Your threats mean nothing to me.

CLAUDE: Do you know what you are?

OSMONDE: I'm not your daughter, anyway. And remember, it never pays to keep people back against their will.

CLAUDE: If you're thinking of your mother, she once implored me not to turn her out.

OSMONDE: Then what is there for you to . . .?

CLAUDE: The next day she was begging me to give her her freedom.

OSMONDE: Well, I know exactly what I want.

CLAUDE: I will not let you throw yourself at this man.

OSMONDE: You can't stop me.

CLAUDE: Your grandmother will take you to Switzerland.

OSMONDE: Now, Father, why not let's talk the thing over calmly and sensibly?

CLAUDE: You're a cold-blooded little monster. Your mother was never like that.

OSMONDE: So much the worse for her, and for all of us,

probably. Now listen. Here is a man who is young and vigorous—chained to a mad-woman. He loves me and I love him. Nothing stands between us except a convention, a falsehood, in which neither of us believes. If I'm a coward and let him down, it's easy enough to guess the sort of company he may turn to for comfort.

CLAUDE: You certainly have no illusions.

OSMONDE: None at all. If I can save him from——

CLAUDE: It's as if you had no conscience.

OSMONDE: Conscience? Rather a dangerous guide, surely. I may be mistaken, even with your example before me . . .

CLAUDE: So that's the lesson my life has taught you.

OSMONDE: The chief thing in life, surely, is not to deceive oneself, isn't it?

CLAUDE: And you think you are not deceiving yourself when you say you are giving yourself to this man out of kindness and charity?

OSMONDE: I said no such thing. Obviously if he didn't attract me I wouldn't do it. All I say is that even from the point of view of being good and helping one's neighbour, and the whole bag of tricks, as Fred would say, my decision is justified. Look at it from that angle if the other shocks you. After all, I'm going to make a home of sorts, even if I don't ask you to give it your blessing. . . . Oh, Father, you remind me of the people in the Swiss Pension, who used to go out on to the verandah every day and look at the Alps through the coloured glass windows. They thought the scenery much prettier seen that way, but it worried them that the effect wasn't a natural one. They would argue about it for hours and never come to any conclusion. You are just the same. You don't know which view you like best, and you make yourself miserable about it. The difference between you and me is that I can't take the coloured glass seriously any more. It may be because all my life I've heard people holding forth about their duty to this and their duty to that, Sunday after Sunday I've been preached at about my soul, with family prayers every day into the bargain. I don't know, but it seems to me there are certain thoughts, certain words which one ought not to hear spoken without feeling a sort of ecstasy, but it was never like that. It was all a matter of routine and your sermons came round every week like the housekeeping. If you had been someone who ever lived in terror or ecstasy . . . But a religion like yours leaves things exactly as they are. It's a painted backcloth, nothing more. And . . . oh, Father, you are so like the good Samaritan in that picture there, the very image of him, really you are! . . . Don't look at me like that, it isn't fair. It's blackmail and it's not worthy of you.

CLAUDE: If you go, I shall have nothing left.

OSMONDE: It would be worse if I stayed. The three of us without any illusions left about one another! Besides, I'm going to do something worth doing. I shall be filling the place of a mother who can never come back. Think of it that way, Father. The coloured glass is *some* good, after all. One mustn't be ashamed of using it.

Enter EDMEE.

EDMEE: Who was here just now?

OSMONDE: M. Mégal came in for a minute.

EDMEE: Who allowed him to come in?

OSMONDE: I had something I wanted to say to him in front of Father.

EDMEE: [*To* CLAUDE] So you were there.

CLAUDE: Yes.

EDMEE: What does all this mean?

OSMONDE: It means that I have taken a decision. I'm quite prepared to tell you what it is, but I warn you that I refuse to discuss it.

EDMEE: You refuse?

OSMONDE: Absolutely. M. Mégal is willing to engage me as governess for his children.

CLAUDE: [*In a low voice*] It isn't even true.

OSMONDE: I shall talk him round soon enough.

EDMEE: [*To* CLAUDE] Are you allowing this? Is that all the authority you have over her?

CLAUDE: [*With sudden violence*] I have no authority over the daughter of M. Sandier. All I can say is that she is following her mother's example.

EDMEE: Claude!

CLAUDE: Now listen to me, Edmée. This is probably the last time you will hear me speak my mind, because I no longer have any intention of standing between you and the interesting invalid who has now become the object of your pity.

EDMEE: Do you mean . . . you're turning me out?

CLAUDE: I should hate to deprive the poor fellow of the care you are longing to bestow upon him.

OSMONDE: Father, you've got the same expression you had just now. You're losing control of yourself.

CLAUDE: [*Brutally*] What are you doing here? Why don't you go and discuss terms with your future employer?

OSMONDE: Discuss terms?

CLAUDE: Unless you think he intends the arrangement to be platonic?

OSMONDE: [*With insulting gentleness*] It's all right. I'm not angry. [*She goes out*]

EDMEE: Claude, why don't you stop her?

CLAUDE: It's for you to use your influence.

EDMEE: You must stop her.

CLAUDE: From today I cease to take any interest in you or your daughter.

EDMEE: You're cruel.

CLAUDE: One of the few things you haven't yet reproached me with!

EDMEE: Have you forgotten that you forgave me?

CLAUDE: You can still in all seriousness use that word! Don't you realise that the very sound of it . . . Oh God! all these explanations make me sick.

EDMEE: So they do me.

CLAUDE: I meant what I said just now. Now that she is

leaving us, there's no reason for us to go on living together. You apparently feel that someone else has claims on you; well, you can go to him with a clear conscience. As for me —I shall probably leave the ministry.

EDMEE: [*In sudden alarm*] You don't mean that!

CLAUDE: I feel that what little power I thought I had left has gone from me.

EDMEE: But you can't suddenly have lost your faith; it's impossible.

CLAUDE: I don't know. Perhaps I've never had the true gift of faith.

EDMEE: The true gift of faith. And yet in the old days, before we were married, it was so wonderful the way you talked about life and religion . . . When you said certain words you sounded so sincere always.

CLAUDE: I was sincere and I was happy.

EDMEE: And the way your eyes used to light up. Sometimes I think it was because of that look in your eyes that I married you. I had never met anyone who looked like that, the faces I knew were like closed books. I had never met anyone who talked like you. The sound of your voice alone, your words, opened up a new world for me.

CLAUDE: And yet, not ten minutes ago, Osmonde was telling me that the constant repetition of these same words had deadened her faith.

EDMEE: Not the same words. They were new then, they were intact.

CLAUDE: You said I opened up a new world for you. What was that world?

EDMEE: I couldn't say, exactly.

CLAUDE: Remember what came afterwards. Those first miserable months of our marriage. The doubts I had to wrestle with. And those long, lonely walks of yours. You would come back exhausted, sombre and depressed, your face set. When I spoke, you hardly answered and I felt you were shutting me out. How I loathed you for it.

EDMEE: You never said so.

CLAUDE: I wonder if I really loved you in those days? And if you loved me? [*A pause*] You had staked your life on a look in my eyes, on a tone of voice, because they held a mysterious promise—of what? . . . a promise which has never been kept—and that is the whole story of our life together. . . . And when I think about God, it's the same. I have thought at times that He was speaking to me, but I may have been simply taken in by my own feelings in a moment of exaltation. Who am I? What am I? When I try to get hold of myself, I escape from my own clutches. A few minutes ago I thought I loathed you, I wanted to hit you, to trample on you, to throw you out. . . . And now, it's all over. . . . He's lucky, don't you think?

EDMEE: Whom do you mean?

CLAUDE: I mean . . . him.

EDMEE: Why is he lucky, Claude?

CLAUDE: Because soon everything will be over for him.

EDMEE: You are not afraid of death?

CLAUDE: No, I don't think so. After all, it is man's only sure blessing, even if it is not a door that opens.

EDMEE: Why do you smile?

CLAUDE: You remember that spot on the hills above Saint-Loup where the ground suddenly drops sheer to the river bed down in the ravine? On clear days you can see the three Becs at the far end of the valley. We could go there one evening after dinner, like in the old days and then we could . . .

EDMEE: [*In terror*] No, no, I don't want to . . .

CLAUDE: Are you afraid of being judged?

EDMEE: Yes. . . . I think so.

CLAUDE: I'm not. . . . To be known as one is . . . or else to sleep.

FELICIE'S *voice is heard in the passage.*

FELICIE: [*Off stage*] It's all right, Mademoiselle, I'll tell the Pastor you've come. [*She enters*]

CLAUDE: What is it, Félicie?

FELICIE: It's Mademoiselle Aubonneau with little René, as she calls him.

CLAUDE: Why did you say I was in?

FELICIE: Well, you are in, aren't you? [CLAUDE *and* EDMEE *look at each other*] Will you come this way, please?

Enter MADEMOISELLE AUBONNEAU *and* LITTLE RENE.

MLLE. AUB.: Good afternoon, Mme. Lemoyne, good afternoon, Pastor. I do apologise for calling at this hour but it was René's half-holiday and we've been out shopping the whole afternoon.

CLAUDE: Not at all, not at all. It's very kind of you.

MLLE. AUB.: We specially wanted to come today because it's the anniversary of your wedding-day.

EDMEE: December twenty-first. So it is.

MLLE. AUB.: Now then, René, wake up, dear, and give the flowers to Mme. Lemoyne. The child's always half-asleep!

RENE *gives bouquet to* EDMEE.

EDMEE: It's far too kind of you.

CLAUDE: Yes, really.

MLLE. AUB.: It's the very least we could do considering all you've done for us. His mother asked to be specially remembered.

CLAUDE: How is she?

MLLE. AUB.: Much the same, really, but she doesn't complain. As she says, if it hadn't been for the Pastor and Madame Lemoyne, Heaven knows what would have become of her.

EDMEE: What do you mean?

MLLE. AUB.: Don't you remember, it was you who got her into the Michel Bizot Hospital.

CLAUDE: Yes, of course. That's where she is.

MLLE. AUB.: With the Deaconesses of the Michel Bizot. She says everyone is so kind to her.

CLAUDE: That's good.

MLLE. AUB.: And she asked me specially to say that she prays for you every day, Pastor, though I'm sure you've no need for her prayers, and for you, too, Madame Lemoyne, and for Mademoiselle Osmonde.

CLAUDE: Thank you, thank you very much.

MLLE. AUB.: There's not many Pastors like you, Sir, that's what I tell them at home.

RENE: Can I go and wish my god-mother a happy Christmas?

MLLE. AUB.: You see, Sir, he won't be here on Christmas Day, he's going to stay with my mother down in Charente for the holidays.

EDMEE: Of course, I'd forgotten that Osmonde was his godmother. [*She goes to the door and calls*] Osmonde!

OSMONDE: [*Off stage*] Yes. What is it?

EDMEE: Your little godson has come to see you, René Aubonneau.

MLLE. AUB.: No—Ferraudon, my brother-in-law's name.

EDMEE: Yes, yes, of course. I'm so sorry. It's the little Ferraudon boy, Osmonde.

OSMONDE: [*Off stage*] I'm in the middle of packing.

MLLE. AUB.: Is Mademoiselle Osmonde going away for the holidays?

EDMEE: No. She's going to take up a position.

MLLE. AUB.: Not really! She is so clever, isn't she? And I suppose it's something very interesting.

EDMEE: It's with a gentleman whose wife has gone out of her mind.

MLLE. AUB.: Good gracious. . . . What shocking things one hears these days.

EDMEE: He has his two little girls living with him.

MLLE. AUB.: Oh, yes. A middle-aged gentleman, of course. I'm sure she'll be a real mother to the poor little dears.

OSMONDE: [*At the door*] Hullo, René. Come along in. How do you do, Mademoiselle Aubonneau. You come in, too, for a minute.

MLLE. AUB.: Oh, thank you, Mademoiselle. It's very kind of you.

RENE: [*As he goes into* OSMONDE'S *room*] Happy Christmas to you, Godmother.

CLAUDE *and* EDMEE *are left alone.*

EDMEE: There you are. . . . Those are the people we shall have to live for now.

CLAUDE: [*Sunk in his thoughts*] To be known as one is . . .

CURTAIN

ARIADNE

English Version
by ROSALIND HEYWOOD

OF

LE CHEMIN DE CRÊTE

a Play in Four Acts
by GABRIEL MARCEL

A Madame Marie-Anne Comnène
respectueusement.

G. M.

CHARACTERS

Jerome Leprieur

Serge Franchard

Bassigny

Philip Varet

Charbonneau

———————

Ariadne Leprieur

Violetta Mazargues

Fernande Mazargues

Suzanne Franchard

Clarissa Beaulieu

ACT ONE

*Violetta's home. It is a somewhat bare studio in a new
house, near one of the gates of Paris. The back wall is
mostly window, through which roofs and factory
chimneys can be seen. In the middle of the room is a grand
piano. There is a door forward R. leading into a little
hall. At the back there are doors R. and L.*

As the curtain rises, VIOLETTA *is playing Bach's
Partita in C Major for violin solo. She is entirely
absorbed in the music and starts on hearing the door
open.* FERNANDE *comes in with* BASSIGNY.

BASSIGNY: Please go on, I wish you would. . . . [VIOLETTA
*makes a gesture of refusal and puts back her violin in its
case*]

FERNANDE: Violetta! Really! When Monsieur Bassigny asks
you to play. . . .

BASSIGNY: Oh, but of course I don't want to force you. . . .

VIOLETTA: [*Stiffly*] I can't play today. I don't feel like it. I
haven't been well all the week.

BASSIGNY: [*With sympathy*] Not well? I'm so sorry. What's
the matter?

FERNANDE: Her liver, as usual. She ought to do a cure at
Vichy.

VIOLETTA: Don't be absurd. You know it's out of the
question.

BASSIGNY: Why?

VIOLETTA: [*Drily*] For lots of reasons.

BASSIGNY: But your sister's quite right. If your doctor
advises Vichy . . .

VIOLETTA: [*still drily*] I haven't seen a doctor.

BASSIGNY: But you ought to. I could ask mine to come and see you, if you like, and I'm sure he'd make you special terms if *I* asked him.

VIOLETTA: [*coldly*] Thanks.

BASSIGNY: He might get you in cheap at Vichy too. All these people hang together.

VIOLETTA: I hate favours.

BASSIGNY: Oh, come now, be practical. Vichy's full of people worth knowing. You might get all sorts of chances, without even playing a note.

FERNANDE: We hadn't thought of that!

BASSIGNY: Many's the career I've seen off to a good start at a watering place. All you've got to do is just pick up with the right man when his liver's ticking over nicely. I wouldn't hesitate a moment if I were you.

VIOLETTA: I don't.

BASSIGNY: [*to* FERNANDE] Does she really *want* to get on? At times, you know, I doubt it. Here am I, all out to help her, but she *must* do a little more herself than merely put spokes in the wheels.

FERNANDE: Indeed she must.

BASSIGNY: Nowadays bringing out artists isn't a profession any longer. It's pure philanthropy. But it's my hobby. I've got it in the blood. My last penny'll go on it, I dare say.

FERNANDE: How very different you are from your colleagues. Violetta and I have noticed that for a long time, haven't we Violetta?

BASSIGNY: I don't want to run anybody down, but how right you are. There are far too many sharks in my profession. And, hang it all, what can you expect if they haven't a real love of art? . . . What were you playing when I came in? I seem to know it.

VIOLETTA: The Partita in C Major.

BASSIGNY: Oh! *That!* . . . Take care, my girl. Don't you go too far. When Stefanesco played the thing last week . . .

VIOLETTA: He didn't play that one.

BASSIGNY: It doesn't matter which it was. You can send the

stalls to sleep with any of 'em. You listen to me, my dear, and give that Bach stuff a miss at your recital. *Never* bore the stalls. That's Rule No. 1, particularly for a beginner like you.

FERNANDE: [*plaintively*] But surely Violetta isn't only a beginner?

BASSIGNY: I know what I'm talking about. She's never played to the real public. Those potty little college concerts simply don't count. Why, I'd never even heard her name before we met at the Serpelliers.

FERNANDE: What luck for us you came to that party!

BASSIGNY: You're right there. It's the kind of thing I give the go-by as a rule. Soft soaping over-fed dowagers is not my line. Give me work or an early bed every time. *My* liver needs attention too, you know, so keep your eyes open for me at Vichy. I don't want to boast, but if anyone's worth knowing, I always know him. Simplest thing in the world for me, an introduction or two at the right moment . . .

FERNANDE: How can we *ever* thank you?

BASSIGNY: That's easy enough. Just follow my advice.

SERGE *comes in from* MONICA'S *bedroom.*

SERGE: Oh! Sorry. I thought you were alone. [*To* BASSIGNY, *stiffly*] Good evening.

BASSIGNY: [*very taken aback*] What's this? A ghost?

SERGE: Monica's hands are terribly hot. Oughtn't we to take her temperature?

FERNANDE: I suppose you've been playing with the child again, and over-excited her, as you did the other day.

VIOLETTA: All right, Serge, I'll come and see. [*She goes into the bedroom with* SERGE]

BASSIGNY: [*dropping his voice*] She still sees him then?

FERNANDE: It's because of the child. She was taken to see him once a week before this bronchitis, but now Violetta daren't let her go out. She's far too fussy, of course. So he comes here instead.

BASSIGNY: It's all very odd . . . and she . . . It's amazingly good of her to have him here.

FERNANDE: Violetta never bears a grudge.

BASSIGNY: He treated her atrociously. . . . Oh, yes, I found out all about it. And I'm told he and the new wife aren't getting on at all.

FERNANDE: She's pretty common.

BASSIGNY: And now all *her* money's gone in the Viellard Bank smash.

FERNANDE: Oh! Has it!

BASSIGNY: Yes, indeed. So he's just as broke as before.

FERNANDE: Anyway, Violetta would never have married him. At least I don't think so.

BASSIGNY: It beats me how she could lose her head about such a creature? There's nothing *to* him. Besides, he deserted her.

FERNANDE: Well, if you want my opinion . . . I don't believe there was ever anything more than friendship between them.

BASSIGNY: [*pointing to the door*] Friendship! Well, well, well, it went pretty far, didn't it!

FERNANDE: No, I only meant . . . In these days, you know, specially among artists—and she was very young and very lost. I was away in a sanatorium, and she hardly knew a soul in Paris. In those little restaurants a girl can't help hearing a lot, and then she reads things, too . . . Naturally I tried to warn her, but what can you do in letters? And we all have to buy our own experience, don't you think?

BASSIGNY: She paid a pretty price that time, anyhow. The child is a sweet little thing, but she'd be far better in the country—from every point of view.

FERNANDE: I couldn't agree more. But Violetta won't be parted from her. It's very hard to struggle against that kind of feeling, you know.

BASSIGNY: Sentimental bosh, I call it! For her own sake the child should go to the country. And that would be a way of stopping these visits, too. After all, they can't be very pleasant for your sister. . . .

FERNANDE: How right you are. Perhaps *you* could use your influence over Violetta to make her see her duty. . . .

BASSIGNY: She seems dashed pig-headed to me. . . . Oh! yes, I know, it's the reverse side of her good points.

FERNANDE: She's a rather unusual sort of person. *You* saw that at once.

BASSIGNY: I hope I've got a *little* flair . . . She can make a career, that's certain. But it's not what I meant. She's got quality, and one doesn't pick that up in every ditch. These kids from the College . . . they're hopeless. And as the streets are not littered with pupils howling for lessons, half of them finish . . .

FERNANDE: On the streets.

BASSIGNY: And there again, believe me, there's terrific competition. I knew one who drowned herself last week. It's true she was as ugly as sin. But even the tolerable ones . . .

FERNANDE: It's terrifying!

BASSIGNY: If you're weak or mediocre nowadays, under you go. Don't mistake me. I'm always the first to lend a hand to a pal in a hole but self-help comes first. *Never* miss a chance, that's my motto.

FERNANDE: And that's what I'm always telling Violetta. But she's still incredibly naïve about some things. She even despises money. That's all very fine, but one can't live on air. In the old days there were still patrons . . .

BASSIGNY: Patrons! They're as dead as the dodo.

FERNANDE: We had a little legacy two years ago. That's how we've been able to hang on till now. But it's nearly all gone.

BASSIGNY: [*pointing to the bedroom door*] That Franchard fellow? You're sure *he* doesn't get money out of her?

FERNANDE: What?

BASSIGNY: Yes, I told you. He's on his beam ends.

FERNANDE: Don't worry. I hold the purse strings. And he knows how much *I* love him. . . . Oh! He's an utter worm.

BASSIGNY: Yes, that's just about it, a worm.

FERNANDE: When I think what he's cost us. . . . If you'd only seen Violetta four years ago.

BASSIGNY: I see her now; she's still delightful.

FERNANDE: She had a skin like a flower. But she's worried so terribly since it happened . . . [*pointedly*] All the same, she's been better lately.

BASSIGNY: Since when?

FERNANDE: I couldn't say, exactly. More or less since we met *you* at the Serpellier's.

BASSIGNY: Ah! Good. . . .

Enter VIOLETTA *and* SERGE.

VIOLETTA: Monica's temperature is 99.8.

FERNANDE: Why, that's nothing, not even a hundred.

SERGE: All the same, it's a temperature. You say *I* excite her, but I don't like finding her as limp as a rag. She didn't even ask for Red Riding Hood.

VIOLETTA: No, dear, but you've told it to her so often she knows it by heart. [BASSIGNY *reacts visibly to the familiarity*]

SERGE: I *must* know how she is. Could you ring me up tomorrow? Suzanne will answer if I'm out. You can't think how I worry sometimes. She's so like my little sister, the one who didn't live.

FERNANDE: Really, you might take a little care what you say. . . .

SERGE: Oh, when anyone's as down on their luck as we are . . .

BASSIGNY: I'll send you Dr. Paulus . . .

SERGE: Oh! yes, please do, I can't do anything, I don't know a soul. . . .

VIOLETTA: Madame Juquier looks after her admirably, thank you.

BASSIGNY: I've no confidence in woman doctors.

SERGE: Nor have I. . . . Of course, it's not logical, I know. But Suzanne agrees with me, what a man says really does carry more weight. Oh! I must be off, I've a lesson the other end of Paris at six. You *will* telephone, won't you. [*He nods to* BASSIGNY *and goes out. A pause*]

BASSIGNY: [*agreeably*] Well? Have you worked out your programme yet?

VIOLETTA: I really am in no state to give a recital this year.

BASSIGNY: Meaning?

VIOLETTA: I'm not in form, for one thing. . . .

BASSIGNY: But my dear girl, you can't give it till the autumn season, anyway, don't forget that. When you've done your cure at Vichy and picked up in the country afterwards—I know a quiet little hole which is just the place—why, you'll be a new woman. . . . You are pretty trying to deal with, you know.

VIOLETTA: I've gone into everything—the hall, publicity— it all costs the earth. I haven't the money for such madness.

BASSIGNY: And do you imagine *I* haven't worked it all out too? The hall's easy, I'll arrange that. You shall have the Salle Fauré for the 18th of October.

VIOLETTA: [*very pale*] What?

FERNANDE: But Monsieur Bassigny . . .

BASSIGNY: It won't be the first time I've given myself . . . such a pleasure.

VIOLETTA: By what right?

BASSIGNY: I call it giving you a leg up, that's all——

VIOLETTA: I said, by what right?

BASSIGNY: What do you mean?

FERNANDE: Violetta!

VIOLETTA: Have *I* been asked? Really, it's fantastic! Do you take me for a child? Do you think I don't see what you're after? You come talking to me about your love of art! Why, you don't know the Chaconne from a Wieniawsky romance. And then you imagine I'm going to let you tie a rope round my neck?

BASSIGNY: The girl's crazy.

VIOLETTA: *Round my neck* . . .

FERNANDE: Violetta! What's the matter with you?

VIOLETTA: That first evening, at the Serpelliers, you looked me up and you looked me down. . . . Oh! I saw what you were after. Those sort of feelings are never wrong, only I haven't the courage to trust them. I should never have let you put foot inside this house, never.

BASSIGNY: Is she often taken like this?

FERNANDE: She isn't well. She told you so herself. She's been sleeping badly . . .

BASSIGNY: Dr. Paulus will come and see you tomorrow evening, and he can have a look at the child at the same time.

VIOLETTA: I won't see him.

FERNANDE: Look here, Violetta, I've had enough of this. At last you've had the good luck to meet a competent man, who not only appreciates you but can help your career . . .

VIOLETTA: My career!

BASSIGNY: [*sharply*] After all, my dear girl, I really must know what's going on in your little head.

FERNANDE: But there's nothing. She lives in the moment. She's a child.

BASSIGNY: Very well then, what do you propose to do? One must eat. I hardly imagine you mean to let yourself be kept?

VIOLETTA: Is that your business?

FERNANDE: Violetta!

VIOLETTA: It's not for *you* to question me about my private life.

FERNANDE: [*to* BASSIGNY] I do hope you won't think . . .

BASSIGNY: Pardon, but that point *must* be cleared up. I'm willing to forget the foul—yes, foul—ingratitude you've just shown me. We'll put it down to, well, say your liver. But after the interest I've taken in you and the risks I'm about to take—hell, yes, I'm taking on considerable commitments—I've the right to know what sort of a woman I'm dealing with.

FERNANDE: Monsieur Bassigny!

BASSIGNY: You're not a tart. One's only got to look at you

to see that. But there are other ways of mucking up one's life, and I feel anything but confident . . .

VIOLETTA: [*ironically*] *How* unfortunate!

BASSIGNY: You realise, if I drop you, you haven't a hope, I won't say to make good, but to avoid beggary. You get me, my girl, *beggary*. Unless . . . Yes, in that case . . .

FERNANDE: [*plaintively*] We never see anyone, we haven't any connections. Oh, if you only knew Violetta . . .

BASSIGNY: I thought I did know her, but after this outburst. . . . Hell, explain yourself, can't you?

VIOLETTA: I thought I'd done that pretty clearly.

FERNANDE: Violetta, think of Monica. . . .

VIOLETTA: *Please* . . .

FERNANDE: I can't understand you. Here is Monsieur Bassigny giving you the most wonderful proof of his confidence and esteem . . .

VIOLETTA: Much too wonderful. . . .

FERNANDE: And you treat it as an insult.

VIOLETTA: It is an insult. You can see for yourself, he straight away makes it an excuse for worming himself into my private life.

BASSIGNY: An artist can't have a private life.

FERNANDE: For heaven's sake show some sense. If he tries to help you with such amazing generosity, surely it becomes his *duty* to . . .

VIOLETTA: You are funny, aren't you?

FERNANDE: Look at all the women who've spoilt their chances by being soft and silly—artists too, real artists. Look at the little Lubinsky, throwing her career down the drain for the sake of a half-witted fool. And here is Monsieur Bassigny prepared to make considerable sacrifices for you . . .

BASSIGNY: Hey! Don't overdo it.

VIOLETTA: I call it an investment.

BASSIGNY: Heaven's above, my good girl, don't kid yourself like that. Investment indeed! It's more like chucking good money to the dogs. Do you think I've any illusions about what you'll bring in? Launching you is a luxury, just a luxury. It's because I know there won't be one penny profit that the thing appeals to me at all.

FERNANDE: [*plaintively*] Why are you so discouraging all of a sudden?

BASSIGNY: Any fool could see that if I didn't like you, and like you very much, I'd never have put my head inside this place. Young talent's a penny a dozen. I'm bored stiff with it.

VIOLETTA: [*to* FERNANDE] You see!

FERNANDE: But then, Monsieur Bassigny, I don't really quite understand . . . I must say it's a terrible disappointment . . .

BASSIGNY: [*roughly*] Why?

FERNANDE: I thought I'd understood that professionally . . .

BASSIGNY: Professionally! That's a good one!

VIOLETTA: [*to* FERNANDE] Have you got there now?

BASSIGNY: Pure, practical friendship . . .

VIOLETTA: And *quite* disinterested.

BASSIGNY: Yes, quite. That's what I am offering you.

VIOLETTA: It certainly is very touching.

BASSIGNY: I don't know if I understand you, but I'm sure you don't understand me. All this nonsense about my hidden motives . . . I have a mistress, Mademoiselle, and she's one of the best-looking girls in Paris—not that I want to brag, of course.

VIOLETTA: No! you'd *never* brag, would you.

BASSIGNY: She's as stupid as an owl, but that's just what I want. And we can both find consolation round the corner when we're bored with each other. But *you're* different. There's nothing crude about my feeling for you.

VIOLETTA: Many thanks for your accurate information. I'll be equally frank. I happen to have a lover myself.

BASSIGNY: What!

FERNANDE: Violetta!

VIOLETTA: But *our* relationship is different. It fills my whole life, so there's no room left in it for your pure, practical friendship. Quite simply—no *room*. I'm sorry. [*She shakes her head in dismissal*]

BASSIGNY: Very well. Thanks. Good luck. I hope he's got some cash. [*He goes out, shutting the door behind him.* FERNANDE *opens it and follows him. She can be heard talking volubly in the hall, but her flood of words is cut short by the sound of* BASSIGNY *shutting the outer door. She comes in again, pale with rage*]

FERNANDE: I congratulate you . . .

VIOLETTA: What an escape!

FERNANDE: Oh, dear, no, don't think you can get away with it like that. You've got to answer *me* some questions first.

VIOLETTA: As many as you like. But first let me see if Monica needs anything. [*She gently opens the bedroom door*] She's sleeping nicely. [*She shuts the door again*] Well?

FERNANDE: To begin with, are you counting on Jerome Leprieur to keep all three of us?

VIOLETTA: That doesn't deserve an answer.

FERNANDE: You don't mean to be kept by Jerome Leprieur? Right. [*Pause*] In two months' time Uncle Amedée's legacy will be gone. How shall we live after that?

VIOLETTA: Now it's my turn. How would things be different if I hadn't kicked out that greasy beast? Did you count on my "recital" to pull us out of the fire? [FERNANDE *shrugs her shoulders*] Well, did you?

FERNANDE: He told you himself he could put your feet on the ladder.

VIOLETTA: That was just talk!

FERNANDE: You think so? Isn't he exactly the right man to get you big fees? Look at the Serpellier's party. That brought in a thousand francs.

VIOLETTA: Did he get me that?

FERNANDE: He could easily get you others like it.

VIOLETTA: I don't believe it. Real musicians laugh at him.

FERNANDE: Musicians! They're most of them starving themselves. If one counted on them . . .

VIOLETTA: Look here, Fernande, don't you realise the price he wanted for his kind of help?

FERNANDE: In the end he would have asked you to marry him. I'm sure he would. [VIOLETTA *bursts out laughing*] Well?

VIOLETTA: You're out of your mind. . . .

FERNANDE: Really, truly, I'm sure he's a man who just wants to settle down in a home of his own.

VIOLETTA: With me to help him! Oh bliss, oh rapture!

FERNANDE: [*grimly*] Very well then, what *are* your plans?

VIOLETTA: I haven't any.

FERNANDE: If you hope Jerome will get a divorce to marry you, you're wrong.

VIOLETTA: I've never contemplated such a thing.

FERNANDE: Ariadne's got him on a string. It's not only her money.

VIOLETTA: Perhaps.

FERNANDE: She's a very remarkable woman.

VIOLETTA: I know.

FERNANDE: He talks of her to you?

VIOLETTA: Very often. Nearly every time.

FERNANDE: That's odd, isn't it?

VIOLETTA: He admires her. And he's right.

FERNANDE: You admire her too, perhaps?

VIOLETTA: From what he tells me, certainly.

FERNANDE: So what?

VIOLETTA: So . . . nothing.

FERNANDE: Then you do see it's a dead end?

VIOLETTA: Life's a dead end.

FERNANDE: That's only words.

VIOLETTA: *I* don't think so.

FERNANDE: Why would you never read her letters?

VIOLETTA: What letters?

FERNANDE: The ones she wrote me when I was ill. And afterwards too.

VIOLETTA: [*with a vague gesture*] They weren't written to me.

FERNANDE: [*ironically*] Obviously not.

VIOLETTA: Please—don't talk any more about her.

FERNANDE: Ah, well! [*Pause*] You know I got a card from her yesterday.

VIOLETTA: Yes, I recognised her writing.

FERNANDE: She says she wants to come and see me. She's looking forward to meeting you. . . . What?

VIOLETTA: Nothing.

FERNANDE: That'll be nice, won't it?

VIOLETTA: Look here, Fernande, what pleasure can it give you to torture me?

FERNANDE: Oh, pile it on!

VIOLETTA: The whole situation is appalling—impossible.

FERNANDE: You don't seem to mind it much, all the same.

VIOLETTA: That's not true. But . . . I *won't* see her.

FERNANDE: What excuse can you make?

VIOLETTA: Oh, anything.

FERNANDE: She may suspect. You can't know.

VIOLETTA: [*drearily*] Jerome's sure she doesn't.

FERNANDE: What a way to say it.

VIOLETTA: It's all these lies—they're so degrading.

FERNANDE: You haven't *got* to lie. Would you rather she knew the truth?

VIOLETTA: If only Jerome were different . . .

FERNANDE: What do you mean?

VIOLETTA: One has to accept it.

FERNANDE: Accept what?

VIOLETTA: Lying. It's our punishment.

FERNANDE: Why do you say: ours?

VIOLETTA: Jerome is more miserable than I am.

FERNANDE: Oh! what's the creature made of? [*pause*] I may as well tell you here and now, I don't intend to be involved in this mess any longer. I'd counted on Bassigny to pull you out of it all.

VIOLETTA: Precisely how?

FERNANDE: I thought you had *some* sense. I thought you'd make the most of your good luck. The friendship of a man like Bassigny's a chance in a million.

VIOLETTA: Be honest. You hoped . . .

FERNANDE: Nothing at all. But if it *had* happened, yes, I'd have been delighted. Being what you are, you'd have broken with this wretched Jerome creature. And then, as I said, Bassigny would have ended by marrying you. . . . [VIOLETTA *stares at her, appalled*] Why do you look at me like that?

VIOLETTA: I'm so ashamed for you.

FERNANDE: I'm glad you've got some shame to spare!

> *Little* MONICA *is heard calling Mummy, from the bedroom.*

VIOLETTA: Coming, coming, darling. [VIOLETTA *goes into the bedroom*]

> FERNANDE, *left alone, goes to a desk, opens it and gets out a postcard which she re-reads with care. She sits down, the card in her hand, and appears to be thinking deeply. The front door bell rings. She puts back the card, shuts the desk and goes to open the outer door. A moment later she returns, followed by* JEROME.

FERNANDE: Does Violetta expect you?

JEROME: No . . . I don't know . . . I've *got* to speak to her.

FERNANDE: Well, don't upset her again as you did the other day. She hasn't slept without dope since, and you know how bad that is for her. She isn't at all well. A friend came in just now. He was horrified at her looks.

JEROME: Where is she?

FERNANDE: With the child. She's not too well, either.

JEROME: Why don't you send her to the country?

FERNANDE: That's easy enough to say . . . but whom to? Whom with?

JEROME: Well, with you. Couldn't you take her?

FERNANDE: What a lovely idea! If she's alone with me for ten minutes she screams the place down for her mother.

JEROME: She'd have to get used to it.

FERNANDE: You *are* the end, aren't you?

JEROME: Well, I can't help seeing that Violetta's worn out looking after that child. And she's worrying herself sick, too.

FERNANDE: You think she'd be happier away from Monica? Do you?

JEROME: If she knew her to be comfortably settled with you, in a healthy place . . .

FERNANDE: You don't seem to realise that a holiday in the south costs money. The journey alone . . .

JEROME: Why go all that way? Why not just the country? There must be heaps of places where one can live cheap. Everyone's broke and lots of people are taking P.G.s. It's just a case of looking around a bit.

FERNANDE: Rather vague suggestions, aren't they?

JEROME: Oh, well, you know, I'm no good at practical things. . . .

FERNANDE: So I've noticed. [*Pause*]

JEROME: [*uneasily*] This friend you spoke of . . .

FERNANDE: Well?

JEROME: Was it Serge Franchard?

FERNANDE: No. [JEROME *looks relieved*] But he did come too, just now.

JEROME: He's always coming here, these days.

FERNANDE: Yes, since Monica has had to stay indoors.

JEROME: Why can't he just telephone?

FERNANDE: They haven't got the telephone any more. We have to get at them through the porter.

JEROME: Why's that?

FERNANDE: Economy, I suppose.

JEROME: Telephones certainly are expensive. I had a bill for two hundred and six francs the other day.

FERNANDE: But that's only the minimum charge.

JEROME: All the same! . . . I don't want the thing at all, but Ariadne likes me to have it. She says she's easier in her mind when she's away.

FERNANDE: How is she?

JEROME: Wonderful. She always is when she first comes

down from the mountains. But she's over-confident and she will rush around and take risks, and at the end of a month she's all to pieces again.

FERNANDE: You must make her go more quietly.

JEROME: How can I? You know she always *will* have her own way.

FERNANDE: Isn't it nice? She may be coming to see me one day.

JEROME: [*nervously*] What?

FERNANDE: Why not? You know we've been in touch for years.

JEROME: Only by letter.

FERNANDE: I saw her every day for a month when I was at Hauteville.

JEROME: But why does she want to see you now? You're not ill any more.

FERNANDE: The Home she founded keeps in touch with ex-patients. Surely you know that?

JEROME: Yes. . . . But *I* can't come again till she's been.

FERNANDE: Why not?

JEROME: She might find me here. How should I explain? . . .

FERNANDE: Invent something. You're a writer. . . .

> VIOLETTA *comes in.* JEROME *goes and kisses her and then looks at her anxiously.*

JEROME: My darling . . . it's true, you don't look a bit well.

VIOLETTA: [*without answering*] Monica was dripping wet. I had to change her from head to foot.

JEROME: We ought to get a doctor.

FERNANDE: Dr. Paulus is coming tomorrow.

VIOLETTA: [*smiling*] Oh, no, I don't think so.

JEROME: Paulus? They say Valentin is very good for children.

FERNANDE: [*roughly*] You know him?

JEROME: No.

FERNANDE: His fee's nothing—just a mere 3,000 francs a visit.

JEROME: Then what *can* we do?

FERNANDE [*contemptuously*] Are those the only words you can say? [*She turns to go out*]

VIOLETTA: Where are you going?

FERNANDE: I haven't bought anything for dinner yet. [*She goes out*]

JEROME: She's right, I'm good for nothing. Oh, God! I feel just about all-in.

VIOLETTA: [*tenderly*] What is the matter, darling? But kiss me first. That one just now didn't count.

JEROME: We should never kiss in front of Fernande.

VIOLETTA: Why not?

JEROME: It's hard to explain. It seems a sacrilege.

VIOLETTA: [*gaily*] I didn't know you took Fernande so seriously.

JEROME: I don't think I've ever detested anyone so much.

VIOLETTA: You're quite wrong. Fernande isn't *bad*. She's only . . .

JEROME: Well?

VIOLETTA: No. I was going to say something horrible.

JEROME: Better get it off your chest.

VIOLETTA: She's someone who ought never to have got well again.

JEROME: What?

VIOLETTA: I think these people who've been snatched back are to be pitied, you know.

JEROME: That's a paradox, if you like.

VIOLETTA: I'm almost sure she used sometimes to envy the patients who didn't get well. Only she's forgotten that. Poor Fernande!

JEROME: When you're with her you keep these compassionate feelings well hidden.

VIOLETTA: I can only be fair to her when she's away. When I'm with her it's impossible somehow.

JEROME: With Ariadne, it's just the reverse. It's when she's away, I can't be fair, but when I see her again. . . . This time I promised myself I'd find all sorts of faults in her. I even imagined I'd noticed them at a distance and only had to verify them. But I was wrong. They just weren't there.

VIOLETTA: My poor love. But it would be pretty low of us to look for something in *her* to justify our behaviour. It can't be justified. At least let's have the courage to face that.

JEROME: No, no I couldn't, ever. You . . . specially you . . . I've got to tell myself all the time : it's her fault—hers, hers, hers!

VIOLETTA: [*sadly*] You know that's not true.

JEROME: But think. In three years, how long has she spent with me in Paris? Six weeks.

VIOLETTA: What was to keep you from staying up at Logny with her?

JEROME: Stay in those mountains! I loathe them. They *stifle* me. . . . And anyhow, you're wrong. Ariadne herself would have hated it. Two years ago when I tried to get accustomed to the climate, the skyline, that world of sick people, it was she who insisted on my going away. Day after day, she went on and on, the way she has. She's so stubborn. Once she gets an idea into her head, it's there for ever. You'd think it was a point of honour. It's odd in such an intelligent woman. All the same, this time she was right. That life would have *killed* me. Some people say they can think better up there, that their minds feel clear and free. But I should have fallen ill, like Hans Castorp in the *Magic Mountain*. And then I should have died. I know it.

VIOLETTA: You know nothing about it, so why dramatise? Anyway, you can't reproach your wife for sending you back to your normal life.

JEROME: I don't reproach her for that. . . . But why must *she* still lead the life of an invalid when she's perfectly well?

VIOLETTA: She's still very frail. You told me so yourself.

JEROME: Frail, yes, but she seems to want to go on being frail!

VIOLETTA: Jerome!

JEROME: Oh, not consciously, of course. But she never will give herself a chance to be an ordinary, normal woman again. She loves the invalid life. She can't do without it. She's probably only come back now to knock herself up, so that she'll have to flit off to those blasted mountains again.

VIOLETTA: But darling, you know quite well that she's not up to life in Paris.

JEROME: If she *wanted* to be up to it, if she said to herself: I'm cured, I'm going to live like any other healthy woman . . .

VIOLETTA: But you don't know anything about it. And the doctors never suggested there was the least possibility of such a thing.

JEROME: Doctors! Can they even agree among themselves? They'll say whatever one wants them to say. . . . Besides, there was no question of living *in* Paris. Look at that heavenly place near L'Isle Adam, you know, Boischabot. It was only twenty-five miles out. I could have gone there whenever I liked. A light, roomy house, as dry as a bone, with a view one could never get tired of. [VIOLETTA *smiles*] I tell you, *I* should *never* have got tired of it. It was a dream, an absolute dream. But would she hear of it? No. In each letter she made a new excuse more feeble than the last. A kind of sub-conscious bad faith . . .

VIOLETTA: It's strange to think that if your wife had bought Boischabot . . .

JEROME: Well?

VIOLETTA: Nothing. Only that life sometimes produces such curious compensations—or maybe one should say, unexpected makeshifts.

JEROME: What?

VIOLETTA: Don't you remember?

JEROME: You can't mean . . .

VIOLETTA: When we met for the first time at Jeanne Francastel's, you rammed Boischabot down our throats the whole evening. You'd just heard your wife wouldn't buy it, and you could think of nothing else. You didn't let us off one single advantage or convenience—like a child. If we tried to talk of other things, back you dragged us to

Boischabot. At last everyone began to yawn and laugh at you. . . .

JEROME: Oh, you're exaggerating!

VIOLETTA: Everyone but me. . . . I don't know why, but I felt . . . And then—you remember?—you began to notice me. As if we'd been *alone* among strangers. But for Boischabot, perhaps we should never have really met.

JEROME: I'll take you there one day.

VIOLETTA: No, Jerome, it might make me too sad. There was no place for me in the life you dreamt of there . . . and it might have been a very happy life, you know.

JEROME: No, I don't think so. I can never, never again be happy with Ariadne.

VIOLETTA: Why not?

JEROME: It's that I'm *sick* of her, you see, and when she's with me I'm sick of myself for the bitter things I've said to her. It's that she's robbed me of something—and you've given it back to me again. Perhaps it's simply peace of mind.

VIOLETTA: *I've* given you peace of mind? I haven't noticed it. No, no, my dear, if there were no more than that between you two, it wouldn't be very terrible. But there is. It's for *our* lies you can't forgive her.

JEROME: Lies, lying, lying, lies. One shouldn't say such words. But sometimes you seem to make yourself *drunk* on them, just to suffer more.

VIOLETTA: Oh, darling, how wrong you are! I loathe suffering. No-one can say sorrow has improved me. But I don't think it's made me bad. It just stifles me like a—a tomb. . . . Jerome, suppose you told her the *truth*, whatever the consequences . . .

JEROME: [*violently*] Never! [*Pause*]

VIOLETTA: [*gently*] Why not?

JEROME: I won't even answer you.

VIOLETTA: [*very sadly*] You know, darling, there's no other barrier between you two. Once it was down . . .

JEROME: That's not true!

VIOLETTA: You know very well she'd forgive you.

JEROME: But that's what I can't stand. I should loathe her from the moment she did it. And you and I, we two, what would happen to us?

VIOLETTA: There wouldn't be any more "us". There would be you and there would be me. . . . No, I'm wrong. There will *always* be us, but only as a memory.

JEROME: But you've just said that unhappiness stifles you. Wouldn't you be unhappy? [VIOLETTA *does not answer*]

JEROME: [*with sudden violence*] Oh! Why not admit outright that you're sick of me and the whole thing. Come on—out with it! You want to get free at any price? Who knows? Perhaps you have other plans?

VIOLETTA: Jerome!

JEROME: Could *I* reproach you? I've ruined your life. . . .

VIOLETTA: I'd already made a pretty fair start myself. . . .

JEROME: Don't talk of that fellow Serge to me. . . . That's another thing I can't bear to think of. Of course I feel sure of you, but when I hear he's been here, like this evening . . . It's like a nail being driven into me, and I can't pull it out.

VIOLETTA: Oh, I can't believe you really *feel* that. You only imagine you do. It's a kind of auto-suggestion. You know Serge far too well. You know just how much and how little he meant to me.

JEROME: [*bitterly*] In fact, you and I are both accusing the other of inventing things to be unhappy about.

VIOLETTA: No, no, it's quite different about Ariadne . . . its terrible. [*Pause*]

JEROME: She's written to your sister that she's coming to see you.

VIOLETTA: Yes. . . . Oh! Jerome, I don't *want* to meet her, she frightens me.

JEROME: She doesn't frighten the people who know her. Far from it.

VIOLETTA: You don't choose to understand.

JEROME: As a matter of fact *I* don't want you to meet her either. I feel it will make everything more difficult afterwards.

VIOLETTA: *You* can't come here any more while she's in Paris.

JEROME: Then where shall we meet? At Jeanne's?

VIOLETTA: Oh, not there! That summer house of hers has got on my nerves.

JEROME: You are unreasonable. It was your idea to go there when Jeanne was away. . . .

VIOLETTA: I can't think how I dared ask her . . .

JEROME: She'd guessed everything, and encouraged it.

VIOLETTA: Sometimes I despise such connivance.

JEROME: Do you know I've been here twenty minutes and you haven't said *one* kind word to me. . . .

VIOLETTA: It's all so awful. Sometimes it prevents me from *feeling* my love for you.

JEROME: [*bitterly*] Why not just say prevents you from loving me?

VIOLETTA: No, Jerome, that's quite different. If I didn't love you everything would be easy.

JEROME: You'd tell me?

VIOLETTA: Of course, of course, at once. It would be a kind of—liberation.

JEROME: You hope for it?

VIOLETTA: [*in a low voice*] No, I can't even hope for it.

FERNANDE: [*outside to someone unseen*] Our staircase is horribly steep and half the time the lift doesn't work. I do hope we didn't come up too fast?

FERNANDE *enters followed by* ARIADNE, *a little out of breath.*

ARIADNE: Oh, how *charming*! . . . It's *so* light and airy! [*She goes to the window and looks out*] And what a lovely view.

FERNANDE: Lovely, yes, of factory chimneys. But you're right, it's airy enough.

ARIADNE: [*turning round to* VIOLETTA] How do you do, Mademoiselle? I'm so glad to meet you at last. I've heard about you for such ages. [*to* JEROME] Good morning again, my darling. Mademoiselle Mazargues told me I should find you here.

JEROME: Yes, I . . .

ARIADNE: [*cutting in as if to prevent him from showing his embarrassment*] How lucky, I've got the car. We can go home together if you want to . . . or rather, no, I think . . . tell Victor to drive you anywhere you like. I'll take a bus home. . . .

FERNANDE: The underground would be easier from here.

ARIADNE: I couldn't. The lack of air makes me ill.

FERNANDE: I understand that. I was just the same when I first came back.

ARIADNE: [*to* VIOLETTA *and* JEROME] I heard from Jeanne Francastel that you'd met at her house. [*to* JEROME] But you never told me. You do love your little secrets, don't you, darling. [*to* VIOLETTA] If Jerome could help you at all I should be *so* glad. I can well imagine what a virtuoso's career must be nowadays.

VIOLETTA: Oh! I'm no virtuoso, Madame.

ARIADNE: Professional, then. [*to* JEROME] You must know heaps of the people who run concert halls.

JEROME: That's where you're wrong. I don't know a soul.

ARIADNE: But a critic . . .

JEROME: You've all sorts of wild ideas about our privileges. Beyond the red card . . .

ARIADNE: What's the red card?

JEROME: It's a pass, that's all.

ARIADNE: Oh, that's not very exciting.

JEROME: All the same, one couldn't do without it.

ARIADNE: Of course not, darling.

JEROME: I'd only come to show Mademoiselle Mazargues a Sonata by Rosenmuller. It's just been published in Germany.

VIOLETTA: [*faintly*] It seems a lovely thing.

ARIADNE: Do you belong to a good library? Music is such a frightful price nowadays, isn't it? I used to buy everything, but now, of course, one can't. But I've found a wonderful library in Basle, and they post me anything I want.... Would you like the address? The subscription is only 40 francs a quarter....

JEROME: Swiss. That's a fortune in our money....

ARIADNE: Of course, darling. How silly of me. I'm so in the way of reckoning in Swiss francs that I never *think* of anything else.

FERNANDE: Life here must seem very cheap to you.

ARIADNE: Not really. You see, the figures look so enormous, and it's only when I work it out ... [*to* JEROME] Listen, darling, while I remember, would you be an angel and do something for me—go in the car and get a lobster at Prunier's? Philip is coming to dinner, and he adores them so. [*to* VIOLETTA *and* FERNANDE] My brother loves his food, and *how* I admire and envy him! I've been two years on macaroni and boiled potatoes. [*gasp of sympathy from* FERNANDE] Oh, now and then I let myself go, but I always pay for it.

VIOLETTA: Then why do you?

ARIADNE: You know, I don't think one must ever be *too* conscientious. Beyond a certain point conscience really becomes a vice.... Oh, I do hope I haven't shocked you.

JEROME: Why not telephone to Prunier?

ARIADNE: It's too late. They wouldn't deliver in time. *Sure* it's not too much trouble? ... Thank you, it's sweet of you. See you soon, darling. [JEROME *says goodbye very awkwardly to the two women.* FERNANDE *goes out with him.*]

ARIADNE: Now, do tell me, how is your little girl? And I do hope you'll let me see her? I adore children. It's a great grief to Jerome and me that we can't ...

VIOLETTA: [*in a muffled voice*] But ... surely there's still time ...

ARIADNE: No, alas, three years ago I had to have an operation.... You don't mind my asking about little Monica, do you?

VIOLETTA: You know her name?

ARIADNE: From your sister.... She told me *everything*. Oh,

you mustn't insult me by thinking I feel in the conventional way about it. On the contrary . . .

VIOLETTA: I felt sure that . . .

ARIADNE: My mother belonged to what they call the B.P.S., you know, the Best Protestant Society. She had *all* the virtues, and in some ways, of course, she was quite wonderful. The New Testament really was her daily bread, and yet, I never knew anyone who made—I won't say Christianity—but what she herself called morality, seem less attractive.

VIOLETTA: I don't think Christianity and morality are at all the same thing.

ARIADNE: How right you are. But it took me a long time to distinguish between them.

VIOLETTA: Why did your parents call you Ariadne?

ARIADNE: A strange idea, wasn't it, and not an easy name to live up to. It was my father. I was born soon after the first night of *Ariadne and Bluebeard,* and that was a work he loved almost to exaggeration. I think it linked up with something that had once affected him very deeply, but he never told me about it. I suppose he didn't want to make me sad for no reason, so young. . . . I think he'd had great dreams of helping humanity and they'd come to nothing. . . . Anyhow, whatever it was, he insisted on calling me Ariadne. But my mother always called me by my other name, Cecily. That was my grandmother's and comfortably prosaic.

VIOLETTA: You've at least an alternative. I'm not so lucky, and Violetta makes me sick. Why my parents chose such a silly name, I don't know.

ARIADNE: I'm sure it wouldn't seem silly if you did know. Perhaps it reminded them of some simple, touching episode in their own lives.

VIOLETTA: I doubt it. My parents were always on bad terms, even before I was born. They were utterly incompatible, and I suffered from it, always.

ARIADNE: Oh, I do pity you!

VIOLETTA: Sometimes my mother would try to make me side with her against my father; sometimes . . . Oh! I can't think why I'm telling you all that. I've never spoken of it to anybody, before.

ARIADNE: [*tenderly*] And then, later on?

VIOLETTA: I must have been *crazy*.

ARIADNE: *I* don't think so. I'll tell you why. . . . [*she stops*] You see, I once knew little Monica's father. We were students together at the College of Music. And—isn't it odd—for a few weeks, or maybe it was months—I really can't remember—I imagined I was in love with him myself. . . .

VIOLETTA: *You?*

ARIADNE: Yes. I used to soak my pillow for hours, night after night.

VIOLETTA: How extraordinary!

ARIADNE: Isn't it? I was just about to throw myself at his feet, and then—I don't know what happened to me. How can I put it? I simply felt it was *impossible*.

VIOLETTA: He'd have married you, and you'd have been terribly unhappy.

ARIADNE: I'm not even sure I ever thought of making him my husband. You see, before my illness my one idea was to defy what I called public opinion. Childish, wasn't it? Since then I've had other things to think about.

VIOLETTA: But when you met . . .

ARIADNE: Jerome? That's different. You see, we never did *meet*. We were brought up together. Our two families had always known each other. He was away at Oxford when I lost my head about Serge Franchard.

VIOLETTA: Then it was when he came back from England that . . . you felt . . .

ARIADNE: Yes, possibly . . . [*Pause*] A few months, perhaps less, a few weeks later, I told him about Serge as if he'd been an attack of measles. I remember it all *so* well. We'd gone for a walk up above Lake Lugano, and it was then we settled the date of our wedding.

VIOLETTA: [*with agitation*] Why are you telling me all this?

ARIADNE: [*without answering*] You couldn't guess it, but all last winter, up there in the mountains, I thought a great deal about you; ever since Jeanne Francastel came to see me at Christmas. She's very fond of you, you know.

VIOLETTA: Do you think so?

ARIADNE: Does it surprise you?

VIOLETTA: Jeanne's one of those people . . . no, I'm sorry.

ARIADNE: Go on.

VIOLETTA: It's that her inquisitiveness about other people seems to lead her astray, somehow. I've always felt that I intrigued her, I always wonder why.

ARIADNE: [*softly*] It doesn't seem to *me* very extraordinary. She had your photograph. She showed it to me.

VIOLETTA: My photograph? . . .

ARIADNE: Only a rather bad snapshot, but I was so struck by your expression. You had the face of a *real* musician. That's why I want to ask you a great kindness. I shall only be here a short time. Could you give me a few lessons in accompaniment? I'm a bit rusty, but I used not to play too badly. I should so love it.

VIOLETTA: [*taken aback*] But . . .

ARIADNE: Do you dislike the idea? You see, I'm in a state when I *must* have music again. I'm always very unhappy in Paris. I feel ill, and the little bit of energy I've managed to scrape together in the mountains soon fizzles away. And in some way music helps to revive me.

VIOLETTA: But can't you . . .

ARIADNE: Play alone? I can, of course, but it's not at all the same thing. To begin with, I get *so* discouraged by my wretched technique. . . . And it's chamber music I love. Playing *together* is the most intoxicating thing I know. . . . I used often to play sonatas up in the mountains with a friend, a young Hungarian. She died last autumn. It was a terrible loss for me. For weeks I haven't been able to open my piano. . . . But I feel that with you—*only* with you—I should have the courage to begin again.

VIOLETTA: Why with me?

ARIADNE: I don't much like the word "intuition." It's been too cheapened. But it's the only word for a kind of certainty which sometimes comes upon me, suddenly. It's more than an idea. I feel possessed.

VIOLETTA: Oh! That's frightening. [ARIADNE *goes to the piano and turns over the music which is lying on it*]

VIOLETTA: What are you looking for?

ARIADNE: The Rosenmuller sonata that Jerome . . . [VIO-LETTA *moves uneasily*] Never mind. Now, do tell me your fees and please don't make them too low. I know how hard life is.

VIOLETTA: [*affronted*] Oh, really, I can't . . .

ARIADNE: You don't want to do me this great kindness? Ah! that's what I was looking for—the first book of Bach Sonatas. Would it bore you very much to play one with me now, right away?

VIOLETTA: [*more and more uncomfortably*] Isn't it very late?

ARIADNE: I don't mind, if you don't. I know my brother. He won't get to us before nine.

VIOLETTA: But why such haste? I'm out of practice and I'd much rather look through the sonatas before . . .

ARIADNE: Oh, you're laughing at me!

VIOLETTA: No, I'm not. I don't think it's a good idea, really I don't. These intuitions . . . I've thought I had them too sometimes. . . . And you don't know me at all.

ARIADNE: I do—far better than you think.

> VIOLETTA, *giving way to a kind of irresistible fascina-tion, takes her violin.* ARIADNE *sits down at the piano and opens the music.*

ARIADNE: Let's play this one, shall we?

VIOLETTA [*almost inaudibly*] If you like.

> *They begin to play the sonata in E Major. At the end of a few bars* VIOLETTA *stops, shaken by uncontrollable sobs.*

ARIANDE *stops too, astonished. She turns round, gets up and gently takes the violin and bow from* VIOLETTA *and puts them on the piano.*

ARIADNE: My dear, why are you crying?

VIOLETTA: I can't bear it . . . I *can't* . . .

ARIADNE: [*with extreme gentleness*] But haven't you realised I know everything?

VIOLETTA: [*staggered*] You *know?*

ARIADNE: I've been sure—quite sure—for some days.

VIOLETTA: But Jerome . . .

ARIADNE: [*firmly*] We won't talk about Jerome yet. We must keep all this to ourselves, just between us two.

VIOLETTA: But that's impossible.

ARIADNE: Jerome's a child. We could do him a lot of harm.

VIOLETTA: But when he discovers that you know! Oh, I can't imagine . . . anything . . . the worst could happen! He'll go, or he might even . . .

ARIADNE: No, no, no. Jerome won't kill himself, he won't go, and he won't find out anything. It all depends on us. You'll see, you'll see.

FERNANDE, *surprised that the music has stopped, half opens the door.*

ARIADNE: [*to* FERNANDE] We weren't quite together [*to* VIOLETTA]. Shall we go back to the beginning, Mademoiselle?

CURTAIN

ACT TWO

Two o'clock in the afternoon at the LEPRIEUR'S. *Every-thing in the room gives an impression of fastidious refinement.* PHILIP, ARIADNE'S *brother, is smoking, but he stops from time to time to sip his liqueur.* ARIADNE *is lying on a sofa. Her eyes are shut.*

PHILIP: Then you've *still* not yet settled when you're going?

ARIADNE: No, not yet.

PHILIP: You seem to be standing Paris better than last year.

ARIADNE: Oh, let's face the facts. I'm just living on my nerves.

PHILIP: Meaning?

ARIADNE: It'll be like all the other times. As soon as I get back to Logny, I shall collapse again.

PHILIP: [*calmly*] Then why go?

ARIADNE: Are you serious?

PHILIP: Couldn't be more so. You ought to stay here. I'm sure of that.

ARIADNE: I don't understand what you mean.

PHILIP: Well, suppose the Villa Gentiane were let, sold, burnt down, anything you like. . . . Suppose you *couldn't* live there any more. . . .

ARIADNE: I should go somewhere else. . . .

PHILIP: Suppose you couldn't go anywhere else. What would happen then?

ARIADNE: That's a silly question.

PHILIP: Do you think so?

ARIADNE: I should very soon have a relapse. I should be on my back again, helpless, for years.

PHILIP: Does your doctor up there tell you that?

ARIADNE: I don't see a doctor any more. . . .

PHILIP: Oh?

ARIADNE: I know myself. And I've paid quite enough for the knowledge, too.

PHILIP: But all the same, if by some incredible chance you were wrong, wouldn't it be worth trying the experiment?

ARIADNE: What experiment?

PHILIP: Simply to take up a normal life again.

ARIADNE: That's just a little too risky, thank you very much.

PHILIP: But the other experiment—the one you've chosen— is that entirely without risk? Listen, Ariadne, we haven't had one quiet moment together since you came home. Either your husband's been around, or one of those pet invalids of yours.

ARIADNE: Philip, you know how I hate that word . . .

PHILIP: And I've made up my mind to tell you exactly what I think.

ARIADNE: I don't advise you to—not on this subject.

PHILIP: Why not?

ARIADNE: Because you can't tell me anything I don't know already. All you can say I've thought out for myself, ages ago.

PHILIP: Yet there are some things you *can't* know.

ARIADNE: Oh! What?

PHILIP: Now I'm not alluding to anything in particular. But tell me: is Jerome or isn't he, having a love affair? I've no idea, and it's not my business anyway. But there's something I'm not at all happy about. When you're away the lad's about as cheerful as a November fog—not to mention some practical problems, but those I find rather embarrassing to talk about.

ARIADNE: What do you mean?

PHILIP: Well, do you give him an allowance for instance? . . .

ARIADNE: Philip, are you mad?

PHILIP: No. But it would be the best solution. You don't see his almost sordid economy. It's always the same—at the

theatre, in a restaurant, anywhere. And look at his clothes.
It's pathetic. He won't spend a penny.

ARIADNE: But I'm *appalled* . . . I'd certainly noticed he
seemed short of clothes, and they were in rather a mess.
But you know how vague and careless he is. I put it down
to that.

PHILIP: [*categorically*] Well, you're wrong. Jerome reminds
me of those students from the provinces, who always seem
to be hanging on, half starved, for their next miserable little
monthly allowance.

ARIADNE: But that's absurd. He has a cheque book. He
knows perfectly well . . .

PHILIP: Now, listen, Ariadne. If you want me to be quite
frank, Jerome doesn't feel *married*. He feels *kept* by a
distant friend. And he doesn't like it. It would be quite
different if you lived together. . . . Oh, I don't say it's
logical, but it's easy enough to understand, you know.

ARIADNE: But he's never hinted . . .

PHILIP: Good Lord! Of course not. He probably won't even
admit it to himself. [*A pause*] I'm sorry if I sound brutal,
Ariadne, but have you never thought that perhaps you
ought to set him free?

ARIADNE: Now, Philip, you know very well that four years
ago . . .

PHILIP: Ariadne, be honest. Four years ago no-one knew
whether you would live or die. Could any man contemplate divorce, or even separation? But now you're quite
well—oh, not strong, of course. Neither are thousands of
people who can't afford to spend nine-tenths of their lives
on the top of a mountain. The thing's as clear as daylight.
Either you lead a normal life—it *always* comes back to
that—or you set Jerome free—free to marry again if he
likes.

ARIADNE: What nonsense! To begin with, you know he
hasn't a penny. He'd starve on what he earns as a critic.
And if he's really the hypersensitive creature you describe,
do you think he'd take help from his divorced wife?

Besides, whatever you say, Jerome never thinks of money
—never. . . .

PHILIP: I'm afraid I'm not convinced of that.

ARIADNE: What you absolutely don't understand is our
relationship. [*tensely*] There are things I've no right to tell
you. But surely you've guessed. Even before my illness,
even when we led this normal life you keep harping on, we
never . . . [*she stops*]

PHILIP: Are you trying to tell me that even then you weren't
husband and wife?

ARIADNE: Philip!

PHILIP: Well, I should have thought otherwise. But, yes, it's
true, there was that car smash soon after you were married.
. . . Did that? . . .

ARIADNE: I can tell you one thing. Jerome needs me. Even
from far away *I* can give him more than anyone else in the
whole world.

PHILIP: Right. But in that case, surely by living with him . . .

ARIADNE: No, no. Then we'd be *lost*. [*There is a knock on the
door*] What is it?

The maid comes in.

MAID: Please, Madame, there's a gentleman and a lady. They
say Madame is expecting them. [*She gives* ARIADNE *a
visiting card*]

ARIADNE: Thank you, Elise. [*to* PHILIP] It's the Franchards.
But I never thought she'd come too.

PHILIP: The Franchards?

ARIADNE: That pianist who was with me at the College of
Music.

PHILIP: I don't remember.

ARIADNE: [*to* ELISE] Will you ask them to come in, please.

MAID: Yes, Madame.

ELISE *goes out and shows in* SERGE *and* SUZANNE
FRANCHARD.

SERGE: How do you do, Madame. I've brought my wife. I

do hope you don't mind. She so much wanted to meet you.

ARIADNE: But how nice. . . . I'm delighted to see you, Madame.

SUZANNE: Serge has talked such a lot about you lately. He was ever so pleased to meet you again at Violetta's.

ARIADNE: [*taken aback*] May I introduce my brother.

SERGE: How do you do, Monsieur. . . .

PHILIP: Who is Violetta?

ARIADNE: Mademoiselle Mazargues, a young violinist, who's giving me lessons in accompaniment. She's very talented.

SUZANNE: I'm so pleased to hear you say that. *I* think it's lovely the way Violetta plays. But my husband says it's only so-so.

SERGE: I don't. I merely say she ought to work harder.

SUZANNE: But you must remember, Serge, her life is ever so difficult . . .

SERGE: No more difficult than for most artists.

SUZANNE: How can you say that? Her health isn't good. She has her sister on her hands. And then there's the poor little girl . . .

ARIADNE: Yes, the child seems delicate too. It's such a pity.

SUZANNE: We're ever so sorry, and we'd like to do more for them if we could. But we're terribly hard up ourselves, worse luck. [SERGE *becomes more and more exasperated*] Of course you know *everything*, Madame?

ARIADNE: [*embarrassed*] Yes, I know . . .

SERGE: Really, Suzanne!

SUZANNE: I don't see why you all want to make a mystery of it.

ARIADNE: But I don't think my brother knows about it.

SUZANNE: Of course it's all very painful. But I've always tried not—not to be narrow-minded about it, you see.

ARIADNE: Yes.

SUZANNE: Besides, Violetta's a lovely girl. She's helped me ever so. Serge can't understand how much. Anyhow, I'm not angry with *him*. He's what he is. Naturally, if the child hadn't been there, one can't tell. . . . We don't often meet because, of course, I'm a little afraid. . . . And it can't be too pleasant for her, either. One can see that. . . . But she never shows a thing. . . . Not many people would have been so nice in her position. [SERGE *gets up during* SUZANNE'S *speech and walks about*]

SUZANNE: What's the matter, darling? You do seem in a state.

ARIADNE: It is a rather trying situation, isn't it.

SUZANNE: Well, who's fault is that?

SERGE: [*exasperated*] Why ask? You all know. I'm a cad, a beast, a heartless brute, a . . .

ARIADNE: Oh, really, please . . .

SERGE: How *can* anyone be so tactless?

SUZANNE: Me! Tactless! How?

SERGE: God! Don't ask me. It's beyond words . . .

SUZANNE: But what have I said?

SERGE: You haven't said one word since we came into this room which hasn't been beastly and tactless and insulting. . . . Oh, she doesn't mean it. It comes naturally. It's her one talent. I never have had a friend—but now even acquaintances avoid us. We live in a vacuum.

ARIADNE: Oh, I really think you're exaggerating. After all, I knew all about it. Madame Franchard is merely showing that she trusts us.

SERGE: Why did she insist on coming with me? [*to* PHILIP] I don't know if you're married . . .

ARIADNE: My brother's divorced.

SERGE: I can well understand that.

SUZANNE: [*vehemently*] And you can understand something else too. You and I will *never* be divorced. It's against our religion, and anyhow, I'd never do such a thing to mother . . .

SERGE: [*ironically*] Would she disinherit you?

SUZANNE: [*cut to the quick*] Oh, you are unkind. . . . [*to* ARIADNE] My mother's banker did a bolt last February with all her savings, so now she's on our hands. Oh, she does help in the house, and she cooks for us too.

SERGE: Some cooking!

SUZANNE: Is your rotten digestion her fault?

SERGE: Yes. She ruined it.

SUZANNE: That's not true. Even before we were married you always said you couldn't digest cabbage or onions or . . .

PHILIP: [*getting up*] I'm so sorry, but I've just remembered an urgent letter. [*to* ARIADNE] Can I write in Jerome's study?

ARIADNE: Of course. Only don't take his pen . . . no-one's allowed to use that.

PHILIP: Perhaps I'll see you later then. [*He goes out after having bowed goodbye*]

SERGE: I do wonder what your brother can be thinking of us.

ARIADNE: Don't worry. I'll explain to him.

SERGE: I really must apologise for my wife. She's completely uninhibited.

ARIADNE: Is that a fault?

SUZANNE: I thought that as the gentleman was your brother . . . You see, *you*—somehow you make me feel I can trust you. . . .

ARIADNE: [*following her own thoughts*] Nowadays no-one even tries to control themselves. I notice it more each time I come to Paris, even in my own family. It's as if the pressure of life had become intolerable—as if our very hearts must burst.

SUZANNE: Oh, that *is* so true, Madame.

ARIADNE: At my home up in the mountains I hardly see anyone but invalids.

SERGE: You're so good, so wonderfully devoted. . . .

ARIADNE: It's different for them. In spite of everything they are more sheltered and protected. Even their illness is a kind of screen between them and outside events. But down here . . . you're right out in the open, you're exposed to all the terrible forces that have been let loose upon the world . . .

SERGE: [*gloomily*] One thing's certain—*I* shan't stick it long.

SUZANNE: Don't listen to him. He's much better than before we married. He hasn't had a cold all the winter.

SERGE: Why bother to go on struggling? The game isn't worth the candle.

SUZANNE: Oh! And what would happen to me, I'd like to know? *I* enjoy life, Madame. Is there any harm in that?

SERGE: It's a queer taste.

ARIADNE: [*to* SUZANNE] No, no, you're right. Our life . . . in the long run we get what we deserve.

SERGE: I really do kick at that. Have I deserved this humiliation? . . .

SUZANNE: What's humiliating you?

SERGE: Violetta despises me.

SUZANNE: That's not true.

SERGE: I'm sure of it. And with reason, too.

SUZANNE: But after all, what about her? She's . . .

ARIADNE: [*interrupting*] Please don't go on. I am extremely fond of Violetta Mazargues. She's a very fine person indeed. [*A pause*]

SERGE: [*crushed*] That is true. What do you think of her sister?

ARIADNE: It's hard to say. At one time we corresponded quite a lot. But her letters always seemed so artificial. I'd been able to help her a little and I felt she was trying to please me by writing on what she imagined to be my level— a high spiritual plane, if you like. But it never rang true.

SERGE: She's a nasty little cat. I never could stick her.

ARIADNE: Oh, no, she's a victim too. Please don't judge her.

SUZANNE: You're ever so wonderful!

SERGE [*to* ARIADNE] She hasn't done *you* any harm.

ARIADNE: [*solemnly*] Are you sure?

SUZANNE: [*to* SERGE] You know nothing about it.

SERGE: But she's always hurting *me* with her double meanings and cattish hints. . . .

SUZANNE: You're too touchy, you are. After all, do you wonder she was fed up with you?

SERGE: With me? Why?

SUZANNE: Well, but for you, Violetta might have had a comfortable home of her own by now.

SERGE: A comfortable home! She isn't a tabby cat.

SUZANNE: We women *need* security. It's natural enough, isn't it?

SERGE: Speak for yourself.

SUZANNE: She needs it too, as much as anyone else. . . .

SERGE: [*explosively*] I swear to you I didn't seduce her. I didn't want—I didn't feel I had the right to. . . . And afterwards, no-one knows how I *hated* myself. I wished I were dead.

ARIADNE: [*in a voice conveying the contrary*] I'm not worthy of all these confidences.

SERGE: But I only came to see you to talk about her. Is it my fault if Suzanne would come too? I warned her . . .

SUZANNE: [*exploding*] And you say *I'm* tactless! What do you call coming here because you're crazy about Violetta? Madame Leprieur's the last person to talk to about her . . .

ARIADNE: [*stressing her words*] I don't know what you mean by that. But I must ask you again to stop all these vague hints. I'm sure you know nothing to bear them out.

SUZANNE: [*to* SERGE] Are you kidding yourself you'll get her back? Then you can take it from me you're wrong. She scarcely gives you a thought. And I doubt if you ever did count for much with her, anyhow. Look how easily she took our marriage. The truth is . . .

ARIADNE: Stop! You're going to say something you'll be sorry for. Now, do let's talk about little Monica, shall we?

SERGE: There's trouble to come there too. She's just like my little sister, the one who died when she was five.

ARIADNE: Oh, don't say things like that. It would be far better to think what can be done to make her stronger.

SERGE: Fernande wanted some old nurse to take her away to the country, but Violetta refused. And she was right. I never trust that sort of woman an inch.

Suzanne: All the same, it was the only way for her to get good fresh air.

Ariadne: Perhaps not the *only* way . . .

Serge: It always comes back to this miserable question of money.

Ariadne: That may not be insoluble. Near Grenoble there's a Home, like those Preventive Homes in Switzerland where delicate children are sent before they get really ill. I'm on the committee. I could easily ask them to take Monica for a time.

Serge: But she oughtn't to be with a lot of little consumptives.

Suzanne: Serge!

Ariadne: There's no danger of that . . .

Suzanne: You're ever so kind. How can we thank you . . .

Serge: I must say, it does seem a wonderful idea. . . . But we'll have to see what Violetta thinks.

Suzanne: [*thoughtfully*] That's true. Violetta is sometimes so queer—and suspicious, awfully suspicious.

Ariadne: Need she know it's my idea? Couldn't you tell her it was being arranged by one of your relations? If I were you, I wouldn't have any scruples about a little white lie like that.

Serge: [*uncomfortably*] No, perhaps not . . .

Ariadne: I'll see about it. I'll go into the whole thing. If it's all right I'll send you a line to do as we've said.

Serge: But supposing Violetta asks me for details? . . . Invention's not my strong point.

Suzanne: Don't fuss, Serge. We'll get away with it between us, never you fear.

Philip *comes in.*

Serge: [*to* Ariadne, *on seeing* Philip] I'm so sorry, we've stayed much too long.

Suzanne: Oh dear, yes, it's ever so late. . . .

Ariadne: Not at all. I'm very glad we've been able to have this talk.

SERGE: There's one thing I *would* like to ask you. You'll be seeing Violetta. Could you possibly find out what she's doing about a fellow called Bassigny? . . . I'm not at all happy about it. . . . You'd feel the same if you knew him. . . .

ARIADNE: Of course, I'll do my best.

SUZANNE: Now Serge, don't start off again. Goodbye, Madame, I'm ever so pleased to have met you. . . . [*They shake hands and* SERGE *and* SUZANNE *go out*]

PHILIP: Well! Who on earth are those extraordinary people? And what's it all about? It seems pretty queer to me.

ARIADNE: [*exasperated*] I've told you once already. I went to see an ex-patient, whom I've been helping for some time. And there I met Serge Franchard again.

PHILIP: Who's Violetta?

ARIADNE: I told you—her sister. She gives me lessons in accompaniment. . . .

PHILIP: I got that. But why does this Franchard fellow take such a violent interest in her?

ARIADNE: They had an affair. He's the father of her little girl.

PHILIP: He left her?

ARIADNE: I don't think so. As far as I know they agreed to separate, and then he married this woman.

PHILIP: Tactful, isn't she!

ARIADNE: We don't know . . .

PHILIP: And where do *you* come in?

ARIADNE: What?

PHILIP: How are you mixed up in it all?

ARIADNE: I'm not. Surely that's obvious.

PHILIP: Then why did these people come to see you?

ARIADNE: I was very glad to meet him again and I asked him to come and see me sometime.

PHILIP: Pretty weak at the knees, isn't he!

ARIADNE: He'd much rather have come without his wife.

PHILIP: [*thoughtfully*] It's odd, but . . .

ARIADNE: Well, what's odd?

PHILIP: It all gives me a vaguely unpleasant feeling. . . .

ARIADNE: I don't see . . . [*A pause*]

PHILIP: [*suddenly*] I think I've got it! [ARIADNE *starts apprehensively*] Yes, I felt exactly the same the day I found you talking to Gilbert Deplaine . . .

ARIADNE: But I've explained to you . . .

PHILIP: [*categorically*] You have. But still I shall never understand what you were after. You knew Gilbert was my wife's lover. You knew I was determined to divorce her. You were ill, and seeing no-one. And *yet*, there you were, having a heart-to-heart with this boy whom you scarcely knew . . .

ARIADNE: That's not true. He used to go to Logny to see his sister. We'd had some very long talks . . .

PHILIP: And what did you hope to achieve by seeing him?

ARIADNE: How can I say? I may have been deceiving myself, but I hoped up to the end that you and Clarissa would come together again. I *still* think your divorce might have been avoided . . .

PHILIP: Avoided! That's all nonsense. Do you know what I really think? . . .

ARIADNE: Well?

PHILIP: [*thoughtfully*] I don't think your motive was exactly curiosity. It was something more vague, but *far* more powerful. . . .

ARIADNE: I don't understand.

PHILIP: Call it the need to *assert* yourself, to work yourself into the very centre of other people's lives. . . . It's strange. I know, you make me think of those theatrical producers who won't have any barrier between stage and audience. You can't stand barriers. And look at this affair. I don't know what it's all about, but I'm sure you want to worm your way right into the very middle of it.

ARIADNE: In fact, what you're saying is that I am capable of sympathy. And I'm afraid from the way you talk you're not. That's probably why you did a thing I could never have done in your place.

PHILIP: Divorce Clarissa do you mean? I've never regretted it, not for one moment, believe me. [ARIADNE *makes a gesture of doubt*] You don't?

ARIADNE: Yes, I do believe you. Absolutely. Only . . . Clarissa has a point of view too. You've no idea what she feels about it all.

PHILIP: I suppose she's perfectly happy—and anyhow, I don't care.

ARIADNE: You suppose.

PHILIP: Well?

ARIADNE: I've reason to suspect otherwise.

PHILIP: What do you mean?

ARIADNE: What I said.

PHILIP: Then you've kept in touch with her?

ARIADNE: She has written to me.

PHILIP: *She* wrote first?

ARIADNE: I may have sent her a postcard. I really don't remember.

PHILIP: [*furiously*] Anyhow, her confidences to you don't interest me at all. But you had no business to listen to them, let me tell you, far less to *ask* for them, as you probably did.

JEROME *comes in.*

JEROME: Hullo! What's up? Am I interrupting?

PHILIP: Not in the least. I've merely found out something extremely unpleasant.

ARIADNE: That's most unfair. I've known Clarissa for twenty years. What right have you to prevent me writing to her?

PHILIP: In the old days you didn't think her worth your notice. She only began to interest you when her behaviour . . .

ARIADNE: Oh, please don't talk nonsense.

PHILIP: It's the exact truth.

ARIADNE: And now she's miserable—almost a wreck.

PHILIP: She's plenty to live on.

ARIADNE: You think that's enough for her?

PHILIP: It's certainly the main thing, in her eyes.

ARIADNE: It's generous of you, isn't it, to run her down now?

JEROME: [*very strung up*] Why talk about Clarissa? She's gone out of our lives.

PHILIP: On the contrary, she seems very much *in* them . . .

JEROME: Anyhow, please don't talk about her here. . . . But what I want to know is—did anyone come here while I was out?

PHILIP: Yes, indeed. You missed a very odd visit.

JEROME: The Franchards, wasn't it? I thought so. I've just passed them across the way. They seemed to be having an almighty row.

PHILIP: They seem to go in for rows!

JEROME: Why did they come here?

PHILIP: Ask your wife. I don't know. . . . But I do know that in your place I should most certainly find out. Goodbye. [*He goes out*]

ARIADNE: [*tenderly*] Darling one, you're looking terribly tired.

JEROME: Why should I be tired?

ARIADNE: You seem to work so hard these days. Look at that article on the Ravel festival, how you had to rush it through in no time. . . .

JEROME: [*bitterly*] I'm getting to know the tricks of the trade, you see.

ARIADNE: Of course you are. Up in the mountains I read your articles every week and I noticed how they came more and more easily.

JEROME: You wait. In a year or two there'll be no gossip writer to beat me.

ARIADNE: You—a gossip writer?

JEROME: Yes. What else is a man who scribbles about things he knows *nothing* of? . . .

ARIADNE: Knows nothing of? . . .

JEROME: My technical knowledge is nil, exactly nil, and you know it. What's more, there are times when music bores me stiff.

ARIADNE: Only when you're out of sorts.

JEROME: I'm out of sorts pretty often then.

ARIADNE: Why?

JEROME: [*without answering her question*] It's exasperating the way some people treat music as a religion. It isn't a religion. It's an entertainment.

ARIADNE: Oh, darling, I've heard you, yourself . . .

JEROME: Of course I've sometimes said the opposite. What of it? . . . But music simply devours some people's lives. That's what I can't stand.

ARIADNE: Whose life?

JEROME: [*retreating*] No-one in particular. It often happens, often.

ARIADNE: But aren't all the passions . . . devouring?

JEROME: Passions!

ARIADNE: You certainly don't look at all well. Haven't you got thinner lately?

JEROME: I don't know. I don't think so.

ARIADNE: We must make sure. Do you eat enough when I'm away? I've been looking over the cook's bills. You seem to have ordered the same thing every day. It's really better to ring the changes a little, you know. The fact is, *I* ought to be doing the housekeeping for you.

JEROME: From up there?

ARIADNE: Why not? . . . And Philip has worried me too. Just now he said . . . Jerome, tell me, aren't you just a *tiny* bit too economical when I'm away?

JEROME: Oh, tell Philip to keep out of it.

ARIADNE: That's a lot to ask him. . . . Then it's true?

JEROME: What?

ARIADNE: That you make a point of spending as little as possible?

JEROME: It's very natural, isn't it?

ARIADNE: I don't think so.

JEROME: You needn't worry. I get all I need.

ARIADNE: Oh, Jerome, that's too much! . . . And look at your clothes. We'll go together to Tiercelier tomorrow and order two suits and a dinner jacket.

JEROME: Is that all?

ARIADNE: Don't you see? I want you to do me credit. And

we'll go to that good hat man as well. You know . . . I can't
remember his name.

JEROME: I've just got a new hat.

ARIADNE: I don't like it. I'm sure it's not a good one.
[*Pause*]

JEROME: Ariadne!

ARIADNE: Yes, my darling?

JEROME: Do you really mean all that? Can't you see that the
one thing I want is to stop being . . . being dependent on
you? . . .

ARIADNE: But, Jerome . . .

JEROME: Would I have trailed around as I did to get those
newspaper columns unless I was absolutely determined to
earn my own living?

ARIADNE: Then Philip was right . . .

JEROME: Oh, Lord, can't we leave Philip out of it?

ARIADNE: But, darling, if you hate this work so much, we
really *must* find you something else.

JEROME: Don't be so childish. Can't you get it into your head
that one's dashed lucky these days to have a job with any
pay at all?

ARIADNE: I know, I know, but all the same . . . Oh, it's so
absurd. Why can't you see that my one *real* joy is just to
make life a little easier for you.

JEROME: I'm sorry. But you'll have to gratify yourself some
other way.

ARIADNE: [*brusquely*] You're angry with me!

JEROME: Me?

ARIADNE: You certainly are. But why? Oh, well, I suppose
it's only too natural.

JEROME: Now what are you getting at?

ARIADNE: It's my miserable health. You can't forget it.

JEROME: *I* blame you for your bad health?

ARIADNE: Yes, darling, even if you don't realise it. It's the
only explanation.

JEROME: I did think I'd at least proved to you . . .

ARIADNE: You've been marvellous—so patient. But even patience must wear out in the end. . . .

JEROME: But you're better.

ARIADNE: At what a price!

JEROME: You know, you don't look in the least ill any longer.

ARIADNE: Oh, but one can't trust people's looks. I wish one could.

JEROME: So much so that I've sometimes wondered . . . Couldn't you perhaps try to get back to normal, little by little, of course.

ARIADNE: Exactly what do you mean, darling?

JEROME: Well, what about staying here till I could go away with you?

ARIADNE: That's just what the doctor begged me *not* to do. But, of course, if you'd like it . . .

JEROME: I thought you'd given up seeing a doctor.

ARIADNE: I often meet Doctor Droz with one or other of my patients. Naturally he asks how I . . .

JEROME: Oh, do stop saying *my* patients! It's maddening.

ARIADNE: Yes, I see. You're quite right. If it would make you a little happier, a little calmer . . . Yes, darling, I'll try to do as you ask.

JEROME: But I'm not asking anything, Ariadne. Do understand that. I wouldn't for the world make you have a relapse!

ARIADNE: What *do* you want then, darling? One really must take the consequences of what one does. . . . All the same I'm delighted to find that I am, shall we say—wanted? [*She speaks half questioningly*] Many men in your position . . .

JEROME: Well?

ARIADNE: No, you'd be angry. . . . It was just—most men in your position would have found themselves some amusement or other. And really, who could blame them!

JEROME: [*suspiciously*] Why do you say that?

ARIADNE: I feel more and more certain that one should always look facts in the face.

JEROME: [*very low*] It's not always possible.

ARIADNE: What did you say, darling?

JEROME: [*a little louder*] It's sometimes difficult.

ARIADNE: I can't help feeling you're worried about something. Won't you tell me?

JEROME: [*after a pause*] Worried? No. Why should I be?

ARIADNE: [*ambiguously*] Then that's all right. I wouldn't insult you by thinking you're not telling me the truth.

JEROME: You sound ironical.

ARIADNE: Not in the least little bit, darling. And, after all, if you had a secret, I oughtn't to mind. [JEROME *moves uneasily*] I said, *if* you had . . .

JEROME: I still can't make out why the Franchards came here. What did they want?

ARIADNE: They seemed to think I could help them.

JEROME: Why should they think that? . . . You met them at the Mazargues girls, didn't you?

ARIADNE: I met him. But we know them. You know that quite well.

JEROME: I suppose you've heard the whole story . . . and how vilely this Franchard fellow behaved to that girl. It defeats me how you can ask him here.

ARIADNE: But she has him to her house.

JEROME: Because of the child. But she doesn't speak to him.

ARIADNE: It didn't seem like that to me.

JEROME: What could she do, with you there? . . . And anyhow, why were you? That's another thing I don't see—why you had to throw yourself at that girl's head as you did.

ARIADNE: She's very talented. I wanted some lessons. What's odd in that?

JEROME: There are other talented violinists.

ARIADNE: Why should I prefer them? She has great charm.

JEROME: How do you know? She's very reserved and very difficult to know. . . . She's coming here presently, isn't she?

ARIADNE: Well?

JEROME: That's really too much.

ARIADNE: May I point out that she makes something out of these lessons, quite apart from the pleasure they give me.

JEROME: Oh! Then it's charity, is it?

ARIADNE: In no way.

JEROME: If she thought that, you wouldn't see her for dust. She's very proud.

ARIADNE: You've often been to see her?

JEROME: Oh, four or five times, maybe.

ARIADNE: Not more?

JEROME: I don't think so. I didn't count. . . . She's not really my sort.

ARIADNE: Who's Bassigny?

JEROME: An impresario.

ARIADNE: Does he count for anything in her life?

JEROME: [*violently*] What? [*controlling himself*] How should I know? She doesn't let me in on her private life.

ARIADNE: The first time I saw you with her, do you know, just for a second I wondered . . .

JEROME: Well?

ARIADNE: But, of course, I see now how absurd it was. . . .

JEROME: Congratulations.

ARIADNE: Congratulations? On what?

JEROME: On getting over such an extraordinarily silly idea. [*In another tone*] I'm sorry . . . Yes, yes, I know I'm beastly to you. It's not my fault. I'm weak and unhappy. I suppose I was intended for quite a different life. Oh, I do wish my parents had always been poor. Then I'd have been brought up to it. But when they lost every penny it knocked me out . . . I shall never recover . . .

ARIADNE: Don't be so silly, Jerome, dear. I don't know anyone who cares less for money than you.

JEROME: That's true, maybe, but so's the contrary. Independence, Ariadne, independence . . . I can't do without it, and all the same it frightens me. Perhaps if it were offered me, I shouldn't want it.

ARIADNE: Oh, how you do torment yourself! How terribly miserable you make yourself!

JEROME: Night after night I can't sleep at all.

ARIADNE: Another thing you've hidden from me! [JEROME *stirs uneasily*] But we'll soon cure that. I've just been told about some wonderful tablets. They're made in Czechoslovakia, and they do you no harm at all. I'll order you some at once.

The MAID *comes in.*

MAID: Mademoiselle Violetta Mazargues, Madame.

ARIADNE: Ask her to come in, please. And will you bring us some tea, Elise.

MAID: Yes, Madame. [*She goes out and a moment later brings in* VIOLETTA]

VIOLETTA: How do you do, Madame. I'm so sorry, I'm afraid I'm late.

ARIADNE: Oh, no, I don't think you are. . . . Anyhow it doesn't matter at all. You'll have some tea with us, won't you?

VIOLETTA: Thank you.

ARIADNE: I've some new sonatas you may not know and I'm longing to play them with you. Do you mind if I just get them before tea comes? It'll save time. My husband will look after you for a moment, won't you, Jerome? [*She goes out*]

JEROME: All that's so horribly false. Don't you feel it? Don't you mind? [VIOLETTA *makes a helpless gesture*] We *must* think of some excuse to stop these lessons.

VIOLETTA: It's impossible.

JEROME: The easy way you're accepting all this—it shocks me profoundly.

VIOLETTA: How do you know I do?

JEROME: You could always have said you'd no time. . . . No, the fact is, my wife has grown fond of you. You ought to be horrified, but you're not. You feel flattered . . . you're not the same any more.

VIOLETTA: [*looking fixedly at him*] Jerome, isn't there a very simple way—here and now—to put an end to all these lies?

JEROME: Tell her the truth? God! Never! Never! A shock like that, when she's still so delicate . . . You can't tell what . . .

VIOLETTA: Is that the *only* reason?

JEROME: No, perhaps not.

VIOLETTA: You're not being honest, Jerome. You know it's not even the main one.

JEROME: I haven't got to make a list of reasons for which it's impossible. . . . If I thought she suspected, I don't know what I'd do. Life would be unbearable.

VIOLETTA: Why, Jerome?

JEROME: You don't understand what there is between Ariadne and me. . . .

VIOLETTA: [*with profound sadness*] You're wrong, my dear. What I don't understand is . . . and it would be so simple for you to be brave and tell me. If you think we've made a mistake, you and I, there's still time to face it. . . . I promise you not to be angry.

JEROME: Violetta! You know we didn't make a mistake. If you knew how I've missed you all this week. . . . I've been simply frantic. Come here. [*He kisses her*] And yet . . . and yet, we shall have to . . . you understand . . .

VIOLETTA: [*with sudden revulsion*] Never! . . . It's all so contemptible. If there *is* this link you speak of between you two . . . and now that I know her . . .

JEROME: Your meeting each other was a disaster.

VIOLETTA: And it's a disaster that . . .

JEROME: Is it my fault that life's crazy and incoherent? Why can't we be the same? Violetta, we're *not* different. We're made of the same stuff, we're nothing but contradictions too.

VIOLETTA: I can't feel that.

JEROME: [*passionately*] I do loathe pride. I think I hate it more than anything in the world. We only stop lying to others just to lie to ourselves—and that's *more* contemptible.

VIOLETTA: I don't think you're being fair, Jerome.

JEROME: Is life fair?

VIOLETTA: Life . . . life . . . is it anything but a myth? And perhaps, after all, it's only what we deserve it to be.

JEROME: Deserve . . . [*suspiciously*] You might be Ariadne. . . .

ARIADNE *opens the door rather too carefully.*

ARIADNE: I'm *so* sorry. I couldn't find those sonatas anywhere. I must have lent them to someone, and they've not been returned. [*The* MAID *comes in, carrying a tray*] One moment, Elise, I'll clear this little table for you. . . . Help me, Jerome dear, will you. . . . But what's worse, the tuner let me down, and my piano's all out of tune. I'd have done far better to go to you. Yours is so lovely.

VIOLETTA: I've got to sell it.

JEROME: What?

VIOLETTA: So if, by any chance, you should hear of a possible buyer . . .

JEROME: But you can't . . .

ARIADNE: But your lessons? . . .

VIOLETTA: I don't give them at home as a rule, and I've a friend who doesn't use her upright. She'll lend it to me. It'll do quite well.

ARIADNE: I am so sorry.

VIOLETTA: It's just a matter of necessity. There's nothing tragic about it.

JEROME: [*making a slip*] But I'm used to *that* piano. [*The two women pretend not to notice the slip*]

ARIADNE: Well, if you've really decided . . .

VIOLETTA: Yes, there's nothing else to be done.

ARIADNE: I'll tell everyone I know. I think I've an idea already.

VIOLETTA: Thank you so much. You're very kind.

ARIADNE [*giving her a cup of tea*] I hope it's not too strong. A little more water, perhaps?

VIOLETTA: Thanks, that's perfect.

ARIADNE: And yours, darling, now you've told me you can't sleep, I'll give it to you very weak. . . . And in future you'd better have—well, perhaps cocoa, instead?

JEROME: What an idea!

ARIADNE: Oh, but why not? Dutch cocoa's delicious.

JEROME: Tea has never yet stopped me from sleeping.

VIOLETTA: I think Madame Leprieur's quite right.

JEROME: [*too emphatically*] What's this coalition? [*He get up*] I've just remembered I promised my article on the Spanish Dancers for tomorrow. I must go and finish it. Will you excuse me, Mademoiselle? [*He goes out*]

VIOLETTA: [*in a strained voice*] Really . . . it's impossible.

ARIADNE: What's impossible?

VIOLETTA: I don't understand why I didn't tell him you knew everything, then and there.

ARIADNE: You would have broken your promise. That would have been very wrong.

VIOLETTA: All the same, I'd have done it . . . only . . . Oh, I don't know . . . I felt it wouldn't have helped . . . rather the reverse.

ARIADNE: That's quite true.

VIOLETTA: How can you be sure?

ARIADNE: I felt the same. It was an intuition.

VIOLETTA: Oh, I've no intuition. I'm just a coward, that's all.

ARIADNE: No, I'm sure you're anything but that.

VIOLETTA: I am, a miserable coward. And you . . . I don't understand you at all. Sometimes I admire you more than anyone, but sometimes . . .

ARIADNE: Well?

VIOLETTA: I can't explain. I seem to lose my balance. It's awful, like falling through space. Oh, you don't owe me any explanation. I doubt if you could even give me one if you tried. But . . . it's your incredible generosity . . . and the way you made me promise . . . and now, you're so cool and calm when I'm . . . oh, and lots of other things. I can't tell you how unworthy I feel even to come near you, when I've betrayed you so. . . . But all the same, have pity on me, *please* . . . make me understand.

ARIADNE: You mustn't admire *me*. And this other feeling you can't explain, I don't think you must let that run away with you either. You see, there's something you haven't taken into account. After years of physical suffering, I feel one can't help looking at life—no, that's not the right word—evaluating it, in a quite new way. Yes, that's it, one's *values* are different. I'd almost say that certain moral conventions can only be accepted, or even recognised, by healthy people. Illness, you see, Violetta . . . Oh, I certainly don't want to say that it's a privilege or that it frees us from any responsibility. But I've learnt that it does alter one's attitude to the world, or, rather, to a certain natural order of things. It's as if one became aware of another, unguessed-at aspect of them, another dimension perhaps . . .

VIOLETTA: But if that were true, then it *would* be a privilege.

ARIADNE: No, because there's nothing inevitable about it. I've known many invalids who never rose above the first stage of revolt and despair. They had not been granted the power to lift themselves into this second consciousness, which includes our normal consciousness, but surpasses it. . . .

VIOLETTA: It's so hard to follow you. And I don't see . . .

ARIADNE: It's an experience which cannot be imagined or anticipated, though as a matter of fact I am trying to convey it in a book I'm writing. It'll soon be finished, but it won't be published until I'm dead.

VIOLETTA: I didn't know you wrote. . . .

ARIADNE: I don't think even Jerome has any idea of it. Besides, it doesn't matter. I only wanted to make you understand that I can't judge of things like a woman who has never been lifted up to this other plane. There, even the word judge has no more meaning. I don't judge you. I never have, not for a second—any more than I do Jerome. And when I got the letter which confirmed my forebodings . . .

VIOLETTA: Letter?

ARIADNE: Yes, anonymous. I felt a kind of relief, you know. It was like a terrible load off my mind.

VIOLETTA: An anonymous letter! You never told me about it.

ARIADNE: It's of no importance.

VIOLETTA: Who could have been so low? . . . And anyway, no-one suspected. . . . Ah! . . . no, it's impossible.

ARIADNE: The writer didn't manage to disguise her handwriting very cleverly.

VIOLETTA: You recognised it?

ARIADNE: I think so.

VIOLETTA: Then . . . it's Fernande?

ARIANDE: [*nods assent*] We must only think of it as the act of a sick woman. . . . She must never know you've heard about it. . . .

VIOLETTA: More prevarications! More lies! Oh, how it all stifles me. And these things you've tried to explain . . . they're too difficult and remote for me, really they are. This plane you talk about, is it what they call faith? You see, I'm not a Christian. The people round me have never been Christians.

ARIADNE: The truth I sense is far above any church. . . .

VIOLETTA: But surely it should penetrate everything, like a light. . . . Can truth accommodate itself to all this concealment and dissimulation? I can't believe it. If, in spite of everything, you could speak openly to Jerome, if you really tried—oh, how *can* one put it?—tried to pass on to him this wisdom. . . .

ARIADNE: My poor child, you're being deluded by words. Jerome has been *damaged*. We've no right *ever* to forget that.

VIOLETTA: Damaged? What do you mean?

ARIADNE: I don't know that I ought to tell you.

VIOLETTA: [*bitterly*] It's too late to hesitate now.

ARIADNE: Well, you know that Jerome and I grew up together and, from the very beginning, we'd planned to marry one day. The idea was a part of our lives. We never stopped to think about it. Our families thoroughly approved, except perhaps my father, and I think he felt our belief in a joint destiny was not without its dangers. He had more vision than my mother or Jerome's parents. Yet he never felt he had any right to speak openly of his fears to me. But—and this I didn't understand till later, when I made some enquiries—Jerome ran into a special kind of temptation at the University, and particularly in England, and he only won through after a terribly exhausting struggle. And you see, what saved him wasn't religious conviction or belief in a moral law. It was just the thought of me, of our marriage, of what it demanded of him. I'm quite convinced that, if he'd fallen, he never could have faced me, never. I feel sure he'd rather have killed himself. The day before we were married he tried to tell me, by half hints—I'd no idea what he meant—to tell me I'd saved him. I thought he was warning me of his inexperience as a lover and I was frightened. It's true that . . . [*she stops herself*]

VIOLETTA: Oh, please, please, don't tell me any more.

ARIADNE: And then, after all, though we would neither of us admit it, even to ourselves, our marriage was a bitter disappointment for us both. I adapted myself fairly easily, I don't know why, though I soon fell ill, it's true. But Jerome fretted and fretted, I know, and I'm sure his wretched habit of running himself down to other people—and to himself even—dates from that time. You see how all that has tortured me these dreary years I've been so ill. At times I've felt like his evil spirit . . . almost as if I'd torn him from his real destiny.

VIOLETTA: You can't mean . . .

ARIADNE: Yes, I've even asked myself that. But at the same time I knew he repudiated his own regrets, violent though they were. I knew I still stood for his better self. I've never feared death for myself . . . but twice, when it seemed certain, I was terrified. I couldn't face what might become of Jerome without me. Tell me, do you *now* begin to see why jealousy is the very last thing . . .

VIOLETTA: There's something about all that which makes me feel quite sick.

ARIADNE: Had you never suspected this . . . peculiar tendency of Jerome's.

VIOLETTA: Never!

ARIADNE: If you'd known his early surroundings, you'd be less surprised. You see, I knew his mother and his aunts. They were over-refined, bloodless creatures, and they always wanted to protect him against life. . . . You know, it's very lucky he met you. I think you've somehow released him.

VIOLETTA: [*gently, but with a certain acidity*] We love each other, that's all.

ARIADNE: But that's just *why* you've probably saved him. If your attraction for him had been merely physical—that was hardly conceivable, of course—how could I have told you everything, as I'm doing now?

VIOLETTA: You can't help speaking of it as in the past.

ARIADNE: My dear, you look for trouble everywhere.

VIOLETTA: I don't have to *look* for it. . . . Besides you're right, it *is* past. Your incredible generosity doesn't change a thing. It's all a dead-end. From now on . . . [*She bursts into tears*]

ARIADNE: [*tenderly*] Have I explained myself so badly?

VIOLETTA: No, no, very well. Only too well . . .

ARIADNE: He will need you for a long time yet.

VIOLETTA: [*indistinctly*] And *you* will tell me when the time has come to wean him?

ARIADNE: What did you say? Wean him?

VIOLETTA: You see, I *have* understood . . .

ARIADNE: No, you haven't, dear, or your pride wouldn't be so up in arms. Do you think I don't envy you the part you've been given to play in his life? I do, terribly, and yet I'm not jealous, because in my envy there's not an ounce of bitterness or spite. . . . But, oh, isn't it a little hard for a woman to see herself so frustrated by fate?

VIOLETTA: You have the better part. You can't help it.

ARIADNE: But doesn't whether it's better depend on me? The fact is that one grain of egotism, the least personal desire, would make it utterly contemptible.

VIOLETTA: And do you know that I'm prepared to leave to *you* the privilege of self-sacrifice?

ARIADNE: Violetta, I've never said one word about sacrifice. I distrust it, I don't believe in it. To give up happiness means either to mutilate oneself, which I think wrong, or to lie to oneself, which I hate.

VIOLETTA: But then . . .

ARIADNE: I've seen the people round me sacrifice themselves, and their sacrifices weighed like a curse on the very people they were meant to benefit. Harmony can never be born from sacrifice.

VIOLETTA: I don't understand.

ARIADNE: If I sacrificed myself to your love, I shouldn't know it, but I should want some compensation, some reward. That unadmitted aim alone would be enough to create a fog of lies and equivocation between us three. And if by some miracle I did drive out all hope of recompense, what would happen to me? I should just sink into a state of hopeless despair. And however much I tried, Jerome would soon guess why.

VIOLETTA: There's only one way to avoid the lies and hypocrisy you're afraid of. Tell Jerome.

ARIADNE: That *seems* to be true, but it's not. Oh, don't you understand? They'd be there in another form. Truth isn't an object to be given away, it's not a thing to be communicated. I could never convince Jerome I wasn't sacrificing myself for his sake. And that he could never endure.

VIOLETTA: I'm sorry. Neither have you convinced me.

ARIADNE: There's one tiresome difficulty between Jerome and me. It's very silly, but he will insist on feeling himself in my debt. Many people would have thought themselves freed by my bad health, but he has felt himself bound to me by that even more than by the past.

VIOLETTA: It's quite natural.

ARIADNE: Do you really know men so little as that?

VIOLETTA: Well, it's how I should have felt.

ARIADNE: You're a woman. The more I try to free him, the

more I give him *carte-blanche*, the more I shall only in-crease this terrible, crushing feeling of indebtedness . . .

VIOLETTA: [*with energy*] But isn't a guilty conscience crushing too?

ARIADNE: Only one person can free him from that—you. And you must. I want you to. In a fortnight at latest, I shall go back to the mountains. Then we must find a way for you and Jerome to spend a few weeks quietly together, somewhere where nobody will know you. And we must think about Monica too. I'd meant to have a good talk about her today. Oh! I've just thought of something that might help. There's a wonderful home for children near Grenoble. I helped to found it, and I could arrange for you to spend a month with her there. It's not usually done, but I could fix it. And quite near, only twenty minutes away, I know a nice woman who keeps a little pension. It would be very restful for Jerome there and he'd get the food he likes. . . .

VIOLETTA: But it's out of the question. . . . Look at the coincidence. Jerome would be sure to find out that *you* had wanted—and planned—the whole thing.

ARIADNE: Yes, perhaps you're right. It would be dangerous. We must think it over.

VIOLETTA: But that's not all. I don't like this free hand you're giving us. And if you're encouraging us, it's—it's simply shocking.

ARIADNE: [*with crushing gentleness*] Are you reproaching *me*? . . .

VIOLETTA: You don't want to understand. . . . All the same I know there's something sham—unnatural—in all this. . . .

ARIADNE: Unnatural, Violetta? Yes, that may be. But is nature just? Is she pitiful? May not the state of nature be like a cocoon, that the chrysalis has to break?

VIOLETTA: If only you'd trust me to think for myself—stop guiding me . . .

ARIADNE: That's what I want to do. Only I don't feel you're quite strong enough yet. Just now you spoke of Jerome's guilty conscience, but isn't yours gnawing at you even more? And it's that, and that alone, which frightens me in you, my dear. You say you're not a Christian. Are you sure? Mayn't it, after all, be the fear of having disobeyed some higher law that is tormenting you?

VIOLETTA: No.

ARIADNE: But you insist that you're guilty. So it must be towards me, then?

VIOLETTA: I don't know, I can't explain at all. I feel it's this lie . . .

ARIADNE: But think. Suppose for a moment I tell Jerome that I know everything. Suppose, though it's impossible, that he accepts the position and your liaison goes on. Would you feel any better then?

VIOLETTA: I don't think so.

ARIADNE: Well, then, if you *must* feel guilty, let's call this lie which so weighs on you a punishment inflicted by me—for a crime, incidentally, which I refuse to recognise.

VIOLETTA: I give it up.

A long silence. JEROME *comes in.*

ARIADNE: Your article's finished? [*with slightly artificial playfulness*] You see, we've done no work today. I don't know what took us. We've been gossiping all the time.

JEROME: [*constrainedly*] So I see.

ARIADNE: [*to* VIOLETTA] If you really have to get rid of your piano, why shouldn't I buy it for Logny? [JEROME *moves uneasily*] I don't know what's happened to mine, it's nothing but an old tin kettle.

JEROME: I don't think that's a good idea at all.

VIOLETTA: Nor do I. I really couldn't . . .

ARIADNE: [*laughing*] Why? You'd both of you find it very hard to say. The more I think of it, the better it seems.

JEROME: Then it's clear we don't agree.

ARIADNE: Oh, dear, why will people make life so difficult for themselves? It could all be so easy—so easy. . . .

CURTAIN

ACT THREE

The same scene as in Act One. The curtain rises to discover VIOLETTA *and* FERNANDE.

FERNANDE: I think you're fussing far too much about this bronchitis, Violetta. I told you all along that doctor woman was an alarmist. Women always lose their heads.

VIOLETTA: I don't agree, and I've made up my mind. As soon as Monica is better I shall take her away to one of those Preventive Homes in the mountains.

FERNANDE: If you hadn't had that stupid row with Bassigny, he'd have sent us Dr. Paulus.

VIOLETTA: Any doctor who's a friend of Bassigny's is a quack, and please don't ever mention that revolting man to me again.

FERNANDE: Then may one ask your plans? A Home, yes, quite so—but who's to pay?

VIOLETTA: What?

FERNANDE: Unless you mean a so-called "charity" Home, of course. And she'd soon catch the illness you're trying to protect her from there. . . .

VIOLETTA: You know very well I should only leave her with people I could trust, absolutely.

FERNANDE: That's just talk. The security you want costs money. It's a luxury. How are you to pay for it? On who's goodwill are you counting?

VIOLETTA: I'll manage it somehow. I *must*.

FERNANDE: Does that mean, *he'll* manage it?

VIOLETTA: Serge can't do a thing for us. You know that.

FERNANDE: It wasn't Serge I was thinking of.

VIOLETTA: [*without answering*] You're altogether too ready

to take a hand in this odious blackmail. I shall **never** give in to it, never——

FERNANDE: What blackmail?

VIOLETTA: Never, whatever happens!

FERNANDE: If you mean Bassigny, I tell you flat—you've got yourself into a hole where it's no good being so difficult. Naturally, if you like to sacrifice your child to your own finicky tastes . . .

VIOLETTA: [*violently*] I *won't* sell myself.

FERNANDE: Say rather that you want to choose the buyer. Some one must cough up, and I don't think it'll be Jerome. He seems pretty close, to me——

VIOLETTA: Oh, you are despicable.

FERNANDE: Sell oneself or be kept. It's all one.

VIOLETTA: When have I been kept?

FERNANDE: You've managed to get along without it until now, I agree, but it's a luxury you'll soon have to give up. When the rent's paid we shall have just fifteen hundred francs left.

VIOLETTA: Well, you haven't fooled me with your tricks, let me tell you. I even know you wrote an anonymous letter to Ariadne Leprieur.

FERNANDE: [*staggered*] Me?

VIOLETTA: Yes, you—to separate Jerome and me, because you thought our liaison didn't *pay*. . . .

FERNANDE: My good girl, are you mad? But what's all this? Ariadne's had an anonymous letter? She told you so?

VIOLETTA: As it happens, she did.

FERNANDE: I can't believe it. Did she ask you any questions?

VIOLETTA: No.

FERNANDE: Not even . . .

VIOLETTA: Why should I answer you?

FERNANDE: Then you managed to put her off? . . . Well done! I didn't think you had it in you. You've gone up one in my eyes. But I daresay she doesn't care. It may even amuse her. Nine times out of ten these professional invalids are perverts.

VIOLETTA: Oh, stop it!

FERNANDE: Lesbians, as a rule! Oh! they don't always know it, of course.

VIOLETTA: Oh, *how* I despise you; you can't imagine how I despise you . . .

FERNANDE: One more luxury you won't be able to afford much longer. Did someone ring? It's all right, Madame Juquier's still there. She'll open the door. . . .

VIOLETTA: It must be Serge.

FERNANDE: There's the bell again! [*There is a knock at the door*] Who is it?

SERGE: [*from outside*] It's me.

VIOLETTA: [*drearily*] You can come in.

SERGE *enters.*

SERGE: What did the doctor say?

VIOLETTA: The bronchitis is getting less. But she says there's a danger of re-infection, and she wants Monica to go away as soon as her temperature's down. She thinks she ought to spend a least a year in the country, in one of those Preventive Homes.

FERNANDE: I've told you already what I think of that idea.

SERGE: But how are you going to manage? Suzanne and I do nothing but rack our brains. . . . I must say she's been wonderfully decent. [*Hesitantly. He is clearly reciting a lesson*] She's even remembered a distant cousin on the committee of some Home . . . I can't remember the name, it's near Grenoble, I think.

VIOLETTA: It must be Grancey. I've heard of it.

FERNANDE: These places cost the earth.

SERGE: Suzanne's sure she can get a big reduction through this cousin of hers. I gather her father once did him a good turn.

FERNANDE: You sound exactly as if you were saying your lessons.

SERGE: [*uncomfortably*] I'm not very clear about it all.

FERNANDE: That's a pity. Perhaps the place is really a nerve clinic near Bayonne.

VIOLETTA: Fernande!

SERGE: There's a good chance—at least, fair.

VIOLETTA: Please thank your wife very much. Perhaps she would give me some details about it.

SERGE: She'll write. She's got an awful cold at the moment. Such a bore——

FERNANDE: You do look peculiar.

SERGE: Oh, can't you leave me alone?

FERNANDE: With pleasure! But if I may give you a word of advice, disguise your handwriting better next time. [*She goes out*]

SERGE: What *does* she mean? Well? What does she?

VIOLETTA: Serge!

SERGE: What's she *getting* at? Well?

VIOLETTA: You're putting that on.

SERGE: Well?

VIOLETTA: Don't keep on saying "well"? . . . Serge, *you* wrote that letter?

SERGE: What letter?

VIOLETTA: You know you've never succeeded in lying to me yet, though God knows you've tried often enough. . . . But Serge! I didn't think you could do a thing like that. . . .

SERGE: Well?

VIOLETTA: It's the first thing that I can *never* forgive you.

SERGE: You never have forgiven me for anything. . . . Oh, I don't mean you hate me. Not even that. You just despise me.

VIOLETTA: I used not to.

SERGE: Perhaps that's why I wrote to Madame Leprieur—to give you something to despise me for.

VIOLETTA: It's far simpler than that. It was vengeance. You couldn't endure my little bit of happiness . . .

SERGE: You, happy? My poor girl, look in the glass. . . . She showed you the letter? [VIOLETTA *indicates that she did not*] Then how do you know she ever had one? What did she make of it?

VIOLETTA: Nothing, apparently.

SERGE: Oh! Of course it was damn silly. But you see . . . my life isn't so funny. . . .

VIOLETTA: I know.

SERGE: No, you don't. Not really. Suzanne . . . oh! she's not a bad creature, but, to begin with, she's not an artist. It's not only that she knows nothing about music—though she thinks she does. Do you know, sometimes she advises me. "You're playing too loud" she says, "You're using too much pedal . . ." It's laughable. . . . That doesn't much matter. I'll shut her up in time. But it's her *appalling* lack of tact! The things she comes out with sometimes . . .

VIOLETTA: Neither does that matter, really. She loves you.

SERGE: I don't care for being loved in that way. . . . She exhausts me.

VIOLETTA: Remember, you said that of me too, once.

SERGE: *Please*, Violetta . . . I really can't go into details. . . . But do you know I'm reduced to begging for two nights a week off—and I haven't yet got them! She works herself up so and simply raises hell.

VIOLETTA: Poor old Serge. And *you* talked of delicacy . . .

SERGE: How damned foolish I've been, all the same! No, worse than foolish, disgusting. . . . When I think . . .

VIOLETTA: Remember what we agreed.

SERGE: I can't sleep any more. One can face up to accidents or disasters. But to spoil everything by one's own idiocy, by . . .

VIOLETTA: [*sadly*] I don't think there was much left to spoil, you know.

SERGE: Not only idiocy—caddishness . . .

VIOLETTA: Now what are you going to rake up?

SERGE: Do you remember the evening of your concert at the Schola, how everyone rushed in to congratulate you, and it looked as if your career had begun . . . a *real* career . . .

VIOLETTA: Well?

SERGE: I can't tell you how furious I was! You see, you paid no attention to me at all. And next day too, you were far away, in the clouds . . . I made up my mind life would be unbearable, so that very day I asked Suzanne to marry me . . . It was vile! . . . Can you ever forgive me?

VIOLETTA: Poor old Serge!

SERGE: You see, once—when I got that scholarship—I was ambitious too. I *so* much wanted to do something worth doing . . . and it's clear that if we hadn't lived in these horrible times . . . You're not too angry with me, are you? . . . I don't disgust you more than ever?

VIOLETTA: No, Serge, no. I'd already guessed it . . . and it's brave of you to tell me.

SERGE: It's not brave . . . it's like the letter.

VIOLETTA: Don't let's talk any more about that letter, please.

SERGE: You said you'd never forgive me.

VIOLETTA: That was only showing off. One shouldn't be so arrogant.

SERGE: How do you mean?

VIOLETTA: To forgive has long ceased to be a virtue—for ordinary people, I mean. . . . I sometimes think acquiescence, compliance, is the only real sin.

SERGE: For an artist . . .

VIOLETTA: I'm not talking about artists, but about life. If there's any expression I loathe, it's "one must resign oneself to circumstances." Oh dear, I seem to be doing it myself these days, as much as anybody.

SERGE: Are you hiding something from me?

VIOLETTA: Serge dear, why do you want me to worry you with all my troubles? It wouldn't be kind, and what good would it do?

SERGE: It's about Monica?

VIOLETTA: No, honestly, it's not Monica. . . .

SERGE: And there's something else I'm ashamed of, too. I pretended it was to see Monica I've been coming here, but she was only a pretext. You know what I'm like . . . now I keep wondering whether I brought her bad luck by making use of her illness like that.

VIOLETTA: Poor old Serge!

SERGE: Sometimes I feel I never grew up, only nobody
     guesses it. . . . I say, do you think I stopped developing
     when I won that scholarship?
VIOLETTA: It's true, you did tire yourself out dreadfully then.
SERGE: Sometimes I feel crazy with longing for the old days
     before that time, when I was a boy . . . even for people and
     places I didn't like; an old, half-dotty uncle, whom we were
     taken to see once a year; a little place by the river where we
     used to pick cherries. There's a blaring great factory there
     now. Violetta! I'm going to tell you something . . . Suzanne
     . . . she's never *really* meant anything to me—and even her
     money . . . you know I'm not a money-grubber. But—
     you'll laugh—she was like a maid we had at home long
     ago when everything was lovely, before mama got ill. . . .
     But for that, I'd never have married her.
VIOLETTA: [*emotionally*] My poor, poor Serge . . .

     JEROME *comes in.*

JEROME: [*very drily*] Oh! I beg your pardon. Your sister never
     told me . . . I thought you were alone.
VIOLETTA: [*to* SERGE] I'll go and see if Monica is awake . . .
     [*She goes to the door and listens. The two men look coldly at
     each other*] There's not a sound. She must be asleep still.
     Those bouts of coughing make her very tired.
JEROME: [*in an artificial voice*] Then she isn't any better?
VIOLETTA: Oh, yes. Madame Juquier is more satisfied today.
SERGE: I would have liked to peep at her, but . . .
VIOLETTA: You'd risk waking her.
JEROME: [*very tense*] I've only got a few minutes.
SERGE: [*deliberately dawdling*] I don't quite know when I can
     come tomorrow. My pupil in the Boulevard Voltaire wants
     to change his lesson. And you know how it is, sometimes
     one goes on a bit longer. . . . Would you mind if I came
     about seven-thirty, say?
VIOLETTA: That'll be quite all right.
JEROME: I'd come to ask you myself, *when* you'll be . . .
VIOLETTA: If I'm not there, Fernande can give you the news.

SERGE: Thanks.

VIOLETTA: Or I'll write you a little note.

SERGE: [*tensely*] But it's surely natural for . . .

JEROME: [*to* VIOLETTA] Will you in future very kindly let me know what days and hours you will be engaged?

SERGE: If you're referring to my visits . . .

JEROME: Precisely.

SERGE: You can't talk like that to *me*.

JEROME: [*to* VIOLETTA] You see how very unpleasant these meetings are.

VIOLETTA: [*to* SERGE *in a half whisper*] Listen, I'll be here tomorrow about half-past seven. But do be sensible now, and go away. [*After a moment's hesitation* SERGE *goes out in silence*]

JEROME: It's disgusting!

VIOLETTA: [*drearily*] *Must* you behave like that?

JEROME: You know perfectly well I can't stand the sight of the man. You might at least spare me that.

VIOLETTA: Do you imagine he enjoys meeting you?

JEROME: I couldn't care less.

VIOLETTA: I don't believe you're really capable of pity.

JEROME: Possibly not.

VIOLETTA: That's not very nice, is it?

JEROME: The fellow's a dirty cad.

VIOLETTA: I really wonder by what right . . .

JEROME: There can't be two opinions about the way he treated you.

VIOLETTA: No one but me is in any position to judge that.

JEROME: It isn't because you show such exaggerated charity . . .

VIOLETTA: You know quite well he neither seduced nor abandoned me.

JEROME: He took advantage of your inexperience.

VIOLETTA: He took advantage of nothing at all. I knew more about life than he did. He was a child—he still is. You know it wasn't just because I'd lost my head that I gave myself to him . . . I don't know. It was like a need *not* to safeguard myself or take care of the future. There's a kind of miserly prudence that has always revolted me. . . . Oh, it was probably inexcusable, I know——

JEROME: [*bitterly*] Yet you're proud of it.

VIOLETTA: You're wrong, Jerome, I'm not proud of it and neither am I ashamed of it. But I haven't yet learnt how to judge it, and its consequences, whatever they are, will never teach me that.

JEROME: Well! I think myself that if you showed such misplaced generosity . . .

VIOLETTA: What a way to talk!

JEROME: I can think of no other . . . it was doubly up to him to refuse. . . . He had only to go away . . .

VIOLETTA: Go away? Where? How could he have lived? You're dramatising, Jerome. In real life . . .

JEROME: Anyhow, when Monica was born, he should have married you.

VIOLETTA: Who told you that I would have accepted? It's very odd. You can't find your way about in your own life. You're lost in it, like a child in a wood. Yet you plan the lives of others without giving a thought to the lie of the land or the thickness of the trees—Or is it that you're not even conscious of your own inner confusion?

JEROME: [*sombrely*] I am. It stifles me.

VIOLETTA: But then, Jerome dear, don't you think . . . since we're condemned to live in the dark and to wander without hope, oughtn't we to—oh, how can I put it?—oughtn't we to draw the power to help others from the very darkness of our own despair? They are desperate and they don't know it. They don't even know their darkness for what it is.

JEROME: That's all high-falutin' rubbish. How on earth can our darkness produce light?

VIOLETTA: But if we *know* it, Jerome . . .

JEROME: If we knew it, it wouldn't be darkness.

VIOLETTA: It is and yet it isn't.

JEROME: That doesn't make sense. It's like nothing *I've* ever experienced.

VIOLETTA: It is an experience, all the same . . . like some wonderful change of heart . . . Perhaps conversion is not very different.

JEROME: Has Ariadne been stuffing your head with these outlandish ideas?

VIOLETTA: Ariadne? Certainly not. Being with her, perhaps.

JEROME: Oh, that's too subtle for me.

VIOLETTA: I'm no good at explaining. It's not so much what she says. It's more the fact that she exists—that she is *what* she is.

JEROME: If you've discovered her secret, you're one up on me . . .

VIOLETTA: Who said anything about secrets? The last time we were talking . . .

JEROME: There you are! The music's nothing but a pretext . . .

VIOLETTA: I thought of those glorious mountain tracks in the Vosges I love so much. One can climb from peak to peak for hours. *We* crawl painfully along the valleys, but Ariadne is always on the crest . . .

JEROME: On the crest! . . . In a labyrinth would be nearer the mark.

VIOLETTA: A labyrinth. I don't see what you mean.

JEROME: I suppose it's that silly name, Ariadne. . . . But all your interminable interviews, you will *not* understand how I dislike them. What's more, they've got to stop. I won't put up with them any longer.

VIOLETTA: She'll be going away soon.

JEROME: And how do I know your conversations won't continue by letter?

VIOLETTA: After all . . . [*she stops*]

JEROME: Well, what were you going to say?

VIOLETTA: No, nothing . . .

JEROME: What if she half suspects the truth? She may have hit on this infernal way of separating us.

VIOLETTA: Jerome, you're crazy.

JEROME: She hasn't been the same for some time. I've never felt her so remote. Oh! she's just as affectionate—more so, if anything. But I can't explain, she's queer and over-excited. Of course, I see that doesn't make sense if she suspects. . . . Do you know, I've discovered she's writing a book, a kind of intimate diary—to be given to the world after her death, I suppose. One more head turned by Katherine Mansfield. Has she told you about it?

VIOLETTA: She's mentioned it.

JEROME: Has she read you any of it?

VIOLETTA: Yes, a page or two.

JEROME: It's fantastic!

VIOLETTA: Well, really! . . . [*in another tone*] If she hasn't told you, it's because she knows what you think about that sort of book.

JEROME: She doesn't care a hang what I think or what I write about anything at all.

VIOLETTA: That's not true. She admires your articles very much, she's told me so.

JEROME: And even asked you to repeat it to me perhaps? Do you enjoy the job of go-between?

VIOLETTA: Go-between? Me?

JEROME: It's gone on too long! I've decided to stop it, once and for all.

VIOLETTA: So you've come to say goodbye to me?

JEROME: No. I'm going to get a divorce and make you my wife. [*Silence*] Well, can't you say something?

VIOLETTA: [*in a stifled voice*] That would be mad, and very wicked.

JEROME: Look here, Violetta, it's time to stop all this in-explicable secrecy. If, for some reason or other—not that there's any need for reason—*if* you want your freedom again . . .

VIOLETTA: Freedom! That word doesn't mean a thing.

JEROME: What?

VIOLETTA: Freedom cannot be thrown down and picked up again, like a glove—any more than life or love.

JEROME: Well?

VIOLETTA: If you haven't yet grasped that I gave myself to you for ever and ever, without conditions . . .

JEROME: Very beautiful. But I don't trust beautiful talk . . . it's too often nothing but pride.

VIOLETTA: There's no question of pride, Jerome. You can't decide on that kind of fidelity. You recognise it as a fact, like an incurable injury. I, myself, have bound myself to you, irrevocably. It's not my *will*, that can't affect it.

JEROME: You might be talking of illness or death.

VIOLETTA: There's nothing happy in what's happened to us.

JEROME: Why not? Because we're up to our necks in lies and compromise? But that's exactly what's got to stop. When you're my wife . . .

VIOLETTA: In whose eyes shall I be your wife? You don't believe in God, neither do I. You think the law has some spiritual power. But you're wrong. It can't cleanse anything, or purify anything or consecrate anything—except in the eyes of strangers, and we care nothing for them.

JEROME: Who said anything about spiritual power? It's merely a question of getting things straight.

VIOLETTA: At the price of betrayal?

JEROME: Oh, if you're worrying about Ariadne . . . Our marriage was an out-and-out blunder—I've realised that at last—and there's no point in going on with it. And this mysterious malady of hers, which the doctors can't make head or tail of and don't even try to treat—sometimes they even think it's imaginary—it's an outward sign of our relationship, warped and tainted from the beginning by the most hopeless illusions.

VIOLETTA: Stop, Jerome! . . . You're denying your better self. Without her, who can tell what you might have become?

JEROME: Now what are you hinting at?

VIOLETTA: [*pulling herself together*] Nothing, nothing . . . just an illogical feeling.

JEROME: [*nervously*] Did she by any chance? . . .

VIOLETTA: [*firmly*] Now I know Ariadne, I can see very clearly how much you owe her.

JEROME: [*desperately*] I'm so tired of not being able to understand myself. I can't breathe, I . . .

FERNANDE *comes in.*

FERNANDE: [*to* VIOLETTA] I've just had this express letter. Will you read it, please? [*She hands her a paper*]

VIOLETTA: Who's it from? Oh! . . . *that* can't interest me. I've told you often enough I don't want to have anything more to do with . . .

FERNANDE: Is your friend in on this?

VIOLETTA: Certainly not.

JEROME: What's it all about?

VIOLETTA: Nothing at all interesting, I promise you.

FERNANDE: [*holding out the paper to* JEROME] Perhaps you'd like to read it. [JEROME *takes it*]

JEROME: [*looking at the signature*] Bassigny . . . that impresario fellow?

FERNANDE: It is.

JEROME: If it's an engagement . . .

FERNANDE: Not only an engagement.

VIOLETTA: [*strung up*] Look here, Fernande . . .

JEROME: Why all this mystery? Already the other day . . .

FERNANDE: He takes a particular interest in Violetta. At first she seemed to appreciate it, and then . . .

VIOLETTA: That's not true.

FERNANDE: . . . she suddenly turned on him like a wild cat.

VIOLETTA: That's sounds so like me, doesn't it?

FERNANDE: He's going away for some weeks and he's offering you a last chance to think it over.

VIOLETTA: [*sarcastically*] So good of him.

FERNANDE: Unless your friend here is prepared to support you—and he doesn't show much sign of it, even if he could —you'd better think twice before turning down Monsieur Bassigny's very generous offer.

JEROME: Your sister's right.

VIOLETTA: What do you mean?

JEROME: The choice is perfectly clear. If you refuse *my* offer . . .

VIOLETTA: Well?

JEROME: I repeat: things *can't* go on as they are. If you won't marry me, it simply means you're ready to make terms with that creature.

VIOLETTA: Jerome!

JEROME: [*to* FERNANDE] Thanks so much, Mademoiselle, you've made Violetta's position too brutally clear.

FERNANDE: And if this charming matrimonial project comes off, might one ask how you propose to live? The three of you? You're not hoping, I imagine, for an allowance from Madame Leprieur?

JEROME: Money does *not* come into this.

FERNANDE: Bravo! Magnificent! Most impressive!

VIOLETTA: [*who hasn't been listening*] In fact you're giving me the choice between marriage and prostitution.

JEROME: Dramatise if you like. I can't stop you . . . But something's just struck me. [*to* FERNANDE] Again you've opened my eyes. How helpful malice can be!

FERNANDE: Me, malicious! Not a bit. I'm a little too—well, say practical, that's all.

JEROME: Practical? Ah, yes, and I begin to suspect your sister's hardly less so. [*To* VIOLETTA] I see what you're saying to yourself, Violetta: if you marry me, goodbye to all those nice little opportunities . . . Bassignys swarm like rats in a sewer, and there are some, perhaps, slightly younger and less shop-soiled than this one.

VIOLETTA: Jerome! You really believe *that* of me!

JEROME: It's the only explanation, and besides, it's quite adequate. But the thing I really can't swallow is this sort of moral, or sentimental, alibi you've imagined for yourself.

VIOLETTA: Alibi?

JEROME: Yes. *Now* I see the point of this revolting, unnatural friendship . . . I suppose you've managed to persuade yourself that it's for the sake of Ariadne you won't give up all this lying and marry me——

VIOLETTA: If that's what you think of me, I can't imagine why you want to marry me.

FERNANDE: Don't worry, he banked on your refusal. It's a nice cheap way of salving his own conscience.

JEROME: That's a lie.

FERNANDE: Oh, well, I'm not really interested in your squabbles. [*There is a knock on the door*] What is it? [*She half opens the door. A voice is heard outside*]

FERNANDE: All right. Is it really necessary for you to come back tomorrow, Madame?

VIOLETTA: Was that Madame Juquier going?

FERNANDE: Yes.

VIOLETTA: Will you ask her to try to be here by nine? [FERNANDE *goes out, shutting the door behind her*]

JEROME: Has she always been so malicious? [VIOLETTA *makes an evasive gesture*] Violetta, darling, I do hope all this . . .

VIOLETTA: I feel sure you're sincere, but, oh, Jerome, again you did hurt me so! I'd never have believed you could think me self-seeking.

JEROME: After all, it's very natural for you to think of your future, and Monica's.

VIOLETTA: You've just said that money . . .

JEROME: Oh, that was childish. I only said it because Fernande can't believe in any decent, generous feeling. You see, when I seem to get angry and distrust you, it's just that I feel swamped . . . smothered.

VIOLETTA: Yes . . . .

JEROME: Existence is so tangled and absurd. It's strange, and I feel a little ashamed, that I've only realised it since we lost our money.

VIOLETTA: I don't think you need be ashamed. Thought alone can't get us across all thresholds. Some need an experience like poverty or illness.

JEROME: Yes, but that's horrible and I don't trust it, because, after all, such experiences do leave us deformed. Look at

Ariadne, for instance. . . . And the Christians, they seem to think of the sick and disinherited as privileged; yes—I don't know—as if they'd had an operation for cataract and recovered their normal sight. But I believe *only* in happiness, Violetta. Happiness is so marvellous——

VIOLETTA: Ariadne believes in happiness too.

JEROME: But what does she call happiness? Do you remember that little piece is Schumann's *Kinderscenen* called *Perfect Happiness?* Whenever I hear it I want to cry.

VIOLETTA: I know, I know. So do I.

JEROME: It's so bountiful, so overflowing. One could fling one's arms round everybody and everything, round life itself. That's what I feel when *you* play—a peaceful ecstasy. You give us back our lost Eden. The legend lies, you know. We were never chased out of Paradise. It's here, quite close, too close to be seen. Or rather, life hides it . . . Darling, sometimes I've wanted to *die* with you. Have you never guessed?

VIOLETTA: Oh, Jerome, my dear one. No, I didn't know . . .

JEROME: Only there's Monica. And then I feel that death, if we gave it to ourselves, might keep its purest secret hidden from us.

VIOLETTA: [*her voice trembling*] Yes, yes, you're right. One mustn't *want* to die. [*A silence*]

JEROME: [*with ardour*] Oh, Violetta, at last, at last, I feel we're coming out of a tunnel. Oh, this thing between us, if only we could make it clear. And all that means is, to come out into the open. Then everything might get easier . . . even this awful money business. You don't know how that nags at me. I can't sleep because of it. Yes, even that might solve itself in some unimaginable way. But we mustn't even try to wonder how . . . That would be lack of faith.

VIOLETTA: You don't usually talk like this.

JEROME: It's because she's going away. I've a feeling it won't be like the other times. You and I, *we* can make it different, different for ever.

VIOLETTA: [*very low*] And *her* unhappiness . . .

JEROME: I've given up trying to put myself in her place. It's never been any good. Whenever I did she said that I'd been fooled by my own emotions. Imagine what it would be like to try to locate an image or an event that occurred in an unknown dimension. And I do wonder if, perhaps, Ariadne really does live in another world with which we *can't* communicate.

VIOLETTA: We must take care, darling. It's so convenient to banish her to some inaccessible mountain top so that we don't have to worry about her feelings . . .

JEROME: [*passionately*] Violetta! You will, won't you? Oh, Violetta! It's our only chance. You can't say no, you can't abandon me. [*There is a pause. Then* VIOLETTA *gives him her hand. He takes it and kisses it with meditative tenderness*]

VIOLETTA: There's the bell. . . . Oh, dear, it may be Ariadne. She said she might come and say goodbye this evening.

JEROME: I *can't* see her . . . I'd brought this little toy for Monica. May I give it her myself? I'd go straight away afterwards.

VIOLETTA: Hold on a minute. [*She goes to the bedroom door and half opens it gently*] Duckie, here's your friend, Jerome. I think he's got a little surprise for you.

> JEROME *goes in and* VIOLETTA *shuts the door gently behind him. The bell rings again. She crosses the room R., goes to open the outer door and returns with* PHILIP.

PHILIP: I'm Madame Leprieur's brother, Mademoiselle.

VIOLETTA: Oh!

PHILIP: I've heard so much of you from my sister—she very much admires your playing—that I've come to ask whether you would be kind enough to teach my little boy the violin. He's only nine, and has never yet had any lessons.

VIOLETTA: It's most kind of Madame Leprieur . . .

PHILIP: Jacques has a good ear and he loves music, so I don't think he'd be a boring pupil. I'd thought at first of having him taught the piano, but he hates it, I don't know why. And he loves the violin.

VIOLETTA: That often happens.

PHILIP: Would you say half an hour twice a week to begin with? His governess could be at the lesson and then she could help him practise, don't you think?

VIOLETTA: That would be perfect.

PHILIP: Would you come to us or shall Jacques come here? It's as you like. And your fees? Just say what they are. . . . I do want him to be well grounded.

VIOLETTA: We can easily agree on that, Monsieur. . . . What times would suit you best?

PHILIP: I'll write, shall I? Well, that's splendid. . . . I don't think I've ever had the pleasure of hearing you play.

VIOLETTA: I haven't had the chance to play much in public.

PHILIP: And I go to concerts less and less. Most people choose such dull and scrappy programmes nowadays. I used to hear a great deal of music with my sister, but now she's always away in the mountains. . . . You've only made friends quite lately, haven't you? . . .

VIOLETTA: Yes, I only met Madame Leprieur a few weeks ago.

PHILIP: She's exceptionally fond of you.

VIOLETTA: And I too feel . . .

PHILIP: Yes, she's a very extraordinary woman.

VIOLETTA: And a remarkable musician.

PHILIP: Are you sure that she's really an artist?

VIOLETTA: But . . .

PHILIP: I'm not—indeed, to be frank, I don't think she is. Compare her with my father—he was a real musician—and the difference hits one. Art for her, I think, is mainly a means to an end.

VIOLETTA: I don't quite understand.

PHILIP: It's hard to explain. . . . Besides, my sister isn't easy to know.

VIOLETTA: No, I don't think she is.

PHILIP: Less, perhaps, the more she gives herself up to . . . It's very odd—she can't do without the mountains, and she, of course, is convinced it's on account of her health.

But I doubt it. I think she feels the need to live in surroundings which symbolise, for her, her own aspirations.

VIOLETTA: That's natural enough. . . .

PHILIP: I'm not so sure. . . . We used to travel a good deal together and some delightful places, like Touraine or Alsace, she couldn't bear. They were too easy-going, she said. I never began to understand her likes and dislikes till I discovered . . . But I don't know why I'm boring you with all this psychological analysis. And yet, if . . . it might be of some interest, or even use to you. Without realising it, perhaps, Ariadne refers everything that happens to her to her own conception of herself. Understand me, I in no way mean, opinion—Ariadne's far too intelligent to be vain—I mean a kind of mental atmosphere, a climate, and outside it she can literally neither live nor breathe.

VIOLETTA: It's very strange.

PHILIP: It certainly lies behind her choice of companions, and it's probably the cause of her evident liking for invalids. But, you know, this tendency—it would vanish, of course if she faced up to it—it makes her do foolish things sometimes . . .

VIOLETTA: But . . .

PHILIP: Things which have caused, or may cause, a lot of trouble. We must face facts, Mademoiselle. My sister's taste for—shall we say, peculiar—relationships has in it something of unconscious perversion.

VIOLETTA: I'm afraid I don't understand you, Monsieur. It's all too subtle, and anyway, it's nothing to do with me . . . If you'll be kind enough to let me know about the violin lessons . . . But really, I'd rather not talk any more about . . .

PHILIP: Just as you wish, Mademoiselle. You'll hear from me tomorrow, by the first post. [VIOLETTA *goes out with him R. and opens the outer door. An exclamation is heard and then Ariadne's voice*]

ARIADNE: [*outside*] Well, Philip, I never expected to find *you* here!

PHILIP: [*outside*] Mademoiselle Mazargues will explain.

ARIADNE: Won't you come back a moment?

PHILIP: Sorry, I must be getting home to dress. I'm dining
out. Goodbye, Mademoiselle.

> *There is the sound of the door being shut and* ARIADNE
> *and* VIOLETTA *come back into the room.*

ARIADNE: I'm rather intrigued, you know.

VIOLETTA: [*embarrassed*] Your brother came to ask me to
give lessons to his little boy.

ARIADNE: What a curious idea! . . . But after all, it's quite a
good one. How's Monica?

VIOLETTA: Definitely better. Much less bronchitis.

ARIADNE: Oh, how glad I am. I was so worried about her.

VIOLETTA: Thank you. . . .

ARIADNE: [*studying her*] You didn't like my brother coming
to see you, did you?

VIOLETTA: Well, I don't know him at all.

ARIADNE: I wonder why he came. Did you feel . . . was it out
of curiosity?

VIOLETTA: I would never let myself think such a thing.

ARIADNE: I wouldn't put it beyond him. . . . Even if he
suspects . . . I suppose he didn't hint? No, he could
hardly . . .

VIOLETTA: I felt . . . I didn't really understand, but I did get
the impression that he had another reason . . . *Please* don't
make me go on. I couldn't repeat what he said, even if I
wanted to. It was all so subtle, so . . .

ARIADNE: [*gently*] But you did feel it was said against me? . . .
I'm sure of it, Violetta. You see, things are very strained
between us, and I don't know what to do about it. You
know, of course, that he's divorced. Clarissa and I were
friends when we were girls, so it made me very sad. I did
all I could till the very last moment to try to save his
marriage, and for that Phillip has never forgiven me. Of
course, I realise Clarissa was in the wrong. She told her
husband everything with most unusual frankness. But
really, it was partly Philip's fault. It was he who brought

Gilbert Deplaine to the house and encouraged him to come
whenever he liked. At first he clearly enjoyed his wife's
success with such a clever, smart, sophisticated young man.
And he didn't, of course, realise how attracted to Gilbert he
was himself.

VIOLETTA: You're making me feel most uncomfortable . . .
and none of it's anything to do with me.

ARIADNE: You're wrong, Violetta. It's become so very clear
to me how all these stories, in which we're both actors and
audience, are interlinked, and how they illuminate each
other. That's what the novelists have understood so well,
and it's why they alone can shed such flashes of light on the
real meaning of life. My brother called me unnatural to side
with the guilty ones against him. It's extraordinary how
strong-minded people—he prides himself on that, you
know—are always using words like fault and judgment
and blame. It's a ridiculous kind of counter-offensive on
his part to come and give you some sort of obscure warning
about me. . . . Poor old Philip! He's not happy, whatever
he says—and Clarissa misses her child terribly. She'll get
T.B. one of these days. But it's odd about Gilbert Deplaine.
He seems to be drifting away from Clarissa, now that she
lives alone. One never can tell how much latent homo-
sexuality there is in any apparently normal relationship
between a man and a woman, can one?

VIOLETTA: All that's quite terrifying.

ARIADNE: [*in a different voice*] Clarissa will soon be coming
to stay with me in the mountains. Perhaps later on I might
ask you to go and see her sometime.

VIOLETTA: Me . . . But why?

ARIADNE: I just think you might do her good. And I like
my friends to know each other.

VIOLETTA: Does she suspect?

ARIADNE: I've talked of you. She may have guessed.

VIOLETTA: Oh, it's all so embarrassing.

ARIADNE: I'll write you long letters, but they won't be
very regular. Don't be surprised. I've never been a

steady correspondent. Anyway, my health wouldn't have allowed it.

VIOLETTA: I *must* tell you . . . Jerome came in just now. He was very depressed and very strung up.

ARIADNE: He's always like that when I'm going away.

VIOLETTA: There's something else. I've no right to hide it from you . . . [*she stops*]

ARIADNE: Don't be afraid, my dear. You know I can face anything.

VIOLETTA: He said—for the first time—that he was going to get a divorce and marry me.

ARIADNE: He said that seriously?

VIOLETTA: Absolutely.

ARIADNE: And you?

VIOLETTA: I tried to make him see it was impossible.

ARIADNE: Why impossible?

VIOLETTA: And then . . . I can't even explain how it happened . . . But he certainly felt that I would agree.

ARIADNE: And would you?

VIOLETTA: [*very low*] I don't know. Perhaps . . . that depends on you.

ARIADNE: [*after a long silence*] My dear, after all . . . could you have given me better news! That this should have happened . . .

VIOLETTA: But nothing's happened.

ARIADNE: I couldn't with honesty say I've *wanted* it. To begin with, since I've been so ill, I don't very well know what to want really means any more. . . . And then, you see, one isn't so strong as one would like to be. . . . And in the life which has ended today—though at times it was heartbreakingly sad—there were hours which I remember with the deepest gratitude.

VIOLETTA: Why don't you say: with the bitterest regret?

ARIADNE: No, Violetta, really not. Once, long ago, I may have felt regret, but that was before I'd gone through the ordeals which force one—eventually—to grow up. But now I don't feel bitter. It's just that something has come to

an end. I feel solemn . . . I think I could almost say religious.
. . . It's how I shall feel when I'm dying, I'm sure, if I'm still
conscious, of course——

VIOLETTA: Oh, you soar at such heights—and I trail in the
mud and stumble against every stone.

ARIADNE: Heights! Oh, don't think that of me, Violetta. I
should feel I'd been play-acting if you did.

VIOLETTA: If I were in your place and you in mine, I'm sure
you'd disgust me. . . . I should say to myself: "She's got
what she wanted at last."

ARIADNE: You wouldn't. And your place, my place, what
does it mean? In my place you'd have my painful past.

VIOLETTA: I'm so ashamed . . .

ARIADNE: That's the last thing you should be. . . . When you
complained of being at a dead-end I *knew* there was no
other way out. But the decision had to be Jerome's,
Jerome's alone, and we couldn't hurry it. But that I couldn't
tell you. You know how you'd have taken it.

VIOLETTA: Now I only feel sad—terribly sad.

ARIADNE: No, no, you don't mean sad, only bewildered. . . .
But I *would* like to know . . . what do you think put this
new idea into Jerome's head?

VIOLETTA: [*uneasily*] I really can't quite make out . . . He
couldn't bear this equivocal situation any more.

ARIADNE: What do you mean by equivocal, Violetta?

VIOLETTA: This intimacy between you and me.

ARIADNE: [*sharply*] You naturally didn't tell him I *knew*
about you two?

VIOLETTA: No . . . I'd promised you not to. But . . . he could
feel I was being deceitful, and you can't think how unhappy,
how tense it's made him. Only just now he said the most
horrible, hurting, unfair things to me . . .

ARIADNE: But I don't really understand. Why were you more
deceitful than he was? What right had *he* to criticise you?
Don't you think, perhaps, that . . . couldn't his tenseness
be a little due to jealousy?

VIOLETTA: Jealousy?

ARIADNE: Of me.

VIOLETTA: [*weakly*] Yes . . . I see . . .

ARIADNE: And you do see, don't you, that he must *not* take a serious decision like that from momentary, childish resentment. I wouldn't put it beyond him, you know.

VIOLETTA: How can one tell?

ARIADNE: You're an acute and intelligent woman, Violetta. You'd know at once whether his decision was serious, I mean, genuine, or not. You'd have no doubt at all.

VIOLETTA: I had none at the time . . . but now . . .

ARIADNE: Then you certainly mustn't question it now. . . . Do you think Jerome will talk to me before I leave? You know I'm going the day after tomorrow.

VIOLETTA: He didn't say anything.

ARIADNE: Knowing him, I think he's more likely to write. . . .

VIOLETTA: [*questioningly*] *You* couldn't take the first step, I suppose?

ARIADNE: *Quite* impossible. I'd have to speak of this conversation, and that would give away what he must never know . . .

VIOLETTA: Even after . . . ?

ARIADNE: Never, Violetta, never, believe me—for your own sake. Jerome can be vindictive. If he discovered there'd been this kind of complicity between us—I'm sorry, I can't find another word for it—he's the kind of man who might never forgive you.

VIOLETTA: You're probably right. . . . But a letter . . . I'm afraid . . .

ARIADNE: That's only a detail, surely.

VIOLETTA: But you, *you* . . . you're so calm and self-controlled. . . . Jerome was right, you seem to live in another world.

ARIADNE: He said that? Oh, now, every moment, I'm feeling more and more at peace, *really* at peace. At first . . .

VIOLETTA: You didn't show anything.

ARIADNE: You see, a part of my task may be finished now. You know I nearly died some years ago. The doctors gave me up and I felt quite desperate about Jerome. So I prayed —it's a thing I hardly ever do—the only selfish prayer I can remember, not to get well, but just to be allowed to live until he could do without me. It wasn't my instinct that prayed, it was my mind, my reason. . . . Now I need never again ask that of God. It was, after all, a little blasphemous.

VIOLETTA: But you're quite well now.

ARIADNE: Only, I think, for the moment. . . . Some symptoms have come back, the last few days . . .

VIOLETTA: Oh?

ARIADNE: But now it doesn't really matter any more.

VIOLETTA: But Logny, the mountain sunshine, surely that will get rid of them? . . .

ARIADNE: Perhaps. . . . But there's something important we really *ought* to talk about today. It's your future—and money. Jerome, of course, hasn't a penny, and we all know how insecure an artist's life is in these days. And Jerome can't stand even the amount of insecurity normal people can take in their stride. Now I have a little money . . .

VIOLETTA: I don't know what you're going to say, but *please* . . . This business of money, it's a nightmare.

ARIADNE: Only if you won't face it. It's taking these miserable material details too seriously, to avoid them. One must face them, and that's what I want *you* to do with me, Violetta. Together we must find a way out. If Jerome's life with you is precarious and full of worries, it means disaster, I know it does. So we must think of a way I can help you both, without Jerome knowing.

VIOLETTA: It's impossible!

ARIADNE: You mean practically?

VIOLETTA: To begin with . . .

ARIADNE: I don't believe it. If one is determined to do a thing, one can.

VIOLETTA: Not only practically.

ARIADNE: Take care, Violetta, we must go carefully here. At any price we mustn't let false self-esteem destroy everything.

VIOLETTA: I call it self-respect.

ARIADNE: It comes to the same thing.

VIOLETTA: But then, that means more lies—*more* lies coiled in the very heart of our life. Deceive Jerome . . . Oh, no, no, it's atrocious.

ARIADNE: My dear, I've long ago learnt that wisdom is just the art of right emphasis.

VIOLETTA: No, no. It's not we who place the emphasis. I've lied too much already.

ARIADNE: May one not have to sacrifice a personal scruple to a higher, impersonal end?

VIOLETTA: Such sacrifices sound to me like betrayals.

ARIADNE: Well, after all, we needn't decide anything now. But it's a more serious risk than you know, and I can't help feeling afraid for you.

VIOLETTA: How sure you are he's weak and cowardly! How you despise him! And you've no right to. If anyone spoiled him, wasn't it you?

ARIADNE: Oh, dear, I should never have told you I was afraid . . . and after all, how can one tell? Something may turn up, some unexpected way out. . . . The free play of events allows of almost infinite possibilities.

VIOLETTA: [*exasperated*] Oh, first you baited me, and now you're trying to pacify me. . . . But the plain fact that you could suggest this odious plan shows our marriage is impossible. It oughtn't to be and it can't be. And you know it . . . And I wonder if this isn't just a mean and circuitous way to convince me too? Why couldn't you say, quite simply: I refuse, I won't have it. How far more brave and more honest that would have been! . . . Or is Jerome really right? Do you already belong to another world? Do you see shining a light to which we are all blind? Tell me, have you really passed on beyond the rest of us? Its incomprehensible, but if it's true, I don't envy you. And I don't believe it. I can't. Your acceptance, your sham nobility, your sham serenity, aren't they all a horrible mixture of deceit and unconscious hypocrisy? But do you know it? Even if one could force you to speak your most secret thought, would *that* be the truth? Should I at last know the truth?

ARIADNE: [*After a long silence*] We cannot see into the future. But I hope from the bottom of my heart that you will never have to regret those words. Whatever happens, you must remember that *I* have forgiven them.

VIOLETTA: *Whatever* happens?

ARIADNE: Even if I'm not there to . . .

VIOLETTA: What makes you think I shall regret them?

ARIADNE: I'm sure of it, and you know it too.

VIOLETTA: If that were true, you would have found the *one* way to make them intolerable to me.

ARIADNE: What ought I to have said, then?

VIOLETTA: Nothing. I can't stand all this noble talk any more.

ARIADNE: [*gently*] I see . . . Well, you needn't worry, you won't have to. I'm leaving the day after tomorrow.

VIOLETTA: [*in a whisper*] How can I do without you?

ARIADNE: [*as if she hadn't heard*] I would have liked to kiss Monica goodbye and specially to give her this little present. . . . But it's too late. . . . It'll be you who will give it to her for me.

VIOLETTA: You're very kind . . .

ARIADNE: No, I'm treacherous and cruel.

VIOLETTA: [*in a low voice*] I wish I were dead.

ARIADNE: Look deeper into your own heart, my dear. I feel very sure that you love life, with passion, and that helps me. When I get Jerome's letter . . .

VIOLETTA: He won't write it.

FERNANDE *comes in.*

FERNANDE: I didn't know you were here. Why didn't you tell me?

ARIADNE: I came to say goodbye to both of you [*to* FERNANDE] I've seen very little of you these six weeks.

FERNANDE: My sister's kept you busy. Besides, *I'm* no longer interesting.

ARIADNE: Don't say such awful things! But I've seldom seen such a perfect cure. Dr. Groz is always telling me how proud he is of you.

FERNANDE: Oh, yes, I'm a fine case. [*to* VIOLETTA] Serge Franchard has asked me to let you know about that Children's Home. It's called Grancey and it's near Grenoble. He says he's sure to be able to get Monica in for next to nothing. Through a friend of his wife's. That fool of a woman certainly has some useful connections.

ARIADNE: But how perfect! I know Grancey well. I'm one of the founders . . .

FERNANDE: What a coincidence!

ARIADNE: And I could *easily* put in a word too, if you like . . .

VIOLETTA: [*shortly*] Thanks very much, but it won't be necessary.

ARIADNE: But surely, if you let Madame Franchard . . .

FERNANDE: All the same, if you would be kind enough . . . it would certainly help.

VIOLETTA: No, no, Fernande. I don't *want* to take advantage of Madame Leprieur's kindness.

ARIADNE: There's no question of that. But I think the Franchards will be glad they can help you a little in this way. . . . You'll let me know how things go, won't you. Promise? Goodbye. [ARIADNE *goes out, accompanied by* FERNANDE *and* VIOLETTA. *They return a moment later*]

FERNANDE: You're bosom friends. It's quite marvellous . . .

VIOLETTA: [*after a pause*] Marvellous . . . Why did she smile when you spoke of a coincidence?

CURTAIN

ACT FOUR

Two months later, in ARIADNE'S *house at Logny. The spacious, well-lighted room has two large bay windows which give on to a vast horizon. On the right is a grand piano. There is a door into the house and a side-door into the garden.* CLARISSA *and a journalist,* CHARBONNEAU.

CLARISSA: My friend is out, Monsieur, and I don't quite know when she'll be back. Can I give her a message?

CHARBONNEAU: I'm afraid it's a very personal matter, and unfortunately I must catch the evening train. Pardon, Madame, but have I, by any chance, the pleasure of speaking to Madame Clarissa Beaulieu?

CLARISSA: Yes, Monsieur. . . .

CHARBONNEAU: Why then, Madame, it'll be easy to explain to you why I've come. I'm a great friend of Gilbert Deplaine's—you know him, I think—and it's he who's shown me part of a book by Madame Leprieur, which you gave him, I understand?

CLARISSA: Yes, Monsieur. But I'm very surprised that he thought he might show it to anyone else.

CHARBONNEAU: It's in no way confidential, Madame, since your friend means to publish her book.

CLARISSA: Later on, though, much later on. She's no thought of doing it while she's still alive. . . . It's true, I hope to persuade her . . .

CHARBONNEAU: You see, then . . .

CLARISSA: But I'm not at all sure I'll succeed.

CHARBONNEAU: The position is that I've come up to Logny to finish an enquiry into the mentality of the very sick. What, for instance, are their daily trials, their pleasures, their distractions? Where do they turn for spiritual support? It's for one of our best-known weeklies. Illness—long, serious illness—is fashionable nowadays, you know, and I'm very anxious to publish these extracts. They're so vivid and personal—in the Katherine Mansfield class, I should say. . . . And mind you, I could very well have used them without asking permission at all.

CLARISSA: All the same, it does seem to me . . .

CHARBONNEAU: Most of my colleagues wouldn't have hesitated, but I don't think that sort of thing is worthy of our profession. Well, that's how it is, Madame. Will you be kind enough to speak to Madame Leprieur for me? I'd be much obliged for an answer by telegram, for the copy is due at the printers as soon as I get back to Paris.

CLARISSA: I can't say anything definite, but I'm nearly certain my friend will refuse.

CHARBONNEAU: I hardly think she'll be so unreasonable.

CLARISSA: I've told you, already, Monsieur, this is to be a posthumous book. It was written to be published *after* her death.

CHARBONNEAU: It wouldn't be the first posthumous book to be published in advance. I'm afraid I must go, now, Madame. Goodbye. [CLARISSA *rings the bell and the manservant appears at once*]

CLARISSA: Will you please show the gentleman out?

CHARBONNEAU *goes out, preceded by the servant.* JEROME *comes in.*

CLARISSA: [*desperately*] Oh, it really is too much . . .

JEROME: Who was that man with you? I heard a name I didn't know.

CLARISSA [*pointing to a visiting card on the table*] You can see for yourself.

JEROME: [*taking the card*] What does the fellow want here?

CLARISSA: Oh, you know journalists always have to poke their noses in everywhere.

JEROME: Not without an excuse. [*A pause.* CLARISSA *looks embarrassed*]

CLARISSA: You know perfectly well that Ariadne's writing a . . .

JEROME: I know nothing about it. She's never said a word to me about her literary efforts.

CLARISSA: It'll be a very unusual book.

JEROME: Splendid!

CLARISSA: Why not ask her to show you a page or two? . . . I'm sure . . .

JEROME: That she'd be kind enough to. Thanks.

CLARISSA: No, that she'd be awfully pleased.

JEROME: How did that fool find out? . . .

CLARISSA: Is he a fool?

JEROME: Yes, a garrulous, drivelling fool, like nine-tenths of his profession. . . . You don't know why he came?

CLARISSA: I . . .

JEROME: Well, I've no doubt you encourage Ariadne's idea that she's a spiritual initiate, a priestess, a God knows what. Such stuff always leads straight to journalism. That's the main drain nowadays for stupid human vanity.

ARIADNE *comes in.*

CLARISSA: [*with nervous tenderness*] How late you are, dearest! You've been out for ages. Aren't you tired? And you must be frozen. The sun's been down at least half an hour.

ARIADNE: [*irritated*] Thanks. I'm quite all right. Quite. Thank you, Clarissa.

JEROME: [*handing her* CHARBONNEAU'S *card*] Do you know this man?

ARIADNE: Not at all. . . . Oh, one minute, yes. They were talking about him at Beausite or somewhere. He's investigating the sanatoria for some Parisian paper, isn't he?

CLARISSA: That's it.

JEROME: [*sarcastically*] And you're classed as a special expert on the world of invalids, no doubt?

ARIADNE: I don't see . . .

CLARISSA: [*in a whisper*] I'll explain presently.

JEROME: It's more and more clear to me that you're a sort of moral empress here. This reporter's visit was one more delightful act of homage, I suppose.

ARIADNE: What nonsense. . . .

JEROME: Well, didn't you manage to get that Franchard fellow an engagement at Beausoleil, just when they were sacking all the other musicians?

ARIADNE: What has that to do with it . . .?

JEROME: Nothing at all. I'm merely impressed by your influence at this delightful half-way house.

ARIADNE: Why half-way house? Logny is nearly five thousand feet up. . . .

JEROME: I wasn't referring to its height.

ARIADNE: Serge Franchard was starving in Paris.

JEROME: Oh, don't exaggerate. He looked fat and flourishing enough to me.

ARIADNE: I was thankful to get him this temporary job. Besides, it's hardly paid at all, but at least he's under a roof and decently fed. And his wife's got work in a Kindergarten, though she knows practically nothing about it, poor thing.

JEROME: It's all *most* providential.

CLARISSA: I wonder why you're being so sarcastic?

ARIADNE: Never mind. Jerome slept badly. Poor darling! You're finding it harder than ever to settle down here this time, aren't you?

JEROME: I always sleep vilely up here.

ARIADNE: You ought to take more exercise. Yesterday you only went out to get the papers.

JEROME: [*pulling out his watch*] They may have come by now. [*He turns to go out*]

JEROME: [*to* ARIADNE] I hope you'll make your friend explain this journalist business to you.

CLARISSA: But it's only an enquiry into . . .

JEROME *goes out.*

ARIADNE: What's the matter, Clarissa? You're quite pale.

CLARISSA: I can't help seeing how your husband detests me. . . .

ARIADNE: Poor Jerome's terribly nervy. He works it off on everyone. He'll get over it.

CLARISSA: [*nervously*] And about the Charbonneau man. . . . Oh, it's obvious I've been very silly. *Please* don't be angry. . . . You know that passage you let me copy from your journal the other day . . .

ARIADNE: Which one?

CLARISSA: About how suffering releases the soul—it was *so* beautiful—I couldn't help sending it to Gilbert. . . . It's all I can do for him these days, to tell him about books and copy bits out. He's very grateful, you know. You mustn't think him hard. He's full of aspirations, only the people round him are *so* dreadful, and he's *so* impressionable . . .

ARIADNE: I know, my dear. You've told me all about it very often.

CLARISSA: He knows what you mean to me—how tremendously I admire you. I almost worship you, you know.

ARIADNE: Oh, come now, Clarissa. . . .

CLARISSA: And I told him how wonderful your book was—far, far better than the Journal of that Englishwoman, Katherine . . . Katherine . . . He thinks a lot of what I say—he knows I'm sincere. And he's right, I simply can't understand snobbery. The passage I sent really did appeal to him. He wasn't well, and then he's always more impressionable . . . his father died of a duodenal ulcer, you know . . . So he showed it to Charbonneau—he's a friend, I suppose. Gilbert has so many friends, I lose count of them. And Charbonneau came to ask your permission to publish it.

ARIADNE: No. . . . No, never!

CLARISSA: I warned him you'd say that. But I've been thinking, darling, you might be wrong to refuse.

ARIADNE: But this book must *not* appear till after I'm dead. You know that.

CLARISSA: I told him so. He answered: "It wouldn't be the

first posthumous book to be published in advance."
[ARIADNE *laughs bitterly*] Why are you laughing?

ARIADNE: I don't know.

CLARISSA: May I say what I really think?

ARIADNE: Of course.

CLARISSA: Is it really brave to wait till after you're dead? Isn't it a little like hiding one's head under the bedclothes?

ARIADNE: How absurd you are, Clarissa.

CLARISSA: If a book can do good, why wait? Is it from fear—but fear of what? Or from modesty? But lots of people here know you're writing a book . . .

ARIADNE: It's you who told them.

CLARISSA: And they all ask me: Do you know when Madame Leprieur's book will be out? Would you believe it, the little librarian at the Chalet Flora said only yesterday: "So we've got our Katherine . . ."

ARIADNE: Mansfield.

CLARISSA: Well, what did you want me to say to her?

ARIADNE: Oh, I don't know. Just shrug your shoulders. . . .

CLARISSA: It would do the place so much good, she said, if it were known. Why, some people would come specially . . .

ARIADNE: *Please*, Clarissa, it's grotesque. . . . You make me feel like tearing the thing up.

CLARISSA: Surely that's a lack of simplicity. It was horribly unfair, what your husband said just now about journalism. . . . It's the kind of thing aristocrats say . . . Surely if one could give *ordinary* people a little food for their souls—Oh, how badly I'm saying it—in materialist days like these. But he wants it all kept for a tiny élite, for the kind of people who buy first editions. *I* think Communism's the thing of the future. So does Gilbert. It's odd, when he used to be so conservative, isn't it?

ARIADNE: I'm afraid you don't have many illusions about the value of Gilbert's opinions. . . .

CLARISSA: Oh, but he is intelligent, Ariadne, really he is.

ARIADNE: I know. . . .

CLARISSA: If only he'd been better guided. . . . If only his parents . . .

ARIADNE: I wish you wrote to him less.

CLARISSA: What harm can it do? I only try to pass on to him a little of what *you* give me. . . . Is that wrong?

ARIADNE: No, but perhaps rather unwise . . .

CLARISSA: I don't understand . . . you don't talk as you used to. Has Philip put you against me? . . .

ARIADNE: Don't be silly. You know very well that Philip and I . . .

CLARISSA: Then you can't forgive me for causing you to quarrel with your brother?

ARIADNE: We haven't quarrelled, Clarissa.

CLARISSA: Oh, goodness, I can't *help* saying things simply. I can't be complicated and [*hysterically*] subtle like all of you. Oh, it's awful. I'm going away. I shall go first thing in the morning.

ARIADNE: Oh, come now, Clarissa, don't be so childish.

CLARISSA: Something's worrying you, and you won't tell me. Is that kind? As if the lovely thing about friendship wasn't just to *share* . . . you wrote something marvellous about that.

ARIADNE: Please, please, Clarissa, don't ever say another word to me about that rubbish.

CLARISSA: They want you to telegraph your answer. . . .

ARIADNE: I shall telegraph nothing at all. It's sheer impertinence. . . . [*There is a knock on the door*] Come in. [*The manservant comes in*] What is it?

SERVANT: Monsieur Franchard would like to speak to you, Madame.

CLARISSA: I'll leave you now, Ariadne, but I must say I do feel terribly hurt. I can't understand you at all today.

ARIADNE: I'm sorry, Clarissa. . . . Don't be angry with me. . . . [*to the servant*] Will you tell the gentleman I'll be free in a moment?

SERVANT: Yes, Madame. [*He goes out*]

ARIADNE: You asked me if I had something on my mind. . . .

Yes, but it's worse than that, I'm very, very worried . . . I'm sorry. I can't say more for the moment.

CLARISSA: I never hid my troubles from you, Ariadne.

ARIADNE: I know, Clarissa . . . but I *can't*. It's something I can't talk about. Later on, perhaps.

CLARISSA: Very well. Then I'll go now. [*She goes out*]

ARIADNE: [*opening the door R.*] Will you come in, Monsieur? . . .

SERGE *comes in. He is very pale.*

ARIADNE: What *has* happened? You look terribly upset.

SERGE: I should think so! Violetta is here, with the child.

ARIADNE: Here?

SERGE: Yes, here, at Logny. She came yesterday evening. Monica isn't well. She's coughing a lot. . . .

ARIADNE: I don't understand.

SERGE: You know I'd had no news for some time. . . . You said yourself she hadn't written to you.

ARIADNE: No, not a line.

SERGE: She decided to come quite suddenly. I met her at Beausoleil this morning.

ARIADNE: They're at Beausoleil?

SERGE: Yes. That's another thing I can't understand. . . . Violetta looks a wreck. I haven't yet seen the child. We only had a word or two. . . . I must tell you now—I've funked it before—you remember our plan about the Children's Home at Grenoble, and how I told her my wife knew a member of the committee?

ARIADNE: Yes, well?

SERGE: I don't know how she discovered. I think Suzanne must have been pretty stupid. Anyhow Violetta found out it was all moonshine, and that it was *you*. . . . She was furious with me, I really can't see why. We had an awful row, and of course that put a stop to Monica going there. They seem to have been living in a little boarding house outside Paris. Monica got worse and in the end Violetta consulted a Dr. Paulus, who said she must go to a sanatorium.

ARIADNE: Did the X-ray show anything?

SERGE: I don't know . . . I think it did. . . .

ARIADNE: Oh, it's terrible.

SERGE: And then, you see, there's something else that drives me frantic. Violetta is very poor. Why does she come to the most expensive sanatorium in Logny? How can she afford it? That man I told you about, you know, that impresario . . . I'm afraid he's got hold of her. Heaven knows, he can afford to pay for a dozen Beausoleils.

ARIADNE: You've no right to suppose such a thing. You see, she has a little money . . . I'll tell you something quite private. *I* bought her piano. But she's no idea of it, of course.

SERGE: [*staring at the grand piano*] Yes, that *is* her piano.

ARIADNE: She thinks it was bought by a friend of mine, whose name I gave her. She's *so* independent. One has to be very tactful with her.

SERGE: I don't understand being so difficult when one's in such a hole. . . . You've been amazingly good to her and to me. . . . Besides, if she comes here she'll see it. . . .

ARIADNE: The way things are, it doesn't much matter if she does. . . . Did she speak of me?

SERGE: No.

ARIADNE: She feels I'm . . . I can't think why she brought the child here, to Logny. . . . There are heaps of other places where they treat her illness.

SERGE: The best doctors are here. . . . And it may be because of you.

ARIADNE: Why because of me?

SERGE: You've been so good. . . .

ARIADNE: She hasn't written me one word for six weeks. I think she *hates* me.

SERGE: It's not possible. . . . She can't have gone mad, suddenly, like that. . . . Or could it be? . . . [*He stops*]

ARIADNE: Go on. Say it.

SERGE: No.

ARIADNE: I *know* why it is.

SERGE: You know!

ARIADNE: As soon as I got back to Paris I knew everything.

SERGE: [*shaken*] It's fantastic!

ARIADNE: My husband has had no news either. He's miserable about it.

SERGE: Oh! him! . . .

ARIADNE: You've no right to judge him. . . . And don't forget he thinks you've behaved disgracefully. . . . None of that matters at all.

SERGE: [*humbly*] You're probably right. You're a very wonderful woman.

ARIADNE: No. . . . There are no wonderful women—or men either. We're all feeble, broken creatures, all of us. . . . [*She looks out of the window*] Oh, there's my husband coming. You'd better not meet him.

SERGE: I'm not afraid of *him*, you know.

ARIADNE: But for *my* sake, please . . .

SERGE: Very well, if you wish it. . . . I wonder—would you let me come and see you one day? There's so much I'd like to tell you—and I want your advice. . . . You've seen my wife . . . I'm not happy, you know——

ARIADNE: No, no. I never want any more confidences, never. . . . That's all over and done with.

> *She pulls* SERGE *towards the garden door and they both go out.* JEROME *comes in with a paper in his hand. He sits down and reads it intently.* ARIADNE *comes back.*

ARIADNE: Is there any news, darling?

JEROME: Only Communism, Communism, all over the place.

ARIADNE: Let's hope it doesn't spread here.

JEROME: Some hope!

ARIADNE: I should have thought . . .

JEROME: Oh, you needn't pretend to take an interest in politics. You've plenty to do improving your beautiful soul.

ARIADNE: Jerome!

JEROME: With the help of your devoted divorcée, of course— Incidentally, is she staying much longer?

ARIADNE: I don't think so.

JEROME: I dined with Philip last week. He's furious with you. He's sure you only invited his wife to annoy him.

ARIADNE: But how does he know Clarissa is here?

JEROME: Because I told him. You ought to know I can't stand all these mysteries.

ARIADNE: Oh, Jerome, why won't you simply admit that you're very, very unhappy?

JEROME: I'm on edge, exasperated, sickened, if you like, but unhappy—no. Why should I be? . . . You needn't count on me to exercise your talents as a comforter.

ARIADNE: Oh, what a horrible thing to say! . . . Why come here if you only want to hurt me?

JEROME: You, you're invulnerable. . . .

ARIADNE: You think so?

JEROME: I came because I was dying of heat in Paris: because the concert season was over; because there wasn't any air to breathe; and because no one talked of anything but upheavals and civil war. . . .

ARIADNE: You could have travelled.

JEROME: I'm as comfortable here as anywhere else.

ARIADNE: Or as uncomfortable.

JEROME: If you like.

ARIADNE: [*after a pause*] I've just had news of Mademoiselle Mazargues.

JEROME: Ah! . . . And what's that to me?

ARIADNE: She's here with her little girl, who's ill.

JEROME: I suppose *you* arranged that?

ARIADNE: Jerome, I told you I've heard nothing of her for six weeks.

JEROME: Have you met her? Has she telephoned?

ARIADNE: No. I heard indirectly.

JEROME: Through that pianist, I suppose. . . . Well, was it?

ARIADNE: That's quite unimportant.

JEROME: Oh quite. . . . So now there'll be more music, I suppose, and more nice little teas?

ARIADNE: No.

JEROME: Why not? Are you angry with her? Wasn't she grateful enough?

ARIADNE: Darling, it's time to stop all this pretence. . . . Besides, you must have guessed. . . . I *do* know what Violetta Mazargues is to you.

JEROME: She's nothing to me—nothing at all.

ARIADNE: [*very gravely*] What she has been then, if you prefer it.

JEROME: Well, what about it?

ARIADNE: You admit she's been your mistress?

JEROME: If you like.

ARIADNE: Jerome, I only ask you to answer yes or no.

JEROME: I suppose you've got, or think you've got, proofs.

ARIADNE: That's not the point. I didn't want a confession— only a simple, honest answer. I sometimes think you're not as brave as I could wish, Jerome——

JEROME: If you think I'm afraid of the consequences, you're wrong. Yes, I've been the woman's lover. I'll say it to anybody you like. That should simplify things quite a bit, if it's divorce you're after.

ARIADNE: I shouldn't dream of divorce, unless *you* wanted it.

JEROME: Not in the least.

ARIADNE: You've never considered it?

JEROME: All sorts of stray ideas go through one's head. I suppose that did too. It doesn't necessarily mean a thing.

ARIADNE: And she?

JEROME: Ask her, if you're interested.

ARIADNE: You've no desire to see her again?

JEROME: Not the slightest.

ARIADNE: Well, I'm not like you. I feel it's essential that we three should talk the whole thing over with absolute frankness.

JEROME: Is that your idea of good taste?

ARIADNE: To me it's essential.

JEROME: She may not think so.

ARIADNE: I shall do all I can to persuade her.

JEROME: It's incredible.

ARIADNE: You're right, there's something about the whole situation . . .

JEROME: Oh, not the situation. That seems to me quite too commonplace.

ARIADNE: Less so than you think.

JEROME: Well, you can leave me out of this . . . conference.

ARIADNE: Surely you'll do *that* for me? You must admit, I've not been very difficult up to now.

JEROME: Depends on what you mean by difficult. . . .

ARIADNE: After our conversation you can do whatever you like. You'll be entirely free. [*She goes to the telephone and picks up the receiver*] One five, please. Is that the Sanatorium Beausoleil? Could I speak to Mademoiselle Mazargues?

JEROME: You're mad, absolutely mad! [ARIADNE *nods her head to reassure him*]

ARIADNE: Hullo! Is that you, Violetta? . . . No, no, don't cut off, *please*. . . . I heard of your arrival quite by accident. How are you? And little Monica? . . . The X-ray's not good? You poor dear! But, you know, children of that age pick up again in no time. You mustn't be frightened. Has she a temperature? . . . Yes . . . oh, but that's very little. She'll be marvellously looked after. Dr. Schmidt is first class; so clever, and so very, very kind. . . .

JEROME: [*under his breath*] And *such* a good business man.

ARIADNE: And he's *so* optimistic, it's lovely the way he cheers one up. Oh, Violetta, I *do* want to see you, I do, as soon as possible. Can't you look in this evening, after dinner? Anyone will show you our house. It's only five minutes from Beausoleil. . . . You don't know how your silence has hurt me. I wrote five or six times, and sent three reply-paid telegrams . . . and no reply. . . . I didn't know *what* to think. . . . In the end I realised you were terribly angry with me. [*Her voice shakes*] I tried to make myself understand. . . . Oh, I've been *so* miserable. . . . I only want to understand, Violetta. Really, I'm not like what you think . . . I . . . I'm *so* unhappy. Come, do come, my dear,

and let's clear it all up. . . . Ah! Then I'll see you this
evening. Au revoir. Au revoir! my dear. [*She turns round*]
Oh, you're still here?

JEROME: Yes.

ARIADNE: What is it?

JEROME: I'm just a little surprised, that's all!

> *The curtain falls and goes up again at once on the same
> scene. The room is almost dark, the only light coming
> from a corner lamp.* JEROME *is sitting holding his head
> in his hands. There is a knock on the door.*

JEROME: [*drearily*] Come in. [*The door remains shut*]

JEROME: [*louder*] Come in!

> VIOLETTA *comes in.*

VIOLETTA: Jerome! . . . She never told me you were here.

JEROME: I don't see that she had to. . . . Does she know
you've come?

VIOLETTA: The servant will have told her. [*A pause*]

JEROME: Do you *realise* what you've done to me?

VIOLETTA: I couldn't do anything else. It was impossible
after what had happened.

JEROME: May I ask what you're referring to?

VIOLETTA: Besides, you must admit things are far better this
way. . . . [*She waves her hand at the room*] Suppose I'd
taken you at your word. Just look at what you would have
had to give up. I've really done you a very great service.

JEROME: Do you think so?

VIOLETTA: And, what's more, *you* are still the noble one.
You made me the most generous offer and I refused it.
You've got a clear conscience and you're still living in the
greatest comfort. What more do you want?

JEROME: And our love, Violetta?

VIOLETTA: It would never have survived all the upheaval.
Don't let's imagine its death pangs.

JEROME: And now? What has become of it now?

VIOLETTA: We can each answer that for ourselves, in our own hearts.

JEROME: And what does your heart tell you?

VIOLETTA: [*evasively*] I can't think why Ariadne doesn't come down.

JEROME: She's in her room.

VIOLETTA: All the rooms seemed dark, except this one.

JEROME: She does sometimes sit like that in the dark. . . .

VIOLETTA: Praying?

JEROME: I think she—meditates.

VIOLETTA: Oh, God! It's all going to begin all over again.

JEROME: I warn you, she knows about us.

VIOLETTA: She told you so?

JEROME: Yes. . . . You don't seem surprised.

VIOLETTA: [*embarrassed*] No. . . . She would have had to be blind, to notice nothing.

JEROME: Why are you talking in that artificial way all of a sudden? . . . Why did you run away and hide—and not answer my letters? That's what I *can't* forgive.

VIOLETTA: I couldn't trust myself. . . . So I had no other way to protect myself.

JEROME: You didn't answer me just now. Do you still love me, Violetta?

VIOLETTA: I don't know.

JEROME: How do you mean, you don't know? . . . Haven't you been unhappy, these six weeks?

VIOLETTA: Yes, desperately.

JEROME: Because of me?

VIOLETTA: Yes, at first, because of you. . . . And then, Monica got ill. . . . You haven't even asked me how she is.

JEROME: But I know, I've heard all about it. . . . I'm so sorry for you, Violetta.

VIOLETTA: Sorry for me! . . . If you really loved me, Jerome, you'd find more to say than that.

JEROME: Monica's the child of a man I loathe. She looks like him. If I . . . It's not my fault, Violetta. *Do* understand: it's *because* I love you. Love isn't just an easy-going, arm-chair sort of feeling, you know.

VIOLETTA: I wonder if it isn't more like an illness.

JEROME: Well, you seem to be pretty thoroughly cured, anyhow. Congratulations. . . .

VIOLETTA: I'm not cured of anything.

JEROME: And what an idea, too, to come to Logny! As if the child couldn't have been looked after somewhere else. It wasn't to be near me. You didn't know I was here. . . . It's incredible, the way you follow any erratic impulse. Your behaviour's utterly unbalanced.

VIOLETTA: You've been blaming me for having recovered my health. . . . Do make up your mind what your grievance really is, Jerome.

ARIADNE *comes in.*

ARIADNE: [*emotionally*] Oh, Violetta, my dear, thank you for coming. I know what it cost you.

JEROME: As if she hadn't chosen Logny to be near you!

ARIADNE: Please, darling, give us a little more light. That lamp, I think, there, on your right. [JEROME *switches on a light and the piano, which had been in deep shadow, is brightly illuminated*]

VIOLETTA: But Ariadne . . . that piano, it's mine! . . . Then the Madame Deslandes who wrote to me—it was an assumed name? It was *you?*

ARIADNE: Don't be angry with me. I meant it for the best. . . . No doubt it was a horrible mistake, like everything else I do.

JEROME: What's the idea of all this *mea culpa?*

ARIADNE: Listen, Jerome. There's something I must say to you now, in front of Violetta—it's better in front of her. . . . It may surprise and upset you—I don't know—but that can't be helped. We *can't* go on like this, any of us. I used to believe there were harmless, even helpful lies. . . . Now I'm not sure . . . or anyhow I can't . . . Upstairs just now, while you two were alone, I prayed to—oh, I don't know

what to call them—the Invisible Powers, to give me
strength. I need it so much, for I'm certain this is the
turning point of our lives. But I don't know if they heard
me. I feel so terribly weak—quite, quite defenceless . . .
and, oh, there's no kindness in your eyes.

JEROME: But what's happened? You're talking as if *you* were
guilty.

ARIADNE: Perhaps I am. Almost certainly I am. Back in
Paris in April, I knew you were lovers. And then I got an
anonymous letter. But I was already quite sure.

VIOLETTA: That letter wasn't from my sister. We were unjust to her.

ARIADNE: I wasn't at all angry, not at all, with either of you.
As soon as I saw Violetta, I loved her. I'd felt drawn to her
even before we met, and before I knew what she meant to
you. I realised at once how miserable she was about what she
felt to be disloyalty to me, and I *had* to try to comfort
her. . . . I . . . I don't think that was wrong of me, was it?

JEROME: So your friendship . . .

ARIADNE: But where I was perhaps wrong was in making
Violetta hide from you what had passed between her and
me. . . . You see, I honestly believed that once you heard
that I knew about you two, things would become impossible. I thought pride would make you break with her, and
with me too, perhaps. Was I wrong?

JEROME: [*dully*] I don't know.

ARIADNE: Perhaps all the same I ought to have run that risk.
I thought I was being generous, but no doubt I just lacked
courage and faith. . . .

VIOLETTA: [*bitterly*] I think you're *still* blinding yourself.
Are you sure those were your real motives? I think what
you imagined to be a gesture of most generous renunciation
was merely a pretext for intruding where you had no right
to be—no right at all.

JEROME: Violetta!

VIOLETTA: You had every right to condemn our love, to
forbid it, to exclude it; but you had no right, by deceit, by

making me admire you, by fascinating me, to insinuate yourself into its very heart, as if you wanted to . . . to taste at second-hand a fruit you could never have yourself.

JEROME: [*appalled*] Violetta! That's horrible!

ARIADNE: [*firmly*] We're here to discover the truth, whatever it may be. Violetta must say what she really thinks, however much it hurts me.

VIOLETTA: Perhaps I'm being unfair, I may have misjudged you abominably. I know, I admit it. But I can't be *sure*. And you can't make me sure, can you? Can you?

ARIADNE: [*miserably*] No, it's not in my power.

VIOLETTA: You can't imagine the effect you had on me that first evening you came. I almost worshipped you. But gradually I found my adoration for you coming between Jerome and me. And yet I couldn't explain to him because of my promise to you. And he felt *something* was going on, and he was bewildered and grew angry with me—and with you too. So the situation between us became impossible. Something *had* to happen. And it did—Jerome asked me to marry him. And you—though you seemed to accept it and wanted to help—you said the one thing which could make me refuse him and hate the idea. And then I thought you'd worked it all out; the one sure way to separate me from Jerome. And you would still appear a heroine and a saint both to yourself and to me. You couldn't give *that* up! And when you said I must remember you'd forgiven me— oh, if you could only know how that tormented me. . . . I dreamt sometimes that you'd had an accident, that you'd stumbled on the mountain and slipped. . . . I'd wake with a start, thinking: Oh God! Was it suicide? We'll never know! I thought out all the arrangements you'd have made. I thought: she'll have left a letter. She'll have done everything to make it seem an accident, except perhaps one little thing . . . there's sure to be one little loophole of doubt. Your forgiveness was like a knife turning in my heart. . . . So I decided never to see him again.

JEROME: [*harshly*] Why did you come to Logny?

ARIADNE: [*to* VIOLETTA] But Violetta, can't you guess?
When I left you that evening, I felt the harm I'd done
you—I felt it terribly, oh, like a physical pain. I couldn't
forgive myself for forgiving you. I *couldn't*. I tried to
telephone you when I got home that night, but there was
no reply. Then I wrote . . .

VIOLETTA: I didn't open your letters, Ariadne.

JEROME: [*harshly*] Because you were afraid of the truth.

VIOLETTA: What do you mean?

JEROME: Because you *wanted* Ariadne's motives to be mean
and low and unmentionable, at any price. That would save
you from having to despise yourself.

VIOLETTA: Jerome!

JEROME: If anyone's been mean and low in all this, it's *you*.
Ariadne . . . I can't judge her. We've said often enough,
she doesn't live in the same world as we do. But you—you
didnt' have to give in to her. You've well and truly made a
fool of me. Why? Why? Was it weakness—or some subtle
scheme that I'm too simple to guess at?

VIOLETTA: Oh, cruel! It's not difficult . . . I was afraid of
losing you, that's all.

JEROME: Evidently you didn't consider the link between us
very strong!

ARIADNE: Now, Jerome darling, you mustn't take my side
against Violetta. If it's anybody's fault, it's mine, mine
alone. I'm as earthly as you, alas, perhaps more so. You must
never forget everything that's been refused me and taken
from me. That's the most terrible thing in life—I've been
thinking so much about it lately—we don't only do without
the things we've lost. Their inverted shadows live on within
us, like dark destructive powers. . . . Now you're thinking
me super-human, Jerome—oh, I know you used to think
me an unbearable egoist—but there's nothing super-
human about me. If now I feel suddenly that the Spirit has
heard me, it's only because I'm being shown the depths of
my own weakness and inadequacy. Oh, how wrong I've
been, how *wrong*. . . . Isn't it proof enough that I told

Violetta the one thing I should have hidden—that before our marriage you were . . . I had no right to tell her, no right at all. Why did I? I don't know. Was I obeying? . . .

VIOLETTA: [*passionately*] Oh! Can't you see? That you told me didn't matter, so long as *he* didn't know. But now, *now,* it becomes deadly. And can't you see what you've done in Jerome's eyes, by blaming yourself? You've set yourself on a pedestal, and made me, by contrast, the more vile and contemptible. After all, it's *you* who make all these accusations. It's not a voice from Heaven, but you, yourself . . .

ARIADNE: Oh, Violetta, how cruel you are! Even when I've flung away all my pride and self-respect, when I've laid bare all my shame and weakness, you *still* accuse me of heaven knows what designs . . .

VIOLETTA: I'm not suggesting you're not sincere.

ARIADNE: Yes, that too I've probably deserved. . . . Oh, poor Violetta! It's not like you to be so cruel and unjust. It's I, no doubt, who've made you so.

VIOLETTA: You're speaking from your heart, I'm sure. But don't you see? If you were playing with us, if you were being utterly cruel and calculating, could you think of any better way to keep Jerome and me apart . . . could you?

ARIADNE: I won't—I *won't* keep you apart. Jerome, it's in your hands. Violetta's worth more than I am. She's more honest, and she's a real *woman.* She's had one child. She can have others. . . . But I. . . . [*She can hardly speak*] I no longer exist. [*She is shaken with sobs.* JEROME *goes to her, sits down by her, takes her hand and strokes it*]

VIOLETTA: [*standing up*] If you'd really meant to play fair— but why should you?—you'd have been jealous, petty, difficult. You'd have treated me as a rival. That was the only way. Anything else was cheating. Your dice were loaded . . . But oh, Ariadne, I am more than grateful to you. You've taught me what I should never have learnt alone— you've taught me the value, the power of cynicism. Now I know that truth and beauty have nothing in common, that no human art can harmonise them. . . . That's the first step, anyhow. . . . The money sent me by *your* friend, Madame Deslandes, will be returned immediately by *my* friend, Monsieur Bassigny, who is paying for our stay at Beausoleil. . . .

JEROME: Then you *do* admit that Bassigny . . .

VIOLETTA: [*in a changed voice*] Goodbye, Ariadne. . . . Oh, I know, maybe I'm a monster of injustice and ingratitude. But since the gift of prayer is yours, along with *everything* else. . . . pray for me sometimes . . . and for Monica, specially for Monica. Because if she doesn't get well . . . then . . . Oh, I don't know. . . . [*She takes* ARIADNE'S *hand, kisses it convulsively and goes out. A long silence*]

ARIADNE: [*after looking at* JEROME] Oh, God! It's all happening as if she'd been right. You didn't even look at her . . . Jerome, are you quite heartless? Have I killed your heart too? . . . And now I shan't even be allowed to die myself. . . . The invalid who buries all her companions and then writes—and writes—and writes. Clarissa! Clarissa! [*She half opens the door*]

CLARISSA *comes in.*

CLARISSA: Yes, Ariadne. I was afraid to come in. I didn't want to disturb you. Has your visitor gone?

ARIADNE: Yes, yes, she's gone. Now Clarissa, tomorrow morning early we must telegraph to that journalist . . .

CLARISSA: That you refuse . . .

ARIADNE: No, no, that I accept, Clarissa, accept, with many thanks. . . . We'll publish my book posthumously in advance. Don't forget, Clarissa, posthumously in advance. . . . After all, I might as well be dead.

CURTAIN

THE VOTIVE CANDLE

English Version
by ROSALIND HEYWOOD

OF

LA CHAPELLE ARDENTE

a Play in Three Acts
by GABRIEL MARCEL

CHARACTERS

Octave Fortier

Andre Verdet

———

Aline Fortier

Mireille Pradol

Madame Verdet

Louise

Yvonne Cambrin

Anna

Little Jacquot

ACT ONE

Time: 1920. *A large drawing room in a country house in France. Doors R. and L. Backstage tall french windows open on to the garden which can be clearly seen.* ALINE *is discovered looking out at the garden through her lorgnettes. Then she goes and rings the bell by the fireplace. There is a pause. . . . The maid,* LOUISE, *comes in.*

LOUISE: Did you ring, Madame?

ALINE: [*sharply, pointing out of the window*] What are those toys doing there?

LOUISE: [*embarrassed*] It's not my fault, Madame. It was Madame Cambrin took me to the loft to go through Monsieur Raymond's things. [ALINE *starts*] She thought there might be some toys for little Jacquot.

ALINE: Oh, but you should have asked me first.

LOUISE: I wanted to, madame, but Madame Cambrin said as I didn't need to, and if I'm given an order . . .

ALINE: *I* give the orders in this house, Louise.

LOUISE: It was for your grandson . . . so I thought it would be all right with you, Madame.

ALINE: Well, please put the whole lot back where you found them.

LOUISE: Madame Cambrin will be ever so cross with me. . . . Jacquot hasn't anything to play with.

ALINE: Why didn't my daughter bring his own toys?

LOUISE: They had a terrible lot of excess luggage, Madame.

ALINE: Victor will be going into the town in half an hour. He can buy the child something.

> MIREILLE *comes in, dressed for tennis and carrying a racquet.*

ALINE: [*affectionately*] Back already, dear?

MIREILLE: It's so hot on the court. The sun's simply beating down.

LOUISE: Will you be changing, Mademoiselle?

MIREILLE: No, thanks, Louise. I'll stay as I am.

ALINE: Don't forget what I said, Louise.

LOUISE: No, Madame. [*She goes out*]

MIREILLE: [*going to* ALINE, *affectionately*] I've hardly said good morning to you . . . Mother.

ALINE: Mother. . . . You *really* want to call me Mother. . . . You're sure?

MIREILLE: Yes, yes, I do. Please let me.

ALINE: I don't know . . . I wonder . . .

MIREILLE: If I'd been Raymond's wife you'd have found it quite natural.

ALINE: Perhaps.

MIREILLE: And now he's gone, somehow you and I seem even closer to each other, don't we?

ALINE: You dear child! [*They embrace*] All the same, don't do it just to please me . . . only if it comes naturally. . . . You see, your parents mightn't have liked it . . .

MIREILLE: But I never even knew them! . . . No, no, I always feel as if *you* were my real mother. [*Silence*]

ALINE: Who was down at the tennis club?

MIREILLE: Oh, the usual crowd, Jeanne and Henriette and their brothers. Robert Chanteuil was there too.

ALINE: He seems to go there every day now?

MIREILLE: Yes . . .

ALINE: Is he as unattractive as ever? [MIREILLE *makes a vague gesture*]—Of course, I only know what you've said about him.

MIREILLE: I suppose he *is* rather dull really . . . he plays tennis very well.

ALINE: Oh!

MIREILLE: But when one arrives he has a way of looking one up and down . . .

ALINE: That's hardly good manners, is it?

MIREILLE: [*hesitating*] Oh, his manners aren't too bad . . .

ALINE: Aren't they? Look at the way he laughed at poor Jeanne Morel the other day. It was positively vulgar.

MIREILLE: What a memory you have! I'd forgotten I told you about it. But I daresay you're right. He makes fun of the Morels' old aunt too—you know, the deaf one. . . .

ALINE: There you are! . . .

MIREILLE: And he's much too pleased with himself. I caught him looking in a pocket glass just now. He's good looking, of course, but *really* . . . Have you never seen him?

ALINE: No, I don't think so . . .

MIREILLE: Many people wouldn't like his black hair and bright blue eyes. It's a curious combination. [*Silence*. MIREILLE, *embarrassed by it, goes on talking*] But . . . yes, perhaps he does look a bit ruthless.

YVONNE *comes in.*

YVONNE: Good morning, Mother. Hullo, Mireille, how are you? [*to her mother*] Do you happen to know where they've put the toys I fished out of the loft for Jacquot?

ALINE: Yes, I do. I told Louise to take them back.

YVONNE: But why, Mother? It's idiotic. The child must have something to play with. He doesn't know what to do with himself all day long.

ALINE: Victor can buy anything you want for him at Ville-neuve. He'll be going there this morning.

YVONNE: Why on earth buy toys when there are lots here already?

ALINE: I'm quite willing to pay for them.

YVONNE: Oh, I don't mind the money. But what point is there in not using the things one has? Why let all those toys fall to bits in the loft? They do no one any good.

ALINE: I'm having a cupboard made for them. I shall set them out in it.

YVONNE: [*sarcastically*] Set them out! What an idea, isn't it, Mireille? [MIREILLE *makes a gesture of dissent*]

YVONNE: [*to* ALINE] Really, Mother, you've got a very curious notion of showing your feelings for the dead.

ALINE: [*in a strained voice*] Please . . .

YVONNE: The past isn't a religion for you. It's a superstition.

MIREILLE: Yvonne!

ALINE: My dear Yvonne, any woman who is capable of going to a *ball* three months after her brother has been killed can hardly . . .

YVONNE: Oh, that wretched ball! Will you ever let me forget it? When I think what . . .

ALINE: Yvonne, that's enough. I've made up my mind.

YVONNE: How very convenient!

MIREILLE: Yvonne, don't. You're hurting your mother. . . . [ALINE *reacts to this*] And me too.

YVONNE: You?

MIREILLE: [*looking hard at* ALINE] One ought to respect that kind of feeling, Yvonne!

YVONNE: One ought to keep some glimmer of common sense. If my husband were here. . . .

ALINE: Yes, that's the kind of thing your husband would say.

YVONNE: It's quite clear this house won't be big enough to hold both you and me for long. If it weren't for Daddy, I'd . . . [*She goes out*]

ALINE: [*bitterly*] You see!

MIREILLE: Oh dear, it's such a pity. . . . But all the same, don't you think it might have been better . . . though you saw I did back you up . . .

ALINE: Oh, if you only did it out of *politeness*!

MIREILLE: No, but I do feel that Raymond would have given these toys to his nephew.

ALINE: Raymond isn't here any more.

MIREILLE: But toys are not . . .

ALINE: Yes, they are. You cannot possibly understand.

MIREILLE: Of course, for me, too . . . they're relics.

ALINE: Oh no, *you* didn't have him when he was tiny, for your *very* own. . . . You can't remember him playing with them in bed and in the garden and lending them and giving them away. . . . He so loved to give.

MIREILLE: [*in a low voice*] Then, surely, for that very reason . . .

ALINE: What?

MIREILLE: Oh, nothing.

ALINE: Yvonne would have grabbed—yes, grabbed— everything, even his school books, *in case* Jacquot might want them. Yvonne will never starve!

MIREILLE: She may have wanted to have something that belonged to her brother?

ALINE: She never cared for him. Oh, I know, it was always darling Raymond this, and dear old boy that . . . but it didn't mean a thing. . . . What did she ever do for him? No, no, it's better to face it. There's no one who cares but you and me. . . .

MIREILLE: But my father-in-law . . .

ALINE: Oh, Octave! . . . [*her eyes wander absently over the table*] Ah, there they are. I nearly forgot to show them to you, and I'd put them aside for you, too. [*She gives* MIREILLE *an envelope*]

MIREILLE: What is it? [*She opens it*] Oh! *Why* didn't you let me see them before? "Dinard, 1902." Is that Raymond there, digging in the sand? Isn't he tall for his age? And there . . . what's he pointing at?

ALINE: [*leaning over her*] Let me see.

OCTAVE *comes in.*

MIREILLE: Oh, do come and look, father.

ALINE: [*seizing the photographs almost brutally*] No, no, give them to me.

OCTAVE: What is it?

ALINE: Nothing. Nothing at all.

OCTAVE: Aline, you've such a good memory. Can you by any chance remember what happened to Captain de Cluny? I think he went to the Twenty-Fourth regiment in February, '18. But afterwards? I thought we'd heard . . .

ALINE: [*coldly*] I've no idea at all.

OCTAVE: Then I must write to the depôt. [*To* MIREILLE] It's for my little book, you see. Captain de Cluny comes into the part about the Frankfort Trench.

MIREILLE: Oh, have you got as far as that already?

ALINE: [*who is intently reading a book*] He's *always* working at it.

OCTAVE: It has to be finished by the New Year.

MIREILLE: Why?

OCTAVE: That's my time limit. It's self-imposed, of course— One should always set oneself a limit.

MIREILLE: It must mean a tremendous lot of work.

OCTAVE: Yes. The worst part is writing to all the families.

MIREILLE: Could I do some of the letters for you? . . . [ALINE *looks hard at* MIREILLE] Yes, Mother dear? What is it?

ALINE: Oh, nothing. I was surprised, that's all.

OCTAVE: People won't answer. I have to go on at them, three or four times. . . . But I worry them till they do. . . . Those poor devils of the Forty-Second were like my own children . . . I *must* know what's become of them. What a regiment! Three years of it and they never turned a hair. . . . If they hadn't been disbanded after the war, I'd never have left the Army.

MIREILLE: Wouldn't you really?

OCTAVE: No, indeed I wouldn't.

ALINE: Octave, I believe there's a parcel for you from Mazaret.

OCTAVE: [*eagerly*] From the printer's? Where is it?

ALINE: [*pointing R.*] I think it was put on the side table in the hall.

OCTAVE: [*as he goes out*] Why didn't you tell me at once? [*He goes out*]

ALINE: Mireille dearest, you'll give up that plan, won't you? . . . unless you want to hurt me very, very much indeed.

MIREILLE: What plan?

ALINE: About the letters you offered to write.

MIREILLE: But surely, mother, if it helps him . . .

ALINE: [*harshly*] Writing those letters gives him something to do.

MIREILLE: All the same . . .

ALINE: [*going up to her*] You see, darling, I loathe the very idea of that book.

MIREILLE: But . . .

ALINE: And I wonder you don't too. We usually feel the same about things. . . . Oh! The Madeleine Redoubt and the Frankfort Trench [*with a sob*] and Hill 36. . . . Oh, Mireille, Hill 36. . . . Those ghastly massacres . . . And he wants to keep their memory alive. . . . How could you want to help him? No, no, darling, you couldn't do such a thing!

MIREILLE: [*taken aback*] I'll think it over . . . I . . .

ALINE: [*calming down*] Then I needn't worry any more.

> OCTAVE *comes in, holding two paper-bound booklets in his hands.*

OCTAVE: [*diffidently*] Here you are. . . . They've not done the printing quite as well as I could wish. . . . People never do just what they're told . . . but . . . well, tell me what you think of it. [*Rather awkwardly he offers one to* MIREILLE *and the other to* ALINE]

MIREILLE: [*looking at hers*] Oh, how lovely! What a wonderful photo . . . [*As she speaks she turns toward* ALINE, *sees her stiffened with ostentatious despair, and stops*]

OCTAVE: Yes, you see, I put his photograph at the beginning . . . the good one by Dupin. . . . The other's too childish looking. Then I put the mentions in despatches . . . and then his letters, the ones he wrote to me. [*He is evidently embarrassed by* ALINE'S *presence. He makes himself go on talking, but his voice gradually fades out*] There are 65 of them, I think, no, 64 . . . yes . . . anyhow, you'll see for yourself. . . . I cut out the personal bits . . . they wouldn't be interesting. . . . Of course this won't be for sale.

MIREILLE: No . . . of course not.

OCTAVE: It's only for friends . . . people who knew him. . . Well, Aline, what have you got to say about it?

ALINE: Nothing . . . nothing at all.

OCTAVE: Nothing?

ALINE: [*with an effort*] The paper's good. . . . It's very . . . clear print.

OCTAVE: [*ironically*] Thanks. I'm glad you find it legible at least.

ALINE: It's really very good.

OCTAVE: Then you're . . . satisfied? [ALINE *does not answer and remains sunk in dreary meditation until* YVONNE *comes in*]

MIREILLE: [*to break the silence*] Fancy seeing his letters in print! What a surprise!

OCTAVE: Yes.

MIREILLE: [*softly*] And it's a wonderful idea.

OCTAVE: [*putting his hand to his ear*] What d'you say? [MIREILLE *does not answer*] Let me have your copy back. I'll have it bound.

MIREILLE: Oh, thank you *so* much.

OCTAVE: [*in a whisper, pointing to* ALINE] Look at Aline. It's so difficult. I do something to please her, and that's the result. . . .

MIREILLE: [*in a whisper*] You show your grief in such *very* different ways.

YVONNE *comes in.*

YVONNE: We're going to sit under the cedar with Nanny and Jacquot. . . . Come and see us somebody. . . . Hullo, Daddy. Have you said good morning to your grandson?

OCTAVE: Have I not! I've been his horse for twenty minutes at least.

YVONNE: Good for you! Won't you come, Mireille? You're a great success with Jacquot, you know.

ALINE: Yes, go with them, Mireille dear. But I'm soon going to see old Madame Noël. I promised to take her some of our cherries. Perhaps you'll come with me? She'd like to see you, poor old thing.

OCTAVE: Tell her I've written again about her son's Military Medal.

ALINE: [*dully*] Oh, have you?

MIREILLE: We'll tell her.

YVONNE: [*as she goes out, to* MIREILLE] The Noël boy was killed, wasn't he? . . . I'd better go and see . . . No, after all, if Mother's going. . . . Come along, Mireille. [YVONNE *and* MIREILLE *go out by the garden window. There is a silence.* ALINE *turns over the leaves of the booklet with shaking hands and* OCTAVE *looks at her with a kind of desperation. She gives a start*]

ALINE: Octave! What does *this* mean?

OCTAVE: [*going up to her*] What?

ALINE: About some conversation with you. You never let *me* see this letter.

OCTAVE: Let me see. . . . [ALINE *gives him the booklet and stares hard at him*] Oh! Yes. . . . [*with embarrassment*] Well, what do you want to know?

ALINE: Why does he say: "I should always have regretted it if I hadn't taken your advice." What advice?

OCTAVE: Well . . .

ALINE: [*reading*] "Thank you for having shown me the right thing to do." Look at the date! . . . [*sharply*] You advised him to go *before* the call-up!

OCTAVE: You must remember the state he was in, surely during my leave in December '16? He was worried to death. He came to me one evening . . . it was just here . . . and he said: "Dad, tell me honestly, what would you do in my place?"

ALINE: So . . . *one word* from you would have kept him at home.

OCTAVE: Aline!

ALINE: At that moment you held his life in your hands.

OCTAVE: He asked for my honest opinion, as man to man . . .

ALINE: [*contemptuously*] Man to man! Look at him. . . . [*She points to the photograph of Raymond on the table*]

OCTAVE: [*miserably*] He trusted me. I *had* to say what I thought.

ALINE: You took advantage of being his father. You knew he was afraid of falling below your standards. . . .

OCTAVE: But I made it quite clear that he was absolutely free to choose.

ALINE: Oh, you hypocrite!

OCTAVE: I swear I made no attempt to influence him.

ALINE: He loathed the very thought of war. It would have been so easy to persuade him not to go.

OCTAVE: *You* did'nt succeed.

ALINE: That was your fault. . . . And, oh, at that time I wasn't myself. I was living in a nightmare. . . . [*silence*] He relied on you to discourage him from going.

OCTAVE: You're insulting his memory. You're making a coward of him.

ALINE: No! Just an unhappy child who saw things as they really were.

OCTAVE: You say he loathed the thought of war. But who didn't?

ALINE: You, for one. . . . Look at what you said the other night to Doctor Morel: "Our finest years . . ."

OCTAVE: That has nothing to do with it. The war itself wasn't glorious. It was the danger and the fellowship in danger. A woman could never understand that.

ALINE: So much the better for her! Then why write your memoirs if you didn't love the war?

OCTAVE: They're not *my* memoirs. They're the record of my regiment. I'm writing them out of loyalty to my friends.

ALINE: Other people never talk about it. They seem almost ashamed of it. But you . . . you can't let even the dead sleep in peace.

OCTAVE: It's my duty to keep alive the memory of their courage and endurance. I . . .

ALINE: Oh, those are only words. And words like that will make it all begin again . . . until there's nobody left.

OCTAVE: Words? You're disowning your own son.

ALINE: And what did *you* do to him? You . . . [*she stops*]

OCTAVE: Say it.

ALINE: No.

OCTAVE: Go on. I know what you think.

ALINE: Ah!

OCTAVE: You think that it's my fault he never came back. *I* didn't take enough care of him. Oh, why did he come to the Forty-Second?

ALINE: As if you didn't encourage him!

OCTAVE: It was his own idea. He asked to come. He chose to come.

ALINE: What else could he do? . . . He couldn't stand up to you. He was pushed into it. . . . It's like that day . . . [*She is shaken by stifled sobs*] and Hill 36 . . . the raid . . .

OCTAVE: The raid? But he begged to go on it, I tell you.

ALINE: What else could he do? . . . He was caught up in the wheels. . . . No, no, Octave, I know what you're going to say, but I won't . . . I won't . . .

OCTAVE: [*very tense*] So *I* didn't love my own son?

ALINE: You loved him less than your own prestige.

OCTAVE: And you don't think *I've* suffered?

ALINE: A man's suffering's nothing but display . . . It's like a medal ribbon. . . . Oh, you can't deny it. . . . I've seen letters you wrote afterwards, full of just one word: pride. "I'm proud . . . We're proud to have given him to our country. . . ."

OCTAVE: [*firmly*] And it's the truth.

ALINE: Well, that proves I'm right! But suffering like mine dries up all those beautiful feelings. . . . Suffering's a hideous thing. You *can't* go making pretty rhymes about it.

OCTAVE: What do you mean?

ALINE: I found your scribbles lying around—and your rhyming dictionary. You'd forgotten to put them away.

OCTAVE: [*his voice trembling with emotion*] Look here, Aline, I'm not just a playboy. I feel Raymond's death quite as much as you do, and I *won't* have you doubt it. And if I choose to write a verse to put on his gravestone . . .

ALINE: [*indistinctly*] No, no, no. I can't bear it.

OCTAVE: . . . when we've brought our boy home, it's to honour his memory, which is sacred to me, even though you do nothing but insult it. And if he can see you and me, as I'm sure he can . . .

ALINE: Oh, stop, stop!

OCTAVE: You can say to yourself . . . [ANDRE *knocks on the french window*]

ANDRE: Good morning, Uncle Octave. Good morning, Aunt Aline.

OCTAVE: Oh, André, I was just going round to your place for news.

ALINE: Of course, you went and saw the heart specialist yesterday, didn't you?

ANDRE: Everything's all right. He says it's only some sort of nervous condition.

OCTAVE: And that breathlessness?

ANDRE: Nothing to worry about, he says . . .

ALINE: And your heart?

ANDRE: Almost normal. He's just given me a little digitalis.

OCTAVE: Digitalis? Then . . .

ANDRE: Oh, it's only an extra precaution. He says the whole thing's due to my overworking last year . . . and if I keep quiet for a bit it will all pass off.

OCTAVE: That's fine, my boy, fine. Your mother must be pleased.

ANDRE: I'm rather relieved myself. I couldn't help wondering a little.

ALINE: Of course.

ANDRE: Is . . . is Mireille around?

OCTAVE: Yes, she's in the garden, with Yvonne and the child.

ANDRE: I saw her in the distance when I passed the tennis club. She plays nearly every day, doesn't she?

OCTAVE: There's so little for her to do here.

ALINE: [*sharply*] Have you ever heard her complain of being dull? She's not a girl who needs *people*. But, of course, she must have air and exercise.

ANDRE: She was with that Chanteuil fellow. He's always playing tennis this year. I gather he means to settle down here . . . and get himself married too, they say.

OCTAVE: Oh, really?

ANDRE: Perhaps he's after one of the Morel girls. . . .

OCTAVE: Hardly likely. They haven't a penny and he's an expensive young man.

ANDRE: [*worried*] Heiresses aren't very thick on the ground in these parts.

ALINE: From what I hear he's a vulgar bore. I can't think why you're interested in him, André.

ANDRE: But, Aunt Aline . . .

MIREILLE *comes in.*

MIREILLE: Oh! Hullo, André. How are you?

OCTAVE: Full of good news. The specialist's given him a clean bill of health.

MIREILLE: [*amiably but without great interest*] Oh! That's good.

ANDRE: [*Looks away and sees the booklet that* MIREILLE *had left on the table. He picks it up*] Oh! I didn't know that . . .

OCTAVE: They've only just come.

ANDRE: [*getting up*] You never told me you were publishing them.

ALINE: Your uncle did it as a surprise for me.

ANDRE: [*doubtfully*] And you think that Raymond? . . . Oh, well . . .

ALINE: What were you going to say?

ANDRE: Oh, nothing . . . I only wondered . . .

ALINE: Go on . . . Say what you were going to.

ANDRE: Oh, really, it's no longer interesting.

ALINE: Did Raymond ever say anything to you?

MIREILLE: [*in an imploring whisper to* ANDRE] Oh, André, what's the good, now?

ANDRE: No, no, not exactly . . . only I remember that when all this publishing of war letters and diaries began . . .

ALINE: Well?

ANDRE: He thought it a bit . . .

ALINE: Indecent? . . .

ANDRE: Not exactly indecent. . . . Say a bit . . . well, not the sort of thing one does.

ALINE: [*to her husband*] You see! . . . [OCTAVE *gives a kind of convulsive shrug.* ALINE *goes out R. and shuts the door gently.* OCTAVE *stands silent for a moment as if expecting* MIREILLE *to speak, but she remains silent*]

OCTAVE: [*flatly*] I'm going to find Jacquot. At least the kid's . . .

ANDRE: [*going towards him*] I'm sorry, Uncle . . . [OCTAVE *goes out without answering*]

MIREILLE: [*bitterly*] Did you *have* to say that?

ANDRE: I didn't want to. . . . She *made* me . . . it doesn't matter, anyhow.

MIREILLE: Doesn't it?

ANDRE: It wasn't said at him, or at anyone in particular. Even if he has been rather silly . . .

MIREILLE: Mother will never forgive him.

ANDRE: So you call my aunt "mother" these days? [*Silence*] I don't see that what I said mattered. [*emotionally*] But something else does. . . . Mireille, does he really mean anything to you?

MIREILLE: He? Who do you mean?

ANDRE: That man you're always playing tennis with . . . that Chanteuil fellow!

MIREILLE: He's very good at tennis.

ANDRE: He only plays because of you. He's crazy about you. He'll ask you to marry him one of these days.

MIREILLE: He's pretty blind if he does. Everyone knows all that sort of thing is over for me . . . over and done with.

ANDRE: [*humbly and happily*] I'm sorry, Mireille.

MIREILLE: After the wonderful happiness I had . . . and looked forward to. . . .

ANDRE: [*in a low voice*] I know.

MIREILLE: [*emotionally*] No, you don't know. . . . There's nobody in the world now, nobody who doesn't seem a contemptible, insignificant worm to me. . . . And this boy you're talking about and who's worth *far* more than people . . . [*getting more and more worked up*] Anyhow, what right have *you* to ask me a question like that? [*She goes to the chimney piece and leans her elbows on it, her head in her hands, her back to* ANDRE]

ANDRE: [*going up to her*] Mireille, I'm terribly unhappy, but you needn't despise me for it. . . . Raymond was my friend, too. . . . I thought the world of him . . . and I miss him too . . . [*in a low voice*] I'm not jealous of *him* . . . but the idea of anyone else . . . I *can't* bear that!

MIREILLE: [*half turning towards him, cruelly*] Chanteuil fought in the war. . . . He was wounded, twice. . . . [ANDRE *looks at her reproachfully and moves away, with a shudder*] Oh! I'm sorry . . . that was hateful of me . . . but if you only knew what the atmosphere is here. . . . Sometimes I think I'll suffocate.

ANDRE: [*astonished*] What? But they all adore you. You're part of the family. . . .

MIREILLE: [*thoughtfully*] Yes, I know.

ANDRE: Aunt Aline can't do without you . . .

MIREILLE: And I can't do without her, either. . . .

ANDRE: Well then? . . .

MIREILLE: When you're *necessary* to someone like that . . . Oh, I don't know what it is . . . You don't feel free. You can't breathe. [*Horrified*] Oh! I never meant to say that, really I didn't. . . . You don't understand . . .

ALINE *appears at the door and pauses to watch them.*

MIREILLE: [*going to her*] Isn't it time for us to go to old Madame Noël?

ALINE: I'm still waiting for her cherries. Alexis is bringing them here. [*Silence*]

ANDRE: It's late. I ought to be going. The doctor said I wasn't to walk too fast.

ALINE: No, naturally you mustn't.

ANDRE: [*To* MIREILLE] Won't you come and see my mother some time, Mireille?

MIREILLE: Why, yes . . . of course I will.

ANDRE: Couldn't we fix a day now?

MIREILLE: [*her eyes on* ALINE] Perhaps.

ALINE: It's for *you* to decide, darling.

MIREILLE: Tell her I'll write to her.

ANDRE: Well, don't put it off too long. . . . Goodbye, Aunt Aline. [*he goes out*]

ALINE: Why was he looking so miserable when I came in?

MIREILLE: Miserable . . .

ALINE: If the doctor really did say he was all right. . . .

MIREILLE: He could have other worries, couldn't he?

ALINE: He always brooded too much about his health. . . . Not that one can blame him for it. He was never strong. But he always fussed so. Raymond used to laugh at him.

MIREILLE: All the same, there might be . . . something else as well. [*She speaks without looking at* ALINE *and her voice shakes a little. Silence*]

ALINE: Mireille, darling, you asked just now if you might call me mother. . . . It wasn't my idea. You know, I'm not sure I even wanted it.

MIREILLE: Well?

ALINE: Let me finish, dear. It's important. I don't want you to do it merely out of kindness. . . . It *must* come from your heart.

MIREILLE: But it does.

ALINE: Then you'll *always* trust me, darling?

MIREILLE: [*rather bleakly*] What else can I do? . . . Everyone else is dead. I've no-one but you. . . . Anyhow I'm not clever enough to have secrets.

ALINE: Don't be silly, dear. There's no question of secrets.

But even a shadow of concealment between us would spoil everything. You know that. Our common loss . . .

MIREILLE: Why must you *say* it?

ALINE: You mustn't think that I live only for our friendship, darling, but all the same it was that friendship which pulled me through. Without it I think I'd have given up. We must never risk doing anything which could harm it, never.

MIREILLE: But there *is* no risk of that.

ALINE: Dearest, there might be . . . if we're not *very* careful. [MIREILLE *moves uneasily*] You see, you're young and you can't be sure you'll never change. And you ought not to be sure, you see, for people do change. It's a terrible thing, but it's a fact. You might even come to . . .

MIREILLE: Oh, please don't go on. I can guess what you're going to say. But that could never happen, never . . . oh, don't you remember what I told you when we went there . . . and saw all those devastated fields and the hills where nothing will ever grow again. . . . [*in a muffled voice*] That's how it is with me.

ALINE: That's a dangerous thing to say, dear, and you may be deceiving yourself. . . .

MIREILLE: How can you say that? It's cruel of you.

ALINE: [*gently*] You're not being very brave, my dear. [MIREILLE *shivers*] At least I promise you that if you ever do have something to tell me, it will never change my love for you, whatever it may be.

MIREILLE: [*vehemently*] You may think that, but it's not true. You couldn't bear it . . . you know you couldn't, and . . . oh, neither could I . . .

ALINE: Mireille dear, as I see it, trust should be absolute and mutual. If one day you do decide to remake your life . . . and why shouldn't you? It would only be natural . . .

MIREILLE: Mother!

ALINE: If you do, it must never be with someone unworthy . . . not after what might have been . . . I know you could never fall so low as . . . as to give your love to some inferior creature like . . . well, like Chanteuil, who . . .

MIREILLE: [*indistinctly*] Why Chanteuil?

> OCTAVE *and* YVONNE *come in by the french window.*
> *On* OCTAVE's *back is little* JACQUOT, *who is shouting*
> *and clapping his hands.*

OCTAVE: [*trying to put* JACQUOT *down*] There, old man, that's
enough now . . .

JACQUOT: No, no, Grandpa, more, more!

OCTAVE: Well, once more round the lawn, but only once,
mind you. . . .

ALINE: If that child's spoilt, Octave, it'll be your fault.

YVONNE: [*scathingly*] Luckily we have you as an antidote,
Mother.

OCTAVE: [*putting the child down*] Tomorrow, old man. No
more now.

MIREILLE: [*going to* JACQUOT] Hullo, Jacquot! Give me a
kiss. [MIREILLE *gives* JACQUOT *a hug, but feeling* ALINE's
eyes upon her, moves away sharply. To YVONNE] The
mosquitoes seem to have been biting him again, don't they?

YVONNE: That's just what I've been saying. If the pond isn't
emptied . . .

OCTAVE: [*To* YVONNE] Then I'll get the book to show you,
Yvonne. [*He goes out R.*]

YVONNE: But as it's against the law here to change *anything* . . .

ALINE: Don't be absurd, Yvonne.

YVONNE: Well, Mireille, isn't it true? Look at all that old
furniture which nobody uses. . . . It's not worth a penny,
and we need it at home. But . . .

> OCTAVE *comes in, very pale.*

OCTAVE: [*To* ALINE, *in a whisper*] Aline, have you taken my
proofs?

ALINE: Yes. [*The gardener knocks at the window*]

OCTAVE: [*controlling himself with difficulty*] May I ask where
you've put them?

ALINE: Later on, if you don't mind.

OCTAVE: You've not destroyed them?

ALINE: No. I've simply put them away. [*She goes to speak to the gardener*] Are those the cherries, Alexis? I've been waiting over half an hour for them. [*She takes the basket*] What are these flowers? . . . Oh, they seem to be for you, Mireille. [*She gives* MIREILLE *a large bunch of red roses*]

MIREILLE: What?

ALINE: Alexis says Monsieur Chanteuil's gardener has just brought them.

YVONNE: Ha! Ha! Mireille, what's all this?

OCTAVE: Chanteuil?

MIREILLE: [*uncomfortably*] I was silly enough to admire his red roses. You can see them from the tennis courts.

ALINE: I'm going to put on my hat. [*to* MIREILLE] Meet me outside, dear, will you?

YVONNE: [*taking* JACQUOT *by the hand and going out with her mother*] Mother, can't you make sure that Jacquot has his lunch punctually at twelve-thirty? . . . [*The rest is lost*]

OCTAVE: [*controlling himself with difficulty*] I wouldn't put it beyond my wife to burn the book. [*He waits for a protest from* MIREILLE *but it does not come at once*]

MIREILLE: [*after a pause, holding the flowers, her thoughts far away*] No . . . no . . . she'd never do that. . . .

OCTAVE: You don't think so? [*with enthusiasm*] Oh, my dear, if you only knew. . . . [*he stops himself*] But you're still holding that great bunch of flowers. I'll have them put in water for you.

MIREILLE: [*roughly and passionately*] No, no, they must be thrown away.

CURTAIN

ACT TWO

The same scene ten days later. MIREILLE *is discovered writing. Every now and then she looks at a notebook which lies open in front of her. She jumps nervously as the door L. opens, but relaxes on seeing* OCTAVE *come in.*

MIREILLE: [*softly*] I've just written these four letters for you. Do you mind reading them? My spelling's so terrible. . . .

OCTAVE: [*who has heard nothing*] Eh? What?

MIREILLE: I said I'd like you to read these four letters.

OCTAVE: Oh, don't worry about that, I'm sure they'll do perfectly.

MIREILLE: I've written to the Depôt at Dreux, as you told me.

OCTAVE: Good.

MIREILLE: But I'm pretty certain I've got to the bottom of that Dupont muddle myself. There must have been two Gaston Duponts in the 8th company, and one of them is not shown in the depôt records. Mightn't he have come straight from the divisional depôt?

OCTAVE: Mireille, you're a wonder. It makes all the difference your doing the letters for me, you know——

MIREILLE: Oh, that's nothing. I like to.

OCTAVE: When I write too long, it gets at me here. [*He points to his forearm*] Rheumatism, I suppose . . . or old age.

MIREILLE: [*vaguely*] How trying that must be.

OCTAVE: [*looking at her*] You're not looking yourself, Mireille.

MIREILLE: Oh, I'm all right.

OCTAVE: But you've got great rings under your eyes.

MIREILLE: I don't seem to sleep very well these days.

OCTAVE: I thought as much. I heard you tramping about

246

down here for hours last night. Look, my dear, don't
worry about any more letters now. . . .

MIREILLE: But I was thankful to have something to do.
When one can't sleep . . .

OCTAVE: Yes, yes, I know. . . . But all the same you can't
work all night, my child. If my wife found it out . . .

MIREILLE: Oh, you mustn't tell my mother-in-law. . . . We'd
better put away these papers. She might come in.

OCTAVE: I thought you'd taken to calling her mother?

MIREILLE: Not when I talk about her . . .

OCTAVE: Does it worry you?

MIREILLE: What?

OCTAVE: Having a little secret from her?

MIREILLE: I don't like having secrets from anybody. After
all, why shouldn't I help you? It's so natural. But she'd be
upset if she did know about it.

OCTAVE: You think she'd be angry with you?

MIREILLE: [*with energy*] No, no. That would be so petty . . .
and, anyhow, I'm free to do as I like.

OCTAVE: Of course you are.

MIREILLE: No, it's just to spare her. She's unhappy enough
as it is.

OCTAVE: She's not alone in that.

MIREILLE: I know no one else who has her capacity for
suffering—she seems to have a special talent for it.

OCTAVE: Don't you think it's more like a lack of decent
reserve? [MIREILLE *moves uneasily*] I mean she doesn't
merely parade her sorrow. She brandishes it, as if she wanted
to crush one with it.

MIREILLE: It hurts me when you talk like that.

OCTAVE: Why should it hurt *you*?

MIREILLE: Anything said against her is said against me too.

OCTAVE: But, my dear child . . .

MIREILLE: I think Yvonne would agree with what you said.

OCTAVE: [*in a different voice*] Yvonne. . . . Oh, that's quite
another matter. . . . But you know, Mireille, my wife was
altogether different in the old days. . . . Before the war we

never . . . But she seems drunk with this disaster. It seems to have poisoned her somehow. . . .

MIREILLE: [*bitterly*] Sorrow isn't a disease. . . . Are you like Yvonne? Do you find the house too dreary too? [OCTAVE *stirs uneasily*] Aren't we picking up the pieces quickly enough? Do you want to *hurry* back to normal?

OCTAVE: [*gently*] That's not really *you* talking, my dear.

MIREILLE: [*working herself up*] Anyhow, I admire her sorrow, with all my heart. It may be terrible too, but nothing else would be so fine. Anything else would be unworthy . . . [*She is clearly on the point of tears*]

OCTAVE: [*watching her intently*] I don't like to see you get so over-excited, my dear.

MIREILLE: I'm *not* over-excited. It's what I really really feel. If sometimes I seem not to . . . Oh, well, I *hate* myself then.

OCTAVE: [*gravely*] But if you agree so profoundly with my wife, why did you offer to help me with this work? . . . You know she doesn't approve of it. Was it simply for my sake?

MIREILLE: [*her eyes downcast*] But you mustn't think I'm just a slave. I told you: I do what I like.

MME. VERDET *is shown in at the window by the maid,* LOUISE.

MME. VERDET: Thank you, Louise. . . . Good morning, Octave.

OCTAVE: Why! . . . Martha!

MIREILLE: Oh, Aunt Martha, I'm so sorry I haven't been to see you. I meant to, but every day something seemed to prevent it.

MME. VERDET: [*in a strained voice*] You'll always be welcome, Mireille.

OCTAVE: Do sit down, won't you. [MME. VERDET *sits down*] André's been round here a lot lately. He seems much better than he was last winter.

MME. VERDET: [*suppressing a sob*] Mireille, dear, don't be annoyed with me, but I must speak to my brother alone.

He can tell you about it afterwards, but it's . . . it's so cruel . . . I can't . . .

MIREILLE: But of course, I quite understand. [*She goes out quietly*]

OCTAVE: Is it about André?

MME. VERDET: Yes.

OCTAVE: He's not ill?

MME. VERDET: Yes.

OCTAVE: But I thought he was doing so well?

MME. VERDET: [*in a colourless voice*] He's going to die.

OCTAVE: What?

MME. VERDET: [*unable to keep back her tears*] He's dying, Octave. . . .

OCTAVE: Oh, come now, that's not possible. You're imagining things. . . .

MME. VERDET: After André's visit the doctor wrote me a most disturbing letter saying he couldn't tell him the truth. So, of course, I rushed off to see him myself.

OCTAVE: And what did he say?

MME. VERDET: I knew at once . . . he looked so grave and he spoke so quietly, as if . . .

OCTAVE: Look here, Martha, that sounds to me just your imagination running riot.

MME. VERDET: No, it's not. André might have an accident at any time . . . tomorrow or in six months . . . or . . . one can't tell. . . .

OCTAVE: Well, what's that. Anyone can have an accident.

MME. VERDET: No, no, the doctor explained. . . . There's something wrong with his heart!

OCTAVE: And if there is? There's something wrong with my heart too. And don't I know it since I left the army. . . . But I'm still alive and kicking.

MME. VERDET: [*in a trembling voice*] Oh, don't, Octave, it's no good. He explained it all to me, I tell you. A valve may stop working at any moment, and if he gets over-tired or upset, or . . .

OCTAVE: But why on earth didn't they find it out before?

It's not the first time he's been to the doctor. He practically lived there during the war. . . .

MME. VERDET: I think it's got much worse these last few months. . . . Oh, Octave, I can't help wishing now that he'd gone to the front as he wanted to. Even if he'd been . . . killed at once he'd have had . . . at least . . . at least . . . [*She cannot go on*]

ALINE *comes in.*

ALINE: What *is* the matter?

OCTAVE: Martha's had bad news about André. . . . She went to see the specialist yesterday. . . . He's . . . well, he's not very hopeful?

ALINE: What! [*she goes to* MME. VERDET] Oh, my poor darling, how dreadful! . . . Oh, Martha, how *ghastly.* [*She gives her a long embrace*] Then André's good news the other day wasn't true?

MME. VERDET: We daren't tell him the truth. It might kill him.

ALINE: [*holding her closely*] Oh! darling!

MME. VERDET: He doesn't even know I went to see the doctor. . . . And look, if he should come in now, please be quite natural.

ALINE: My dear, you know you can trust me. . . . Oh, the poor, poor boy!

MME. VERDET: If only I could feel that he'd had a happy life. But it's been nothing but bitterness and disappointment. No-one can imagine what he went through during the war.

ALINE: [*gently*] Yes, yes, we can.

MME. VERDET: He always felt everyone despised him because he wasn't fighting. . . . When his cousins came on leave he used to keep out of the way. . . . Oh! not Raymond, of course. *He* was always so nice to him.

ALINE: [*thoughtfully*] Raymond was very fond of him.

MME. VERDET: André so often talks about him.

ALINE: Does he?

MME. VERDET: But think of the boy's life, Aline. He never had *any* happiness!

ALINE: Oh, Martha, you're exaggerating.

MME. VERDET: No, no, I'm not. You see, when his father was alive, I had no time to spare for him, and anyhow . . . what *can* one do for anyone else? We're each of us all alone, really.

ALINE: [*solemnly*] Oh, no, Martha, no. We are *not* alone.

MME. VERDET: Oh, thank you, Aline dear. How good you are. . . . It needs unhappiness like mine to appreciate you properly. [OCTAVE *stirs*] I remember so well when my dear Charles died, you were just as wonderful then. [OCTAVE *goes to the window and looks out*]

ALINE: [*solemnly*] We are *all* drawn closer to one another by suffering.

MME. VERDET: Where's Octave?

OCTAVE: [*without turning round*] Here.

ALINE: [*in a muffled voice*] There is nothing real *but* suffering.

MME. VERDET: André always says how deeply you feel things. . . . I suppose I shouldn't say so, but so does he. . . . Even though he's got such wonderful self-control he can't hide from me what he's going through. . . . It quite frightens me sometimes.

ALINE: You're very close to one another.

OCTAVE: [*to someone the others cannot see*] Hullo! Hullo!

MME. VERDET: Who's he talking to?

ALINE: To Little Jacquot. He's playing with Mireille. Yvonne's gone to Villeneuve.

MME. VERDET: Mireille loves children, doesn't she?

ALINE: Yes.

MME. VERDET: It's wonderful for you to have her here. . . . Ah! How well Raymond chose. . . .

ALINE: He didn't choose.

MME. VERDET: [*softly*] Aline . . . I think André loves her too.

ALINE: André!

MME. VERDENT: [*ardently*] Oh, you mustn't be angry with him. He's struggled so hard against it. He hardly dared admit it, even to himself.

ALINE: [*gently*] But why should I be angry?

MME. VERDET: It would be very natural of you. . . . I know
I should be furious in your place.

ALINE: No one can put themselves in my place, Martha.
Besides . . . no, I don't mind at all. . . . Poor boy!

MME. VERDET: Oh, thank you, Aline, dear. You're so
generous . . . so . . . I was afraid it might come between us,
and yet, somehow I felt *compelled* to tell you.

ALINE: Compelled?

MME. VERDET: Somehow, to you, one can't *choose* what one
says. I've often noticed it.

OCTAVE: [*who has not moved from the window*] Funny little
fellow! [*He comes back to the two women, who stop talking*]
Why have you two stopped talking?

MME. VERDET: Ah, Octave, if you only knew!

ALINE: [*instinctively*] Oh, do be careful, Martha.

MME. VERDET: I was just telling Aline, in confidence, of
course . . . [*to* ALINE] Why shouldn't he know too? . . . [*to*
OCTAVE] It's André . . . he's in love with your daughter-
in-law.

OCTAVE: [*with a start*] Why do you say daughter-in-law?
Mireille isn't my daughter-in-law.

MME. VERDET: Oh, yes. . . . She's like your own child. . . .
[*Silence*] He loves her very, very much. But he never thinks
of himself. . . .

OCTAVE: [*coldly*] Do you think it fair to give away the
wretched boy's secret?

MME. VERDET: What do you mean?

OCTAVE: Just when you've heard . . . or anyhow you imagine
that he's . . . I must say I think it's outrageous of you.

MME. VERDET: Octave!

ALINE: But we're not strangers!

OCTAVE: That makes it worse!

ALINE: Anyhow, I'd guessed it already.

OCTAVE: Well, will you kindly talk about something else,
please?

MME. VERDET: Octave, that's not like you.

OCTAVE: [*to Madame* VERDET] But Martha . . . if what we fear is . . . well, if there's something in it . . . can't you see that's it's a heartbreaking mockery for the boy to feel like that?

ALINE: On the contrary, it may be his salvation.

MME. VERDET: Salvation?

ALINE: Love like that could transfigure his whole life.

OCTAVE: Aline, that's either nonsense or it's *monstrous.* I won't allow you to let Martha hope . . .

MME. VERDET: Aline, do you really think it possible that . . .

ALINE: Hope? No, no, you don't understand me. . . . Of course I've no right to imagine that. . . . But for anyone like André, so deep a feeling could be a comfort in itself.

MME. VERDET: I'm so afraid you may be mistaken. . . .

OCTAVE: That's not what she meant. She's just backing out of it.

MME. VERDET: When he comes home from you he won't speak and he won't eat. He seems quite feverish and then, of course, he doesn't sleep.

OCTAVE: [*to* ALINE] Aline, you tried just now to give the impression that Mireille might, out of compassion or . . . I'm sorry, Martha, but we can't risk any misunderstandings about this. It's too serious.

MME. VERDET: [*her face convulsed with grief*] But, Octave . . .

OCTAVE: I couldn't be more sorry for you, Martha. But you're a simple person and you've no idea what . . . Oh, call it suffering if you like . . . what it can do to a person like Aline. . . .

MME. VERDET: Octave!

ALINE: [*smiling*] No, no. Let him go on. . . .

OCTAVE: But *I'm* not blind, luckily for the child . . . and I . . .

MME. VERDET: Oh, I want to go away. . . . Aline, take me to the car.

ALINE: [*in a muffled voice to* OCTAVE] So you think you can . . . Oh, you are contemptible! [ALINE *and* MME. VERDET *go out.*]

Octave: [*after he has calmed down a little goes to the window and calls*] Mireille!

Mireille *comes to the window.*

Mireille: What is it, father?

Octave: Come with me, my dear. The time has come for you to talk to me quite frankly. But not here, your Aunt might come in.

Mireille: No, really, I don't like all these secrets. . . .

Octave: But it's for your own sake, Mireille. It's because I'm afraid.

Mireille: Afraid? Why?

Octave: I thought I'd noticed . . . and . . . well, I know that the other morning you had a talk alone with Chanteuil.

Mireille: We only had a knock-up at tennis.

Octave: Yvonne saw you.

Mireille: What if she did?

Octave: You see, if . . . Well, he's obviously taken with you. Look at those flowers, and the way he talked about you at the Morels. . . . It's as clear as daylight. And, if you felt. . . . I mean, you mustn't be held back by any scruples. . . . You might have an idea *I* didn't like him . . . or my wife, perhaps. [Mireille *moves uneasily*] Fate sent you to live with us here as our child. But that doesn't prevent your being *entirely* free. I'm saying it all so badly because . . .

Mireille: [*bitterly*] Because you're saying it against Mother. You don't have to defend *my* freedom. Nobody threatens it here. And do you know this young man's mistress was staying in the neighbourhood a few weeks ago? . . .

Octave: Who told you about her?

Mireille: Oh, I happened to hear . . .

Octave: Well, I was told definitely that he'd broken with her a year ago. . . . You're no longer a child, Mireille. You know quite well that when a man marries . . . From all I've heard Robert Chanteuil has nothing to be ashamed of. . . .

Mireille: Then you've been making enquiries?

Octave: I just found out, that's all.

MIREILLE: Why? And what cause are you pleading? Why not say outright that it's against *her*, to hurt *her*? . . . Oh, it's a hateful thing to do!

OCTAVE: No. It's because I want *you* to be happy.

MIREILLE: And do you know what kind of happiness I can still endure?

OCTAVE: Mireille, that's not like you.

MIREILLE: Oh, you're torturing me. . . . Oh, if only I could go *away*!

OCTAVE: Go away?

MIREILLE: But I'll never have the courage, never.

ALINE *and* ANDRE *come in*

ANDRE: Mother never told me she was going to see you. . . .

ALINE: She only looked in as she was passing.

OCTAVE: Oh, André, nice to see you.

MIREILLE: Hullo, André.

OCTAVE: And how are you?

ANDRE: Had mother anything special to say to you?

OCTAVE: No . . . er . . . no. [MIREILLE *moves uneasily*]

ANDRE: To ask you about then? . . . I was puzzled. She always tells me where she's going, and she looked awful just now.

ALINE: [*too quickly*] She had a bad headache.

ANDRE: Headache? She hardly ever has a headache. Did you see her, Mireille?

MIREILLE: [*embarrassed*] Yes . . . no . . . only for a moment.

ANDRE: Why only a moment?

MIREILLE: [*hesitating*] I . . . Yvonne went to Villeneuve and I had to look after Jacquot.

ANDRE: You all look very odd. What's the matter?

MIREILLE: The matter?

ALINE: Don't be absurd, André!

OCTAVE: Yes, it's ridiculous.

ANDRE: [*going to* ALINE, *in a whisper*] Mother didn't tell you, did she? . . . She had no right to . . .

ALINE: [*indicating* MIREILLE] Ssh! André.

MIREILLE: What did you say?

ANDRE: *She* knows all about it.

OCTAVE: André, my boy, be careful.

ANDRE: I couldn't bear you to think . . . and now he's going away, I can face anything.

MIREILLE: [*pleadingly*] André . . . please . . .

ANDRE: [*to* OCTAVE *and* ALINE] I've guessed right, haven't I? That's what mother came to talk about? And her face when she left! But Good Lord, I swear I've put the idea right out of my head . . . [*to* MIREILLE] You don't believe me. You think I sent her! . . . Oh, now I shall lose the little I had. Oh, why did she do it? Why? Why?

MIREILLE: [*going to him*] André, I didn't know . . .

OCTAVE: Look here, there's not a word of truth in all this . . .

ALINE: [*to* OCTAVE] Why do you deny it?

MIREILLE: [*to* ANDRE] But everything will be just the same, André, I promise. . . . I know, I *do* know you're speaking the truth.

ANDRE: I want so little, really . . . and when I heard he was going away . . .

OCTAVE: Who are you talking about?

MIREILLE: André!

ANDRE: Forgive me for being afraid . . . of *that*.

MIREILLE: [*in a miserable whisper*] Oh, you've no decency. [ANDRE *tries to take her hand*] No, no, don't touch me!

OCTAVE: Who's going away? You don't mean Chanteuil, do you?

ANDRE: Yes.

OCTAVE: Why's he going? [ANDRE *watches* MIREILLE *who has cast down her eyes*]

OCTAVE: [*to* ANDRE] And what can it matter to *you*? Answer me, please.

ALINE: But, Octave . . .

OCTAVE: Oh! *You* . . .

ANDRE: [*passing his hand across his forehead*] Oh, I don't

know why I let myself go like that. It was childish . . . I . . .
[*He staggers*]

MIREILLE: What's the matter?

ANDRE: Nothing. I'll be all right in a minute. . . .

ALINE: We can't let him go away in this state. . . .

ANDRE: I'll go and sit down in the garden a moment.

ALINE: Shall we come with you?

ANDRE: No, no, I'll be all right. [*He goes out into the garden*]

OCTAVE: [*to* MIREILLE] Now listen to me, Mireille. We didn't
tell him the truth. My sister never dreamed that . . . She
came to tell us that the poor boy can't live very much longer.

MIREILLE: [*shaken*] Oh!

OCTAVE: And I suppose my wife didn't want him to guess,
so she let him think . . . [*to* ALINE] You were quite wrong
to do that, you know. There was no need to give him any
reason at all. You've upset him very much.

MIREILLE: [*very gravely*] So . . . he's going to die, is he?

OCTAVE: That's what his mother understood. But, of course,
she always sees the blackest side of everything.

ALINE: [*gravely*] I'm afraid this time she's right.

OCTAVE: What do you know about it?

MIREILLE: And he believes . . . oh, it's appalling.

OCTAVE: It's very lucky that so far we've been able to keep
him in the dark . . . If he felt that knife hanging over his
head . . .

MIREILLE: Yes, yes. But it's so humiliating to be made a fool
of like that. It's degrading. . . . I know that in his place I . . .

OCTAVE: I don't know if André's strong enough to face the
truth. . . . I doubt it, to be honest.

ALINE: [*sharply*] Do you think it's very generous to dis-
parage him at a time like this?

OCTAVE: I'm not disparaging him, I'm merely seeing him as
he is.

MIREILLE: Wouldn't a little pity be . . .

OCTAVE: Oh, I *pity* him all right. But once you start pitying
people . . . [*he realises he's in dangerous waters and quickly*

changes the subject] Did you know Chanteuil was going away, Mireille?

MIREILLE: [*uncomfortably*] No.

ALINE: How could she have known?

OCTAVE: Didn't he mention it the other morning?

ALINE: [*sharply*] You've been talking to him, then?

MIREILLE: [*in a low voice*] We had a knock-up the day before yesterday.

ALINE: You never told me.

MIREILLE: [*still uncomfortably*] I didn't think of it. . . . You know he's always at the tennis club.

OCTAVE: It's extraordinary, his going off like that. He was telling everyone he meant to settle down here.

MIREILLE: [*with an effort*] It may only be for a few days.

OCTAVE: But André seemed to think . . .

MIREILLE: [*indistinctly*] What does he know about it? [ALINE *meanwhile has sat down at the table, and has opened a book that she doesn't read.* OCTAVE *watches her and recognises a familiar expression*]

OCTAVE: Well, I'm going to see if André's feeling better. [*He goes out.* MIREILLE *stands as if not knowing what to do, then, as if impelled, she goes up to* ALINE]

MIREILLE: Mother. . . . [ALINE *does not answer*] What are you reading?

ALINE: I don't know.

MIREILLE: You don't know?

ALINE: [*putting down the book*] Mireille, this is the first time you've ever *really* hurt me.

MIREILLE: Hurt you?

ALINE: [*her voice trembling*] And I didn't think you were capable of such . . . [*she cannot go on*]

MIREILLE: Go on!

ALINE: The word doesn't matter. It's not only that you were so careful to keep this conversation from me. . . . It was your voice and your face when you said: "We had a knock-up the day before yesterday." You were trying to put me off.

MIREILLE: I don't have to account to you for *everything* I do, Mother.

ALINE: Don't call me that, Mireille. It's a mockery.

MIREILLE: If I have a reason for not mentioning a particular conversation . . .

ALINE: Then you ought to tell me so quite frankly.

MIREILLE: You would have accepted that?

ALINE: Of course.

MIREILLE: I don't know how to stop at half-confidences.

ALINE: [*gently*] You mean it's easier to lie.

MIREILLE: That's insulting.

ALINE: Oh, Mireille . . . I think now you've said the only thing that could still hurt me.

MIREILLE: [*blazing*] I want to be *free*. I won't be . . . coerced.

ALINE: Who's talking of coercion?

MIREILLE: I'll be nobody's slave, nobody's. . . . If I'd told you that I'd refused to marry him . . .

ALINE: He asked you then?

MIREILLE: It's because I said no that he's going away. If I'd told you about it I'd have felt I was currying favour with you, and that I couldn't bear . . .

ALINE: Darling! . . .

MIREILLE: It was perfectly natural to say nothing about it. . . . Any ordinary woman would understand, but . . . oh, I don't know, you seem to be a sense short! I've often noticed it, and then . . . But I want to be *free*, don't you understand, or I should despise myself. And I shouldn't *be* anything. And then I should hate you. . . . Oh, when I feel like this I want to go right away and never, never come back. [ALINE *moves uneasily. There is silence*]

ALINE: I'd noticed you seemed rather depressed lately.

MIREILLE: You're always watching us.

ALINE: I'd even wondered if it had anything to do with that man . . .

MIREILLE: I can't bear the way you always know everything.

ALINE: But I was quite wrong, you see, because for a moment I was afraid you rather liked him.

MIREILLE: I was crazy. I hate to think of it. . . . [*working herself up again*] But why be afraid? If the impossible had happened and I had . . . well, even if I had loved him . . .

ALINE: From what I know, I think it would have been a disaster.

MIREILLE: What *do* you know?

ALINE: Never mind, since it hasn't happened. You've refused him, so it's clear you couldn't have cared for him. [MIREILLE *makes some agitated gestures as if to extricate herself from an invisible net*]

MIREILLE: But do you understand? . . . If I *had* accepted him, I couldn't have stood the least hint of disapproval from you.

ALINE: Naturally, I should have done my best to hide my feelings.

MIREILLE: I don't think you'd have succeeded. You've far less self-control than you think, you know. And if you'd tried to stop me, once I'd decided, I'd never have forgiven you.

ALINE: But darling, you're upsetting yourself for nothing, since it didn't happen.

MIREILLE: [*in a whisper*] Even the idea of it drives me quite crazy.

ALINE: [*after a silence*] You see how right I was the other day when I begged you to trust me.

MIREILLE: Oh, that was just futile talk.

ALINE: But what has happened has made me realise something. . . . Life here with us is beginning to oppress you. I can feel it.

MIREILLE: No, no, it isn't. Only your unjust accusation bowled me over. It was *so* unjust . . . and then that dreadful thing too.

ALINE: You mean about André?

MIREILLE: Yes. [*Silence*] Did you know he was in love with me?

ALINE: I guessed it.

MIREILLE: Poor boy! But why was he so meek and humble just now? And in front of you he should never have . . .

ALINE: But he thought his mother had told us.

MIREILLE: All the same . . .

ALINE: And I think he feels that he doesn't really count for anything. Perhaps it's having been so humiliated during the war.

MIREILLE: That should have stiffened his pride.

ALINE: No, he was so ashamed not to be fighting, you see . . .

MIREILLE: He could have gone to fight . . . if he'd wanted to?

ALINE: Your uncle often says he'd have been sent home in twenty-four hours.

MIREILLE: [*thoughtfully*] Yes, that is true, I'm sure . . . all the same, such humility in a *man* . . .

ALINE: But when it's genuine . . .

MIREILLE: I never realised you had such a good opinion of him. [ALINE *makes an evasive gesture*] Then Aunt Martha didn't even hint about . . .

ALINE: She only said that André was very fond of you.

MIREILLE: [*shuddering*] But why did she say that?

ALINE: I don't think she had any special motive. It was just that she couldn't keep it to herself any longer.

MIREILLE: But how could she have imagined, seriously . . . how *could* she?

ALINE: No. [MIREILLE *looks at her anxiously*] Of course she couldn't.

MIREILLE: [*sharply*] Oh, it's awful!

ALINE: What do you mean?

MIREILLE: I can never be sure what you're *really* thinking . . . or getting at . . .

ALINE: All the same, if I have so very little self-control . . .

MIREILLE: [*bitterly*] You've far too much . . .

ALINE: Besides, what could I be getting at, as you call it? You asked me if my sister-in-law could really contemplate that you and André . . . [MIREILLE *moves nervously*] No, I don't think she could. . . .

MIREILLE: But you, can *you*?

ALINE: Darling, what's the point of all these questions? Are you . . . feeling your way?

MIREILLE: [*violently*] Then do you imagine I've thought of committing suicide that way?

ALINE: Mireille!

MIREILLE: Yes, I mean it—*suicide*. And it doesn't revolt you? You can calmly approve of me—*me* being married to that semi-corpse. What could I feel for him but a little pity—and contempt, perhaps?

ALINE: My dear, you're dramatising.

MIREILLE: Dramatising?

ALINE: It's not for me to approve or disapprove of what you do. You haven't asked my opinion. And it's surely obvious that I would never want to influence you.

MIREILLE: [*under her breath*] You couldn't do that.

ALINE: I could have tried to help you to know yourself a little better.

MIREILLE: [*still under her breath*] Thank you.

ALINE: You see, you may be a little mistaken when you say that for André you only feel . . .

MIREILLE: Then you think you know me better than I know myself? . . .

ALINE: Possibly.

MIREILLE: [*intensely*] If *only* my parents were alive; they would never allow this. They would save me from myself.

ALINE: From yourself. Then it's . . .

MIREILLE: *They* would consider my happiness!

ALINE: [*sorrowfully*] Mireille!

MIREILLE: I'm sorry. But you don't value happiness enough. Oh, of course I feel now that I could never bear to be happy again. But suppose I'm wrong, don't you see, suppose I'm wrong.

ALINE: [*after a silence*] I'm sure of one thing. If marrying André . . . [MIREILLE *starts*] seems to you like committing suicide, we must wipe out all thought of it.

MIREILLE: How do you expect *me* to know?

ALINE: When I saw the idea cross your mind, I said to myself: *that* may be the solution.

MIREILLE: You always *will* do other people's thinking for them.

ALINE: I felt that for a nature like yours, which has been matured by suffering . . .

MIREILLE: Matured, do you call it?

ALINE: I felt that for you true happiness could only be found in . . . in sacrifice. . . . [*Silence*] But, perhaps I was wrong. . . . [*in a whisper*] You're so young. . . .

MIREILLE: I've got that feeling about sacrifice too. . . . Only I want to be sure that it's more than . . . Oh, I don't know . . . more than just aspiration.

ALINE: You don't trust yourself. . . . But you know that true life consists in giving.

MIREILLE: But am I worthy to feel that? It might be only a passing, sham enthusiasm . . . and have I even the right to marry him? . . . [*she shudders*] Perhaps, if I didn't know that . . . that it wouldn't be for long . . . I might never have thought of it. But think how disloyal I should feel, *waiting* for the end . . . feeling impatient, perhaps, if it were delayed. Oh, it's horrible!

ALINE: [*hugging her*] But darling, ideas like that are just phantoms of your own imagination. Life will drive them away.

MIREILLE: Life! . . . If I could at least be sure that the idea of sacrifice was my *own* . . . and that I was really worthy of it . . .

ALINE: [*in a whisper*] Darling, I didn't know you thought so deeply. . . .

MIREILLE: [*sharply jerks herself free*] Perhaps I've been *infected* with it.

There is a silence and OCTAVE *comes in.*

OCTAVE: André feels better. He wants to go home. But I don't think it's wise to let him walk. . . . Is the car there?

ALINE: You know Yvonne took it to Villeneuve.

MIREILLE: Stop a moment. . . . I want to speak to him before he goes. [*she goes out*]

OCTAVE: [*suspiciously*] Now what's going on? . . . What have you been saying to her? You haven't . . . ? Good God? No! She's too normal, she's too much sense. . . . Aline!

ALINE: I can't tell you. It's not my secret.

OCTAVE: Then you have! But I won't allow it! Damn it, no, that's too much. . . . [*he starts to go out*]

ALINE: [*very calmly*] Be careful, Octave.

OCTAVE: What do you mean?

ALINE: You don't seem to realise how violently Mireille clings to her independence.

OCTAVE: Well?

ALINE: If you rush in and interfere, you may drive her into doing just what you want to prevent.

OCTAVE: Then she hadn't made up her mind?

ALINE: I know nothing about it.

OCTAVE: This is just a trick to stop me speaking to her.

ALINE: A trick? . . . Really, Octave, what do you take me for?

OCTAVE: I won't allow you to do it.

ALINE: Then you're suggesting that . . .?

OCTAVE: You dominate her! Yes, you do. You've made a slave of her.

ALINE: If she heard you say that! . . .

OCTAVE: She half knows it already. I'm going to open her eyes.

ALINE: I doubt if she'll thank you. Besides . . . it isn't true. No one could respect other people's freedom more than I do.

OCTAVE: That's about the last straw! . . . Look here, are you serious?

ALINE: Do you realise you're shouting at me?

OCTAVE: I don't give a damn. . . . Do you think I don't see what you're up to.

ALINE: Octave!

OCTAVE: You're condemning that wretched child to prison. . . .

ALINE: Octave!

OCTAVE: You are. Morally, you're imprisoning her for the sake of a poor boy who's no longer here to prevent you or to *repudiate* what you're doing.

ALINE: That's enough, Octave!

OCTAVE: You hold that girl in a vice. . . . And you call your tyranny kindness. . . . Mother, she even calls you Mother!

ALINE: I said, that's enough, Octave!

OCTAVE: And then . . . oh, that's the most damnable thing of all . . . you open the prison door just a crack because the man's all but dead already.

ALINE: Oh, you're intolerable!

OCTAVE: [*violently*] Yes, because he's half dead . . . I was watching you with Martha just now. You've never been able to stand her before. You seem to thrive on misery and death. . . . [*in a muffled voice*] If you hadn't found a wretched moribund creature for Mireille you'd never have let her even begin to rebuild her life.

ALINE: That's utterly untrue. I've told her twenty times . . .

OCTAVE: It's not what you *say*, you know that.

ALINE: I've promised her . . .

OCTAVE: That you'd make allowances? Could there be any more certain way to hold her? You ought to have encouraged her to marry some normal, healthy boy. . . . She's made for life and . . . and love . . .

ALINE: So Raymond . . .

OCTAVE: No, no, no. Don't pretend you're doing this for your son. It's for *yourself*. It's for your own . . . Oh, words can't describe it. . . . You've made chains of her sorrow and her scruples and her admiration for you. . . . And now, when for a moment she had the illusion that she might escape, look what you've done . . .

ALINE: You've very eloquent, Octave. But unfortunately *you* have good reasons to forget, and for wanting everyone else to forget. But *I* remember—everything. That's my great crime in your eyes, and naturally you hate me for it. Yes, you do hate me these days, Octave. . . . Otherwise you wouldn't accuse me . . . *me*, of treachery.

OCTAVE: Well, perhaps it isn't treachery. . . . Perhaps you don't even realise what you're . . .

ALINE: [*contemptuously*] Oh, please don't try to explain. It isn't worth it. I've only one more thing to say to you. Mireille's longing for *absolute* self-sacrifice is a thing a man like you could never even begin to understand.

OCTAVE: Mireille? She's in love with Chanteuil. That's the real truth.

ALINE: It's not.

OCTAVE: I assure you it is.

ALINE: Then let her tell me so, to my face.

OCTAVE: You'll only get from her the answer you want. I tell you, you've made a slave of her.

ALINE: It's not possible.

OCTAVE: *You* can never know her real thoughts. That's the punishment of all tyrants. Very likely when she's with you she no longer knows them herself. . . . Now, listen to me . . . as it's come to this, there's only one thing left for me to do. I shall go away this evening and I shall *not* come back. [*He puts his hand suddenly to his breast, and stands quite still, looking desperately unhappy. He seems to be waiting for* ALINE *to speak, but as she does not, he goes out, hastily*]

ALINE: [*stands still and silent for a few moments. Then she repeats* OCTAVE'S *words with intense indignation, as if fighting against them*] Me! Treacherous! It's not true . . . it's *not* true. [*Yet she grows more and more miserable and finally falls on her knees in despair*]

MIREILLE *comes in, very pale.*

MIREILLE: [*in a whisper*] I had to tell him that I loved him. . . .

CURTAIN

ACT THREE

A year later. Four o'clock on a November day in
ANDRE's *and* MIREILLE's *drawing-room. It is very
light, with two windows opening on to a balcony. The
curtain rises to discover* MIREILLE *knitting in an arm-
chair and* OCTAVE, *still in his overcoat, sitting R. and
holding a little parcel in his hand.*

MIREILLE: But you really ought to take off your coat. I'm
so afraid you'll catch cold when you go out again.
OCTAVE: Thanks. But I'll only be staying a minute.

A MAID *comes in.*

MAID: Did you ring, Madame?
MIREILLE: Anna, will you please bring a cup of coffee for
Monsieur Fortier? He's so cold. And will you draw the
curtains? It's nearly dark already.
MAID: Yes, Madame. [*She goes out*]
OCTAVE: What are you knitting so furiously?
MIREILLE: Socks for the babies at my orphanage.
OCTAVE: [*in a hostile tone*] Do you ever do anything but good
works?
MIREILLE: We're having a sale next month. I'm counting on
you for a subscription!
OCTAVE: Oh, you are, are you. But you know I've no use
for young women turned philanthropists. That sort of
thing's for the old. Do you ever meet anybody but church-
going old frumps and nuns at your orphanage?
MIREILLE: I'm very fond of nuns.
OCTAVE: You must be, seeing the kind of life you're living.
MIREILLE: Are you *trying* to hurt me?

OCTAVE: No, no, of course not.

MIREILLE: As a matter of fact, you wouldn't find it so easy these days. Do you remember how suspicious I used to be and how quickly I lost my temper? But I hardly ever do that now.

OCTAVE: More's the pity.

MIREILLE: It proves I've found my right road.

OCTAVE: [*detachedly*] Yes, yes. . . .

MIREILLE: And peace of mind too.

OCTAVE: My dear, I've brought you the book. . . . It came out this morning.

MIREILLE: [*with emotion*] Oh! Our book! . . .

OCTAVE: Our book? Oh, no, that was all very fine once upon a time. But not now. [MIREILLE *wants to open the parcel*] No, no. Open it later. Only . . . look here, my dear, don't show it to *him*.

MIREILLE: You mean to André?

OCTAVE: Yes. You see, he was never at the front. He wouldn't be interested. And he'd say things . . . Oh I don't know. You do promise, don't you?

MIREILLE: If you like. All the same . . .

OCTAVE: Yes, I do. Ah well, that's that. Now I can pack up in peace.

MIREILLE: Oh, Father!

OCTAVE: No, no. You mustn't call me that any more. I say, do you still call her Mother? Not that it's my business.

MIREILLE: Oh, I can't bear to see you so . . . so desperate.

OCTAVE: Come, come my dear, there's nothing to make a song and dance about. What have I to live for, anyway?

MIREILLE: [*stammering*] There's Yvonne. . . . [OCTAVE *shrugs his shoulders*] Well, little Jacquot then. . . .

OCTAVE: Jacquot. Yes, at first I tried. I thought . . . But he's not enough like our . . . like my . . . Oh, you'll see, he'll sell motor-cars like his father. . . . One should learn to change one's ways, but it's difficult at my time of life, you know, very difficult. To get the reading habit, for instance—I don't mean an occasional magazine, but reading for days on end . . .

MIREILLE: [*gently*] But that's so tiring for one's eyes, isn't it?

OCTAVE: And after a minute or two I don't pay the slightest attention. It's very odd. . . . You know, my dear, if *you* had a child, why then I might . . . Six weeks ago I had a hunch that something was in the wind. [MIREILLE *moves uneasily*] I don't know why, I'm sure. [*Silence*] Well, how's André?

MIREILLE: [*with artificial brightness*] Last time I saw his doctor he was definitely encouraging. He said that if we were very careful and went very gently we might really hope. And André looks much better than he used to.

OCTAVE: [*detachedly*] Oh!

MIREILLE: If you weren't determined to think otherwise you'd have noticed it yourself.

OCTAVE: I'm not determined to think anything.

MIREILLE: [*working up*] Oh, yes, you are! You want things to go from bad to worse with us. Because you once dreamt of some sort of absurd and impossible happiness for *me*— yes, it was, *quite* impossible—you can't bear to admit that *now* my . . . my spirit is at peace.

OCTAVE: Oh, your *spirit*! . . .

MIREILLE: And yet it's true. I do really *exist* now that I'm needed by somebody. I read a thing that struck me so much the other day: "We do not really begin to live until we have risen above ourselves". Don't you feel how wonderful that is, and how true?

OCTAVE: I've no use for quotations.

ANDRE *comes in, a little out of breath and holding a telegram in his hand.*

MIREILLE: [*reproachfully*] André, how naughty of you. You didn't take the lift!

ANDRE: I'm all right, darling. Good evening, Uncle Octave.

OCTAVE: [*coldly*] Good evening.

MIREILLE: What's that telegram?

ANDRE: [*giving it to her*] They've just given it to me down-stairs. [*dropping his voice*] It's from Aunt Aline.

OCTAVE: [*putting his hand to his ear*] What?

ANDRE: [*louder but embarrassed*] It's from . . . Aunt Aline.

OCTAVE: [*coldly*] So she's back?

ANDRE: She arrived this morning.

OCTAVE: And she's all right, I suppose?

MIREILLE: [*detachedly*] As far as we know.

ANDRE: She's coming to dinner with us.

OCTAVE: [*getting up*] Ah! Then I must be off.

ANDRE: [*shyly*] I . . . I say, Uncle Octave. . . .

OCTAVE: What is it?

ANDRE: We simply hate . . .

MIREILLE: André, please . . .

ANDRE: To feel that Aunt Aline and you . . .

OCTAVE: Well?

ANDRE: To . . . to feel this misunderstanding between you.

OCTAVE: Misunderstanding? There's never been any mis-understanding.

ANDRE: Don't you think that with a little goodwill on both sides? . . .

OCTAVE: [*ironically*] Goodwill! Ah! Yes! Quite! quite!

ANDRE: If you both really *tried* to understand each other? . . . I mean . . .

OCTAVE: Look here, young man!

ANDRE: It seems so awful at your age . . .

OCTAVE: [*exploding*] Will you kindly mind your own business and let me mind mine.

ANDRE: If *we* could do anything. . . . *You* think I'm right, Mireille, don't you?

MIREILLE: [*expressionlessly*] Of course.

OCTAVE: Goodbye.

MIREILLE: When will you be coming again?

OCTAVE: I'll look in one of these days. . . . Oh, but that won't do, now *she's* back. . . .

MIREILLE: But you can wire . . . or telephone. Please do. . . .

OCTAVE: Hm! I'm not much good at the telephone.... Well, we'll see. But look here, André, no more of that nonsense, please, or I shall clear out, and for good.

ANDRE: Oh, uncle, how stubborn you are.

MIREILLE: André!

OCTAVE: [*controlling himself with difficulty*] Goodbye. [*He goes out*]

ANDRE: Well, I'm very surprised you didn't back me up.

MIREILLE: [*ignoring this*] I've had your hot-water bottle put in your bed. It's time for you to rest. Why do I always have to remind you about it?

ANDRE: I don't need a rest to-day. Why won't you answer me?

MIREILLE: Well, if you want the truth, I didn't think you were exactly tactful.

ANDRE: Tactful!

MIREILLE: They haven't asked us to arbitrate . . .

ANDRE: Who spoke of arbitration?

MIREILLE: Or to interfere with them in any way.

ANDRE: I don't agree with you. Think of how lonely poor Aunt Aline must be. . . . Put yourself in her place.

MIREILLE: That's very difficult. [*Silence.* MIREILLE *sits down rather wearily*] Oh, André, I'm so glad to have a few minutes' peace before she arrives.

ANDRE: Would you like me to read to you?

MIREILLE: No, no. Just come and sit here near me, and hold my hand.

ANDRE: Do you know what I saw this morning in the Avenue Victor Hugo? A second-hand piano, really very cheap. . . . . You wouldn't like to go and try it?

MIREILLE: [*gently*] No, thank you, darling. You know what I told you, I don't seem to need music these days.

ANDRE: [*after a silence*] You're not unhappy, are you?

MIREILLE: [*flatly*] Of course not.

ANDRE: I'm always so afraid you may blame me for what happened.

MIREILLE: Nonsense!

ANDRE: You told Uncle Octave about it?

MIREILLE: No.

ANDRE: [*with feeling*] That's good. I don't like him to know when things go wrong.

MIREILLE: Nor do I.

ANDRE: And Aunt Aline?

MIREILLE: Well?

ANDRE: You haven't told her about our disappointment?

MIREILLE: She didn't even know we were hoping for a baby.

ANDRE: [*softly*] But . . . I wrote to her.

MIREILLE: André! Without telling me?

ANDRE: Why make a mystery about anything so normal and so wonderful. I knew how glad she'd be . . . but I haven't dared tell her what's happened. She's always so *very* anxious for us to be happy, isn't she?

MIREILLE: She is indeed, far too anxious. I don't like people to feel like that.

ANDRE: [*reproachfully*] You call Aunt Aline people?

MIREILLE: Oh, don't be silly.

ANDRE: [*bitterly*] It's odd, but I sometimes have an idea that that you don't feel the same towards her as you used to do.

MIREILLE: That's not true . . . but if it were . . .

ANDRE: I should mind that very much.

MIREILLE: What does it matter to you?

ANDRE: You see, you don't deny it . . . I feel there's a kind of link between Aunt Aline and me.

MIREILLE: [*very seriously*] Yes, that's very true.

ANDRE: Oh! . . . What a way you said that!

MIREILLE: You frightened me.

ANDRE: But Aunt Aline does count for a great deal in our life.

MIREILLE: Oh, I know that!

ANDRE: It may seem odd to you, but I think she counts for more than mother, even.

MIREILLE: [*with a sigh*] I dare say she does.

ANDRE: She needs us so much. . . . We're the only people who belong to her now.

MIREILLE: That's equally true of Uncle Octave.

ANDRE: Oh, but he doesn't feel things like she does. He's so thick-skinned, don't you think so? . . . I thought you'd be *so* delighted to see her again. . . .

MIREILLE: I am, of course I am . . . only . . .

ANDRE: Well?

MIREILLE: Somehow I'm a little afraid . . . One never quite knows what Aunt Aline will bring with her.

ANDRE: Bring with her? What do you mean? She's always the same.

MIREILLE: When she's there, or as soon as she's anywhere near even . . . I don't feel the same. Everything looks a different colour somehow . . .

ANDRE: [*very worried*] What *do* you mean?

MIREILLE: Oh, nothing. It doesn't matter.

ANDRE: You know, I'd like to try to be . . . a little like the son she's lost. I always feel that she's adopted me, don't you?

MIREILLE: [*with hidden irony*] Yes, I do. I've felt that from the beginning. [*There is a knock on the door*]

ANDRE: What's that? [*He goes to the door and finds* ALINE, *who comes in*]

ANDRE: Oh, Aunt Aline, it's you! We didn't hear you ring.

ALINE: My dears! My dears! [*She kisses them both*]

MIREILLE: [*mechanically*] Mother!

ALINE: It's seemed *such* a long time to me. . . .

ANDRE: And to us too!

ALINE: Now then, let me have a good look at you both. [*to* ANDRE] Why, André you're a little fatter than three months ago, I do believe.

ANDRE: Yes, I'm *very* well now.

ALINE: [*with enthusiasm*] Oh, I'm *so* glad!

MIREILLE: [*moves uneasily*] Hmm! *Very* well. Don't exaggerate, André. As a matter of fact he looked better last month.

ALINE: [*to* MIREILLE] And you, my darling. How are you? [*She looks at her carefully*] You don't look . . .

MIREILLE: Oh, I'm all right. . . . [*Pause*] I gather André wrote to you . . .

ALINE: [*with excessive emotion*] Then it was all a mistake?

ANDRE: [*humbly*] We had a disappointment.

ALINE: What . . . an accident?

MIREILLE: That's a rather pompous word, isn't it?

ALINE: [*in a voice shaken with emotion*] What happened then?

MIREILLE: [*more and more irritated*] We haven't got to make a *tragedy* of it, have we?

ANDRE: We went to dine with some cousins in the rue Marcault . . .

ALINE: [*disapprovingly*] You went out at *night*?

MIREILLE: And then on the way home André complained of feeling tired. It isn't an easy district to get taxis at night. I saw one empty and ran after it.

ANDRE: I tried to stop her.

ALINE: You should never have gone there at all.

MIREILLE: But one can't shut oneself up *all* the time. . . . And I don't like André to go out without me. I always worry till he comes back. He nearly fainted the other day. . . . He didn't tell me. Someone else did.

ALINE: Oh, I feel quite, quite heartbroken. . . . [*to* ANDRE] Oh, André, if you only *knew* how happy I was when your letter came . . .

ANDRE: Of course you were!

MIREILLE: It simply shows one shouldn't talk about such things too early.

ALINE: I'd made so many *wonderful* plans.

MIREILLE: That's never a good thing to do, you know.

ANDRE: But after all, in a few months . . .

ALINE: Let's hope so . . . [*to* MIREILLE] But darling, *do* be sensible next time.

ANDRE: She means to go and work in that orphanage again tomorrow. It's far too soon.

ALINE: Do you work for an orphanage?

MIREILLE: I must fill my life somehow.

ANDRE: You do agree with me, don't you, Aunt Aline?

MIREILLE: [*dryly*] I'm sorry, but I'm going back.

ALINE: [*after a silence*] You know, I haven't seen your flat yet.

MIREILLE: Well, we're not settled in yet, really.

ANDRE: But we're getting on. Come and see it now.

ALINE: I never imagined your drawing-room was so large. Of course, when you have a piano . . .

MIREILLE: We're not going to have one.

ALINE: Why not?

MIREILLE: André doesn't like music. . . . And I'm too rusty . . .

ALINE: But what a pity to give it up. . . .

MIREILLE: [*bitterly*] A pity? What's the good of playing for oneself alone? . . . And anyhow, when have I the time to practise?

ALINE: You've time for your orphanage.

MIREILLE: [*with energy*] That's different. There, I'm some *use*.

ALINE: [*to* ANDRE] I do see what she means.

ANDRE: Yes, it's the sort of the thing you'd do yourself. [MIREILLE *moves uneasily*]

ANDRE: [*to* MIREILLE] Aunt Aline finds that kind of thing quite natural. I remember Raymond once saying: "Mummy seems to love unhappy people. It's so odd." Then he added: "But they always frighten me." [*Silence*]

MIREILLE: [*forcibly controlling herself*] And what's the news of Villeneuve?

ALINE: Oh, nothing seems to have happened down there.

ANDRE: How are the Morels?

ALINE: I think they're all right. I don't see them any more.

ANDRE: And what about that man I disliked so much?

ALINE: [*uncomfortably*] I don't know who you mean.

ANDRE: Why, Chanteuil. What's become of him?

ALINE: [*taken aback*] But . . .

ANDRE: Well?

ALINE: I . . .

ANDRE: Has something happened to him?

ALINE: Don't you read the papers?

MIREILLE: The papers?

ALINE: [*too low*] A motor accident.

ANDRE: What?

ALINE: He had a motor accident.

ANDRE: Well? [ALINE *makes a gesture*] He's dead?

ALINE: Yes.

ANDRE: Poor fellow! [*He turns towards* MIREILLE, *whose face hasn't changed*] Did you hear that?

MIREILLE: Yes, it's very sad.

ANDRE: He must have been driving like a lunatic.

MIREILLE: [*in spite of herself*] What do you know about it?

ANDRE: He always looked like a road-hog.

ALINE: [*with reserve*] I don't think he was driving himself.

ANDRE: Was anyone else killed?

ALINE: She was terribly injured.

ANDRE: She?

ALINE: The . . . the woman who was with him.

ANDRE: Oh! His mistress, I suppose. [*Silence*]

MIREILLE: [*controlling herself*] But you've told us nothing about yourself or your plans? [*She passes her hand across her forehead*] I always seem to have a kind of headache these days.

ANDRE: Shall I get you an aspirin?

MIREILLE: No, thanks. I'm all right.

ANDRE: [*to* ALINE] I've been to see that little flat in Rue Oudinot for you.

ALINE: Oh, thank you. But I'm not going to take it after all.

ANDRE: I'm glad of that. It was an absolute dungeon.

ALINE: I'm going to look for a nice boarding-house somewhere.

ANDRE: Umm! But you do so hate noise and clatter. . . .

ALINE: Oh, I shall only go down for meals, of course.

ANDRE: What a life!

MIREILLE: Lots of people have to lead it.

ANDRE: What'll you do until you find one?

ALINE: Go to an hotel. I can stay on where I am now.

ACT THREE 277

ANDRE: [*with energy*] Good Lord, no. We can't have that. We've got a room empty.

ALINE: But André . . .

ANDRE: No, no, *of course* you must come to us. . . . I'll go and tell them to make up the bed now. And we'll send for your luggage at once. [*He starts to go out*]

ALINE: Wait, André, wait, don't be so absurd. [*The door shuts after* ANDRE] He's so impulsive! But Mireille, darling, that accident of yours was dreadful. I can't bear the thought of it. . . . And how is André really? He's looking so pale.

MIREILLE: If he takes things very quietly. . . .

ALINE: Yes, yes, oh, dear, so long as . . . [*she stops*]

MIREILLE: [*with dreary irony*] . . . as we have time to have another, you mean. . . . [*Silence.* MIREILLE *looks at* ALINE *with loathing, but* ALINE *doesn't notice*]

ALINE: When I rang the bell just now, you can't imagine how anxious I felt . . .

MIREILLE: Oh, yes, I can . . .

ALINE: I'm sometimes so terrified that you're not happy . . .

MIREILLE: [*dryly*] André is very kind. He loves me very much and I've the life I chose . . . [*with sudden violence*] the life that I chose for *myself*.

ALINE: [*in spite of herself*] You're quite sure of that?

MIREILLE: Don't you *dare* to doubt it.

ALINE: [*as if struck in the face*] Oh, God!

MIREILLE: [*in a voice more and more shaken by sobs*] I married André because I knew . . . that elsewhere I'd only find disappointment . . . and bitterness. I hadn't the energy or the wish . . . for . . . for certain satisfactions. I didn't *want* them. All I wanted was calm . . . and peace of mind. And I have that . . . I have . . . [*she ends in a flood of tears*]

ALINE: But Mireille, you're crying. Oh, my poor darling, you're pretending to yourself. [MIREILLE *stirs*] Oh, my poor little Mireille! Then it *was* true. And it's all my fault. Perhaps that wretched Chanteuil . . .

MIREILLE: [*in a kind of rage*] Now what are you trying to make me say? Now you're going to do as much damage by your remorse as you did then by your tyranny. Oh, I *hate* you! How I hate you.

ANDRE *comes in.*

ANDRE: There, I've arranged it all. Why, what's the matter?

ALINE: It's about your disappointment.

ANDRE: [*more and more distressed*] But look here, the thing's not a major disaster, after all.

ALINE: No, no, of course not.

ANDRE: It's not as if we'd lost a child. And we've still our whole life in front of us.

ALINE: [*with artificial enthusiasm*] Yes, yes, of course you have. [ANDRE *stares at her, and then shrinks away*] Mireille, darling, don't you feel that too?

MIREILLE: Oh, do let's stop all this talk. Look, could you be awfully kind and leave me alone a little? I can't bear any more, I can't . . . *really.* [MIREILLE *sits down by the fireplace and stares into the fire. After some wordless dialogue between* ALINE *and* ANDRE, ALINE *signs to* ANDRE *to stay and goes out quietly*]

ANDRE: [*to himself with great distress*] Our whole life! [*Silence. He goes to* MIREILLE, *kneels down by her and looks at her with intensity*]

MIREILLE: I did ask you to leave me alone for a moment.

ANDRE: But I don't understand. You're not talking as you usually do.

MIREILLE: I'd warned you.

ANDRE: But it's not Aunt Aline's fault. *She* hasn't changed.

MIREILLE: [*bitterly*] That's true. [*Sharply*] You've just asked her to come and live with us.

ANDRE: Only for a few days.

MIREILLE: Well, *I won't have it,* even for a few days. Do you see?

ANDRE: Why not? [*Silence*] Why not, Mireille?

MIREILLE: It's no good trying to explain. You'd never understand.

ANDRE: [*with energy*] But I want to understand. At least you won't deny that we owe her a great deal.

MIREILLE: [*violently*] No, we don't. We owe her *nothing* . . . nothing at all. And what's more, life here is only endurable if she's far away.

ANDRE: [*his voice trembling*] What! Then . . . then you *have* got a grievance against her?

MIREILLE: Nothing in particular. But she swamps everyone. No one can *exist* when she's about.

ANDRE: You mean she has too strong a personality?

MIREILLE: If you like.

ANDRE: Stronger than yours?

MIREILLE: Possibly.

ANDRE: Isn't that rather petty of you?

MIREILLE: Very well. Then I'm petty.

ANDRE: But why are you so different when she's here? Just now you seemed miserable. I even felt as if you didn't love me. Or . . . or . . . perhaps that's the truth.

MIREILLE: André!

ANDRE: Tell me. Is that what it is? Don't you love me?

MIREILLE: Don't be so silly. No . . . it's just that she's *too* afraid, don't you see, that everything isn't quite, quite perfect for us.

ANDRE: That's only because she loves us so much.

MIREILLE: She too *obviously* wants us to be happy.

ANDRE: You object to that. How horrible of you!

MIREILLE: Her reasons for wanting it are too good.

ANDRE: What on earth do you mean?

MIREILLE: [*controlling herself*] Look André, doesn't it strike you as odd? You and I never quarrel, but before she's been back one hour . . . well, look at us now. It's as if she can't help being destructive . . . it's not what she does. It's what she *is*. . . . You know, I think it's that she's suffered *too* much, so that . . .

ANDRE: You haven't answered me. Why are her reasons too good?

MIREILLE: Oh, don't take casual words so seriously.

ANDRE: [*gently*] Mireille, this time you *are* lying.

MIREILLE: But can't you see, if we didn't . . . if things went wrong with us she might reproach herself for it.

ANDRE: Why? Why should it be her fault?

MIREILLE: I didn't say it would. I only said she might imagine it was.

ANDRE: I don't understand.

MIREILLE: Oh, well, never mind. [*Silence*]

ALINE: [*gently from outside*] Can I come in?

ANDRE: Yes, do, Aunt Aline. We want you.

MIREILLE: Oh Lord!

> ALINE *comes in. She has clearly been crying and her voice is muffled.*

ALINE: Listen, my darlings. I want to say something to you. Please don't interrupt me. I feel that if I let you persuade me to stay with you, even for a day or two, we should probably regret it, all of us. It might be the . . . the end of something between us.

ANDRE: [*roughly*] Why?

ALINE: [*taken aback*] But . . .

ANDRE: . . . Then Mireille's attitude doesn't surprise you?

ALINE: [*faintly*] What attitude?

ANDRE: Good Lord! What a way you look at each other!

ALINE: [*stammering*] You . . . you see, I remind her too much of past unhappiness. She needs to live sheltered from the past.

ANDRE: Oh, no, it's not that.

MIREILLE: [*in a strained voice to* ANDRE] Are you trying to *make* us hurt each other, André?

ANDRE: [*miserably*] Then there's something you *can* hurt each other about. But in the old days . . . It feels as if there's something for which Mireille *can't* forgive you. And even you yourself don't seem too sure . . . [*sharply*] Aunt Aline, did you *press* Mireille to marry me?

MIREILLE [*with downcast eyes*] No, she didn't.

ALINE: I thought you'd be so happy together.

ANDRE: We are. [MIREILLE *makes a gesture of assent*] Well then! [*In an artificial voice*] We can look forward to a happy life . . . unless we have bad luck. . . . Of course, people can have accidents. . . . Look at Chanteuil.

ALINE: [*in spite of herself*] Why talk of Chanteuil?

ANDRE: But why not?

MIREILLE: [*with sudden vehemence*] Mother! Did you come back into this room to make sure you'd *quite* destroyed us? Were you afraid you might have left us one tiny little bit of life? No, no, don't look so pitiful. . . . Oh, you're dreadful. First you break our hearts, and then you come and force us to apologise because they're broken.

ANDRE: [*despairingly*] Mireille, Mireille . . . then you loved Chanteuil as much as that?

MIREILLE: Oh, I don't know, I don't *know*.

ALINE: Goodbye.

MIREILLE: Yes, go! I can see what you're counting on. You think I'll soon be sorry and ashamed. . . . Oh . . .

ALINE: Goodbye. I am not angry with you.

> *She goes out.* ANDRE *remains silent, deep in gloomy thoughts.* MIREILLE *goes to him gently and puts her hands on his forehead.*

MIREILLE: [*in a trembling voice*] It's all right, Andre. . . . Everything will be just like it was before. . . . Nothing at all will be different, really it won't.

ANDRE: [*with visible irony*] Oh, no, nothing.

MIREILLE: You'll see, with a little time.

ANDRE: Time. . . . It needs time. It *would* need time. [MIREILLE *moves uneasily*] Mireille, would you have married me if I hadn't been a sick man?

MIREILLE: Oh, come, André, don't be so silly.

ANDRE: You've answered me. Thank you.

MIREILLE: You don't understand.

ANDRE: Yes, I do. I'm just beginning to. I'm done for, isn't that it?

MIREILLE: [*with energy*] You're going to live. I'll take such care of you. *And* . . . [*she whispers in his ear*]

ANDRE: [*sadly*] Let's hope so . . . Oh, I said that the way *she* does. . . . Mireille, do you really think she's a wicked woman?

MIREILLE: No . . . no. She's just a poor, pathetic creature.

ANDRE: [*after a silence*] I didn't like the way she said good-bye.

MIREILLE: [*much agitated*] Oh, André . . . You can't mean that! . . . Oh, no, that's not possible . . . she could never . . .

ANDRE: But . . .

MIREILLE: She's suffered so much. . . . And after all, what is there to stop her? . . . She's no religion . . . and if she . . . André, if she killed herself . . . [*with terror*] life would be unbearable. Oh, I must prevent that . . . at any cost I must. . . . [*Silence.* MIREILLE *goes to the desk and searches feverishly*]

ANDRE: What are you looking for?

MIREILLE: [*with helpless resignation*] Her telephone number.

CURTAIN

About the Author

GABRIEL MARCEL was born in Paris in 1889. Philosopher, dramatist, teacher, musician, he is popularly regarded as the foremost exponent of what has been called Christian Existentialism, though the fundamental issues of his thought were articulated before his reception into the Roman Catholic Church in 1929. In the words of Professor James Collins, he prefers to regard his speculative enterprise as "a concrete philosophy centered upon the mystery of being, although he grants that it is both compatible with Christianity and naturally disposes the individual toward receiving such a revelation from God."

Marcel is notoriously unsympathetic to the elaboration of a rigorous philosophic system, and his characteristic *Metaphysical Journal*—anticipating in considerable detail the later themes of Sartre and Camus—first appeared in 1927 (the same year as Heidegger's *Being and Time*). His Gifford Lectures (Aberdeen) of 1949–1950, published as *The Mystery of Being*, constitute perhaps his closest approach to a consecutive statement. M. Marcel has visited Japan and the United States, where his William James Lectures—delivered at Harvard in 1961, and drawing heavily on the testimony of his dramatic experience—were later published as *The Existential Background of Human Dignity*. His major speculative works also include *Being and Having, The Philosophy of Existence, Homo Viator, Man Against Mass Society, The Decline of Wisdom*, and *Creative Fidelity*.

Professor Collins in *The Existentialists* and Professor Ronald Grimsley in *Existentialist Thought* offer exemplary and lucid expositions of Marcel's philosophic stance. Dr. David Roberts, in *Existentialism and Religious Belief*, examines it within a more explicitly Christian context.

R. H.

DRAMABOOKS

71
72
74
75
76
77
79
83
85